INTERACTIVE BOOK

Marko Rubel

Contact Information:
Marko Rubel's Office:
1-800-600-7997
1-866-598-2030
Support@MarkoRubel.com
www.MarkoRubel.com

This is an Interactive Book with Free Training Videos!

**START NOW – DOWNLOAD YOUR COMPLIMENTARY
FINANCIAL FREEDOM MATRIX**

go to

www.MarkoRubel.com/book

Before you read this book, please download this free tool that will help you achieve your financial goals. Remember to take advantage of hours of free video training and resources available exclusively for the readers of this book.

Copyright © by Marko Rubel. All rights reserved.

This publication is intended to provide accurate and authoritative information with regard to the subject matter covered. It is offered with the understanding that neither the publisher nor the author is engaged in rendering legal, tax, or other professional services. If legal, tax, or other expert assistance is required, the services of a competent professional should be sought.

> *From a Declaration of Principles jointly adopted by
> a committee of the American Bar Association and
> a committee of Publishers and Associations*

This book is intended for instructional purposes only. Every effort has been made to reflect the applicable laws as of the date of the publication of this book. However, this is a dynamic field of endeavor in which new laws are enacted, old laws revised and/or reinterpreted on a continuing basis, and where statutes, rulings, and precedential case law are constantly changing. Readers are advised to proceed with the techniques described herein with caution. Neither the author, publisher, licensees, nor distributors make any warranties express or implied about the merchantability or fitness for any particular use of this product.

I dedicate this book to my wife, Tammy, who has been my partner in life and business, since 1996. I love you.

Statement of Integrity

Our organization lead by Marko Rubel does not believe in get rich programs—only in hard work, adding value, and taking action with real strategies that can get you results. The proven strategies you will be learning about in this book and in our training courses have been personally used by Marko and numerous students nationwide to effectively invest in today's real estate market. As stipulated by law, we cannot and do not make any guarantees about your ability to get results or earn any money with our ideas, information, tools, or strategies. We don't know you, and besides, your results in life are up to you.

Our team is here to support you in your endeavors and can be reached any time by calling :
1-800-600-7997 *or emailing* **support@MarkoRubel.com**.

Earning Disclaimer

EVERY EFFORT HAS BEEN MADE TO ACCURATELY REPRESENT IDEAS IN THIS BOOK AND THEIR POTENTIAL. THERE IS NO GUARANTEE THAT YOU WILL EARN ANY MONEY USING THE TECHNIQUES AND IDEAS PRESENTED. EXAMPLES ARE NOT TO BE INTERPRETED AS **A PROMISE OR GUARANTEE** OF EARNINGS. EARNING POTENTIAL IS ENTIRELY DEPENDENT ON THE PERSON USING OUR PRODUCT, IDEAS, AND TECHNIQUES. WE DO NOT PURPORT THIS AS A "GET RICH SCHEME."

YOUR LEVEL OF SUCCESS IN ATTAINING THE RESULTS CLAIMED IN OUR MATERIALS DEPENDS ON THE TIME YOU DEVOTE TO THE PROGRAM, IDEAS, AND TECHNIQUES MENTIONED, YOUR FINANCES, KNOWLEDGE, AND VARIOUS SKILLS. SINCE THESE FACTORS DIFFER ACCORDING TO

INDIVIDUALS, WE CANNOT GUARANTEE YOUR SUCCESS OR INCOME LEVEL. NOR ARE WE RESPONSIBLE FOR ANY OF YOUR ACTIONS.

NOTHING IN THIS BOOK IS A PROMISE OR GUARANTEE OF FUTURE EARNINGS. ANY FINANCIAL NUMBERS REFERENCED HERE OR ON ANY OF OUR SITES ARE SIMPLY ESTIMATES OR PROJECTIONS AND SHOULD NOT BE CONSIDERED EXACT, ACTUAL, OR AS A PROMISE OF POTENTIAL EARNINGS—ALL NUMBERS ARE ILLUSTRATIVE ONLY. WE INCLUDED THE ACTUAL CLOSING DOCUMENTS OF EXAMPLES USED. HOWEVER, WE CANNOT VERIFY WITH COMPLETE ACCURACY THEIR STATEMENTS, SO YOUR RELIANCE ON THEM IS AT YOUR OWN RISK.

THERE CAN BE NO ASSURANCE THAT ANY PRIOR SUCCESSES OR PAST RESULTS AS TO INCOME EARNINGS CAN BE USED AS AN INDICATION OF YOUR FUTURE SUCCESS OR RESULTS. MONETARY AND INCOME RESULTS ARE BASED ON MANY FACTORS, INCLUDING LOCAL MARKET CONDITIONS AND MARKET TIMING. WE HAVE NO WAY OF KNOWING HOW WELL YOU WILL DO, AS WE DO NOT KNOW YOU, YOUR BACKGROUND, YOUR WORK ETHIC, OR YOUR BUSINESS SKILLS OR PRACTICES. THEREFORE, WE DO NOT GUARANTEE OR IMPLY THAT YOU WILL GET RICH, THAT YOU WILL DO AS WELL, OR MAKE ANY MONEY AT ALL.

REAL ESTATE INVESTING AND FORECLOSURE BUSINESSES AND EARNINGS DERIVED THEREFROM HAVE UNKNOWN RISKS INVOLVED AND ARE NOT SUITABLE FOR EVERYONE. MAKING DECISIONS BASED ON ANY INFORMATION PRESENTED IN OUR PRODUCTS, SERVICES, OR WEB SITE SHOULD BE DONE ONLY WITH THE KNOWLEDGE THAT YOU COULD EXPERIENCE SIGNIFICANT LOSSES OR MAKE NO MONEY AT ALL. AS WITH ANY PRODUCT OR SERVICE, WE KNOW THAT MOST WHO BUY THIS BOOK OR OUR PROGRAMS NEVER USE IT, AND THEREFORE, WE BELIEVE THAT MOST NEVER MAKE ANY MONEY. BUILDING ANY BUSINESS TAKES HARD WORK.

ALL PRODUCTS AND SERVICES OFFERED BY THE AUTHOR AND HIS AFFILIATED COMPANIES ARE FOR EDUCATIONAL AND INFORMATIONAL PURPOSES ONLY. USE CAUTION AND SEEK THE ADVICE OF QUALIFIED PROFESSIONALS. CHECK WITH YOUR ACCOUNTANT, LAWYER, OR PROFESSIONAL ADVISOR BEFORE ACT-

ING ON THIS OR ANY INFORMATION. USERS OF OUR PRODUCTS, SERVICES, AND WEB SITE ARE ADVISED TO DO THEIR OWN DUE DILIGENCE WHEN IT COMES TO MAKING BUSINESS DECISIONS AND ALL INFORMATION, PRODUCTS, AND SERVICES THAT HAVE BEEN PROVIDED SHOULD BE INDEPENDENTLY VERIFIED BY YOUR OWN QUALIFIED PROFESSIONALS.

YOU AGREE THAT OUR COMPANY IS NOT RESPONSIBLE FOR THE SUCCESS OR FAILURE OF YOUR BUSINESS DECISIONS RELATING TO ANY INFORMATION PRESENTED HERE.

Compliance with Law

SINCE LAWS ARE CONSTANTLY CHANGING, YOU MUST CONSULT WITH YOUR OWN ATTORNEY TO DETERMINE THE TECHNIQUES, PROCESSES, AND IDEAS PRESENTED IN THESE COURSE MATERIALS ARE LEGAL AND IN COMPLIANCE WITH YOUR LOCAL REAL ESTATE LAWS, FORECLOSURE LAWS, AND OTHER LAWS.

IT IS YOUR OBLIGATION TO INVESTIGATE ALL OF THESE LAWS OR REGULATIONS AND TO ENSURE THAT ANY IDEAS, WEBSITES, OR SERVICES OFFERED BY THE AUTHOR AND HIS AFFILIATED COMPANIES COMPLY WITH THOSE AND ANY OTHER LAWS.

INTRODUCTION
— READ BEFORE YOU START

Read This Important Message to Start and Get Your Free Gifts

This book is different from all the other books you've ever read. It reveals an investing strategy completely unknown to the general public and unknown to the majority of the investor community.

The general public unfortunately thinks the only way to make money in real estate is to buy property, sit on it for 20 or 30 years, rent or lease it, then constantly be hassled by bad tenants, plugged toilets, and negative cash flow, and then wait for the market to go up, so they can sell it for a profit. I'm going to show you that their thinking and strategy simply aren't true. You'll learn proven strategies that can quickly turn single-family houses into cash, almost overnight, without using any of your credit or savings, and build real wealth over a few years ... instead of a few decades.

On the other hand, the investor community overwhelmingly believes that the only alternative to being a landlord and hassling with tenants is wholesaling "ugly" houses or rehabbing them. In my opinion, this is the same type of suffering as dealing with ungrateful tenants, just more intense … since it's condensed down to just a few months vs. a few decades.

> **This book is NOT about having TENANTS.**
> **This book is NOT about WHOLESALING houses.**
> **This book is NOT about REHABBING HOUSES.**

In this book, you'll learn a totally new and different approach to investing in real estate. This is the one approach that can eliminate both the tenant hassles and ugly houses, all at the same time. It is the result of countless years of learning in the school of hard knocks, and I've found it way more profitable than flipping ugly houses.

My goal is to show you my hidden strategy that's created so many millionaires, and even though it's available to anyone with a pulse, most have never heard of it. And my goal is to inspire and motivate you, both at the same time, to finally take action and improve your life. It's time to …

Think Bigger – Invest Smarter – Live Better

Starting back in 1997 when I got downsized from a corporate job and started learning about creative real estate and all the way up till now—I've participated in hundreds of transactions as a full-time investor, starting with wholesaling, then some fix-and-flip deals, to finally figuring out the most powerful strategy in real estate that there is, which I'll describe to a T in this book.

Over the recent years, I've been invited as a guest speaker to over 50 different real estate seminars and conferences nationwide, I've presented in numerous real estate investment associations and clubs in different cities, and I can say without any hesitation that **most investors have never heard** of these strategies, and the few who have, have only heard parts and have an incomplete understanding of the whole. By reading this book, you'll be decades ahead of them by understanding one of the most potent wealth-generating business models in existence.

On another subject—the reality is that most people never complete the books they read. So what have I done? I intentionally separated this book into 3 major sections that work as stand-alone sections. They're easy to read, and I hope you finish this book for your sake, as well as for your family's.

Here's what you do—**Read at least Section 1**, which is the first 100 pages or so. This will give you a good understanding of this powerful, but little known business model. It'll also motivate you to continue reading.

If you're holding this book in your hands right now, you owe it to yourself and your family to read at least Section 1.

Then the next section, **Section 2, is another EXCITING section—because it gives the PROOF**. In the book I introduce you to a small group of my coaching students and their private deals. *(I hope I don't upset those that I didn't include—but unfortunately, I have limited space and can't include everyone, even though I tried.)*

I'm going to break down their real estate deals and how they applied what you'll be learning in this book, so you can generate massive financial gains in your immediate future. Some of my coaching students are making more money than they ever thought possible, and they'll tell you that in the video training that came with this book.

Listen, my biggest problem when reading, buying, and applying any wealth-building information I've come across over the last 20 years has been the issue of proof—I always ask myself, *"**Is this really possible?**"*

When you get to Section 2, I give you the proof via real-life examples, and to further enhance your experience and your excitement, I did something very special—I interviewed each of the 10 investors and even provided you with a link where you can get **FREE access to those video interviews full of tips, advice and insights**.

Not only that, you'll get to see the houses and the documents used to make these deals happen. You'll hear from each of them first-hand, and as I like to say, "Truth exists for those who can prove it."

In **Section 3**, we'll explore other investing strategies, such as Wholesaling, Lease Options, etc. and I'll explain how these strategies fit in our business model. You will learn why those strategies should be part of your investing business but NOT your main strategy.

FREE TRAINING → Go to www.MarkoRubel.com/book

DON'T FORGET—this is an interactive book with hours and hours of FREE training, priceless resources, and precise real estate tools, so remember to go to the website listed above and take advantage of all the resources that are yours FREE. As a bonus, you can also join our weekly investor newsletter (eZine).

In summary, there are lots of ways to make money in real estate, but what you can learn in this book is a much more potent business model than wholesaling ugly houses, fixing them up by babysitting contractors, or renting them out to ungrateful and unappreciative tenants.

It is far faster and extremely more profitable to follow the advice I give you in this amazing book if you want to be a real estate investor that makes money. HOWEVER, write this down in your memory—I will not be supplying the work and the determination you need to be a raving success. Those attributes are up to you. If you make a commitment to yourself and your family to act on the strategies presented in this book, you'll succeed no matter your background or your location. Success is 90% getting started and 10% not stopping, no matter the setbacks. Without that type of commitment, neither this nor any other book, course, or seminar in the world can help you.

Let's make it happen for you!

HERE'S WHAT THIS BOOK IS NOT...

The purpose of this book is to inform and introduce you to a very profitable niche in the real estate investing business.

However, let me be very clear here. This book is not a guide to building a million-dollar business that the described business model definitely has potential of. It is unrealistic to expect that you can create a profitable business based on 300+ pages of information. Even though this book provides a huge learning potential and some amazing financial discoveries, it is still just a start in the right direction. And it's certainly not the end of your learning curve of the methods presented in the sections.

This is <u>not</u> a get rich quick book.

If you believe there is a shortcut to wealth without work, then this book is most likely not for you. Getting wealthy requires lots of learning, lots of implementing, some failing along the way, then dusting yourself off, and getting up and learning from your mistakes. All successful people know that if they can persist through their challenges, they're going to be super successful.

However, it's all worth it in the end. You too, like many investors you'll meet in this book, have a dream of a better life or you wouldn't be reading this now. The investors you'll meet here are achieving their dreams, so why wouldn't YOU? Why get scared of a little work that's involved when you know at the end of it all, there's lots of fun and the result is what matters.

Let me ask you ...

How would you feel if you did a deal and cashed a $115,393.52 check like this?

What would you do with the money?

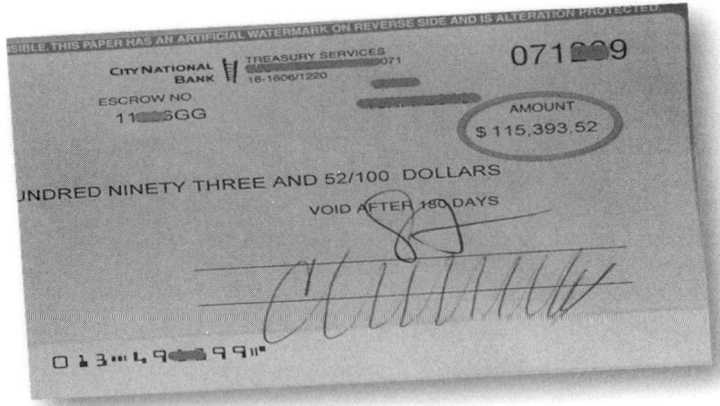

If the thought of putting this money into your bank account excites you, then I'd advise you to not let this book out of your hands for the next hour because this is how long it will take you to learn what might be the biggest financial discovery of your lifetime. As already stated, "The general public has no clue about this business model." YOU ARE ONE OF THE LUCKY ONES.

→ **When I asked the investor who generated this check the same question—"How did you feel when you cashed this check?"—This is what she said:**

"YOU KNOW, MARKO, THIS WAS THE HAPPIEST DAY IN MY LIFE EXCEPT FOR GETTING MARRIED AND HAVING OUR SON. I LOVED IT!"

(These are the exact same words you'll hear directly from this investor in the video interview at **www.MarkoRubel.com/book**)

Watch the video interview with the investor from the previous page.

Want proof? You'll get plenty of proof that you can start making more money than you've ever made before, no matter what your situation is currently. So even though it is not what we'd call "overnight riches," it is well worth your effort.

Talk Is Cheap, Marko—Where's the Proof?

I agree with you. Talk is cheap, and that's why **I've included 25 (TWENTY FIVE) real-life examples of deals** accumulating hundreds of thousands of dollars in generated profit—and all these deals will be explained in Section 2. Not 1 deal, not 2, but 25 documented deals!

And not only will you see the actual documents for each deal, you'll be able to actually see and hear those investors on a Skype interview I conducted with each one of them. **They are my coaching students and you'll hear how they did it**, and learn what was important to each one of them and how they felt about the process. And some of them became millionaires.

These are the coaching students you will meet in this book, and hear about their results:

$1,200,000.00 - 24 Deals   Got Paid to Buy   251 Deals Completed $25,000 + $926/mo.

   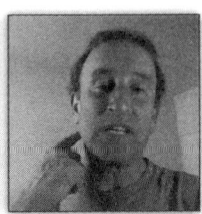

$115,393.52 Check $70,200.00 CASH   25 Houses in 18 Months $106,973.00 Profit

$20,000 CASH $0 Down to $20k Cash   20 Houses worth $1M+   15 Deals in 15 Months

$47,693.15 Profit $10,000.00 CASH   Got Paid to Buy   Got House for Only $10

*Results presented are not typical—Read the Earning Disclaimer

Marko, Have you Done What You Teach Successfully?

That's a simple answer—yes, I have. What I teach you has made me a millionaire. I guarantee you—this book is not about theory.

As Tom Cruise yelled, *"Show Me The Money!"* in the movie *Jerry Maguire*, I'm going to do the same for you. I'm going to show you my gross profits from 12 consecutive months in the amount of **$1,404,899.85** dollars - I'll show you the checks because that is the ultimate proof. It is the proof you've been looking for, and with that proof you know you are learning from a bona fide millionaire and your time will not be wasted.

At first I was a little hesitant to show you my earnings. I was afraid you would look at it like I'm bragging because you don't know me yet. And I understand your skepticism. You don't know that I am still the same humble guy that I've always been. I respect where I am currently and where I came from.

I was also hesitant because I didn't want to come across as a know-it-all and have you thinking this business is super easy and that you'd be making lots of money overnight. Let me be very clear on that. My results are not typical, and there are many other factors involved that make those results not typical—**so make sure you read the Earning Disclaimer** for the full story.

Here's the big reason WHY I've decided to show you one of my best years, despite all of the above—

I want to make sure you believe what I am writing about because if you don't, then I've wasted hundreds of hours of my time writing this book and your time as well by your reading it.

My goal is simple. I want you to be sure you have no doubts about the strategies presented here, so you can actually make some informed decisions and take action on them as fast as humanly possible. When you act with good information, it helps benefit you and your family.

The last reason I decided to show you the checks in this book is that I know for a fact that many self-proclaimed "experts" write books, teach seminars, and sell you DVDs, etc. but have no real experience on the subject they write about. I've met many pretenders that "talk the talk" but do not "walk the walk." Now I'm not saying anything bad about them, but it may be their friend or family member who has done the investing, not them. I believe its wrong for them to write from that perspective because unless you've been in the trenches, you <u>never know the details and the nuances involved</u> in making it happen with real estate.

Sure, I've been invited as a real estate expert to the local **FOX**, **ABC**, and **NBC** TV stations to talk about real estate numerous times. I even got nominated as the expert in front of the **National Real Estate Investor Association**—the organization that governs most of real estate investing clubs, covering over 40,000 investors nationwide, but that doesn't change my outlook on what I'm covering here. Those things are proof that I know what I'm talking about, but the checks offer the real proof that I've done the work and had some really good success doing it.

Here are the checks issued by the closing companies payable to my company or my name:

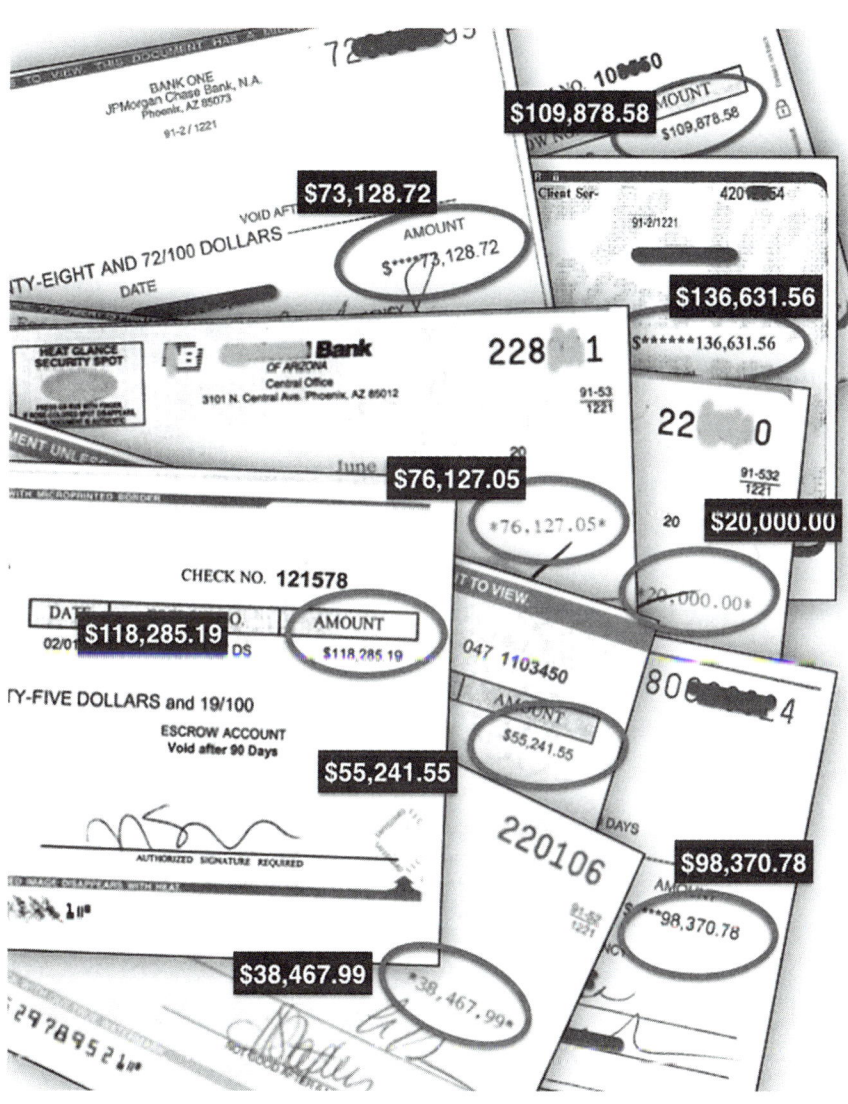

... and more checks... totaling **$1,404,899.85** dollars over

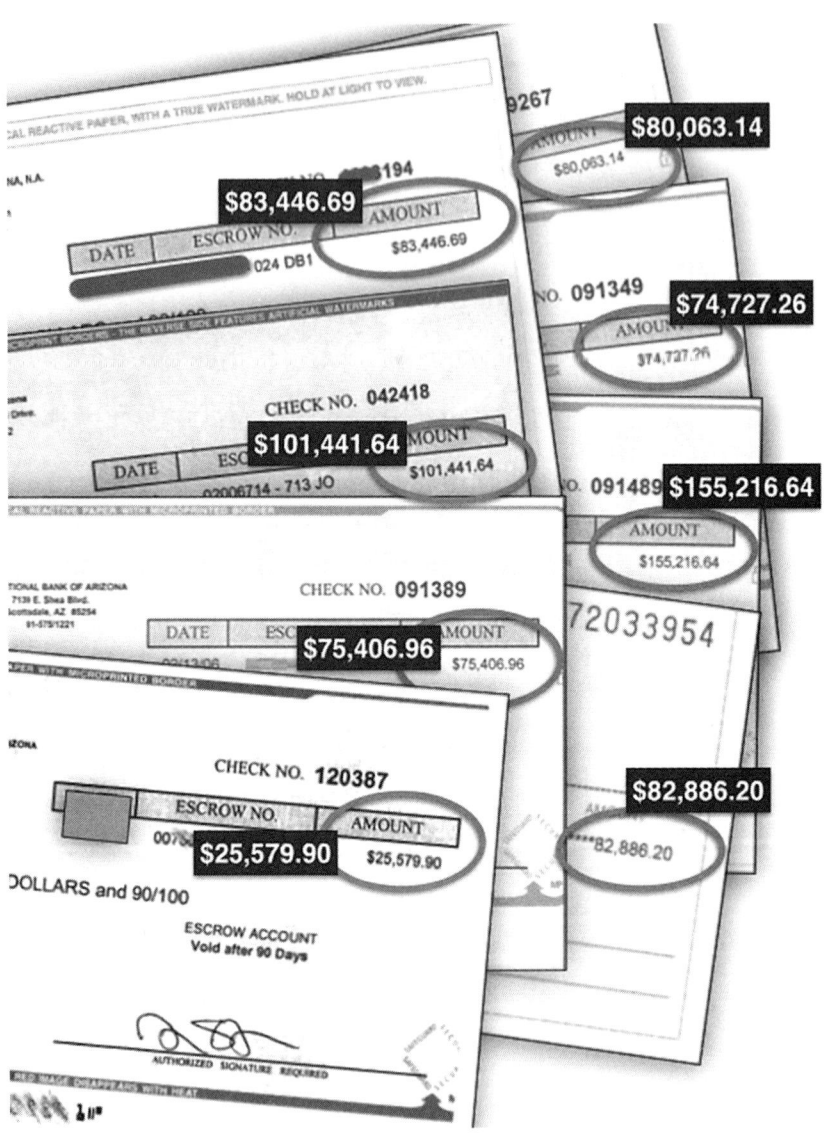

A few comments on these checks:

- *Title company information & the account numbers are blacked out for privacy*
- *Dates are blacked out intentionally to not give excuses to those who will say that the strategies worked x number of years ago, but not currently or x number of years from now. The fact is—these same strategies will work 10 years from now ... as long as there are people who live in houses.*
- *These checks are AUTHENTIC and could be verified by any authority in the United States. I have too much to lose to make up stuff like this, and rest assured, I would never do that.*

As I said before, my results are <u>not</u> typical and this is <u>not</u> a get rich quick business. I personally don't know of any "get rich overnight" opportunity, but I sure have seen plenty of "get poor overnight" examples. You can read the Earning Disclaimer at the start of this book—as it will tell you that individual results will vary greatly and in accordance to your input, determination, hard work, knowledge, various other skills, your ability to follow directions, to view market conditions and numerous other factors completely out of my control. In other words, you as an investor and a reader are responsible for your success! It cannot be given to you!

So now that you know that this is for real, let me answer WHY I am writing this book ...

* * *

I've shown you a lot of the checks. You now know that you're learning from a bona-fide millionaire, but if you're like a lot of people, you still may have some burning questions in your head ... or you just might be a little skeptical.

Here are a few of the questions that I get asked a lot:

– If you really are rich, Marko, why are you sharing your strategies with me of all people?

– Why did you bother writing this book?

– Why do you bother teaching people your real estate strategies?

Maybe you don't have questions like that, but I know I would have them if I were in your shoes, so let me answer a few of them, so we can jump into a lot more exciting subjects, the stuff that actually matters to you.

By writing this book I benefit in two ways. Yes, there will be a small financial benefit, but the bigger WHY is the emotional aspect.

Some people reading this book will see the financial portion as the most important aspect while others will realize that when you're already doing really well financially, a very important part of your work becomes the emotional satisfaction it can give you. Let me explain.

Through my decades of hard work, failure, resetting, learning, and slowly building and creating success, I found myself in a position where I have such a healthy financial well being that I can devote my time and energy to supporting others in their quests for success. I've worked hard enough to now have the luxury to pursue emotional satisfaction in my work, and I get that from helping people achieve their goals.

It's hard to describe the feeling of happiness that overcomes me when I see a student improve their life, their family's life, and their finances. It is also impossible to describe the emotional feeling when they come and thank me in person at a live event for saving or changing their family's future or their legacy.

It's hard to describe the feeling of love I get from their tears, hugs, and handshakes at my events and meetings.

Don't get me wrong. I have plenty of love in life from my wife and my kids, but it still feels good to me when one of my students sends me an email that says, "I love you, Marko. Thank you …" I hope you can understand what I'm saying.

In the videos you'll hear a lot of them say, "Marko cares" or "Marko goes out of his way." If it were only the financial reward that I was after, I would only do what I was required to do. In other words,

I wouldn't go out of my way like I do to make sure you are a success. But you know what? I do, and I do it out of love for and my need to give back to my students. I still remember days when I couldn't pay rent, and what real estate did for me and my family.

I already know, this book will change lives and that's why I wrote it—to help as many people as I can achieve their goals in life and in business.

And all I'm doing is what Maya Angelou, the famous writer and poet and also Oprah Winfrey's coach, told Oprah to do, and that is:

> "WHEN YOU LEARN, TEACH.
> WHEN YOU GET, GIVE."

No part of this book has been written by a ghostwriter like many of the books that you see in print. For me, this insider information is too important for my students and readers to miss, so I would never delegate the writing of this book to anyone.

These are my thoughts and my words.

My wife can tell you how many hours I've spent in front of my computer writing this book. Sure you'll see some of my funny English in places (I am from Croatia, you know), but I did have an editor proofread it, just to make it better for you.

Enjoy the book, and I'll see you at an upcoming seminar. Make sure you introduce yourself when you see me in person, and let me know what you think of the book.

xxiii

Your Mindset Is Your Success

> "Your attitude, not your aptitude, will determine your altitude."
>
> —Zig Ziglar

As you are already realizing, this is going to be a very exciting book. Literally life-changing.

However, before we dive into the investing strategies that this book is all about, let me reveal the most important ingredient for your success and that ingredient is—your MINDSET. Do not downplay this important ingredient.

You should have an open mind when you're learning these strategies, but more importantly, you have to have a mindset that doesn't take NO for an answer. Then you must persevere until you find or get what it is that you're looking for.

1 – PERSERVERANCE

Running a business is not easy—if it were easy, everyone would have their own business. Many dream about having their own business, but very few have it. When you have the knowledge—it's not hard. It's actually a lot of fun.

Becoming a millionaire is NOT easy—if it were easy, everyone would be a millionaire and then being a millionaire would mean nothing. But when you become one, life is amazing.

In the process of getting your investing business up and running and all the way to becoming a millionaire, I know without a shadow of a doubt, you will encounter a lot of obstacles. That's what we call business. Many people will stop in the middle of getting started and just give up. The secret to your being successful is this—the few people who do persevere will get the life that only a few can dream of.

I encourage you to persevere in your endeavor because of one reason—it's awesome at the top and a whole lot better than being at the bottom. It's worth the effort.

Quick Warning: When you get impatient with your progress, always ask yourself this question:

"Where am I going to be in 6 months financially if I don't do this?"

I don't know how you'll answer, but I know one thing for sure: You will be 6 months older. The 6 months will go by anyway, but if you get your first deal going during those 6 months, your life is going to make a turn in the right direction. So will it be worth it? You bet.

2 – DETERMINATION

On another point …

This is "creative" real estate investing. This is not "conventional" real estate investing. Those points are not the same.

We are in creative real estate investing because it offers higher profits and an expedited path to wealth, without our having to have a lot of starting capital. That's why you're reading this book. However, creative real estate investing comes with its own challenges. For example, you need a *motivated* seller for these strategies to work, so those people who are not motivated—will not agree to what you're offering. No problem—NEXT …

Another example is that not every title/closing company will close your deal because it is not what they're used to doing and most importantly—it's not conventional.

Many of them have a lot of business and make plenty of money doing conventional closings, so they really don't care about closing a few deals that are out of the norm. However, there are always other title/closing companies who are starving for business and will happily accommodate your requests.

So here's the mindset I want you to have. Remember it:

SW – SW – SW – SW
Some Will—Some Won't—So What? —Someone's Waiting

What does that mean? It means that not every seller will go for your deal, but you'll find plenty who will, and some can't wait for you to show up at their house to help them solve their problem.

The same goes with the title or closing company who refuses to close these kinds of deals. Don't stress about one company that won't close the deal. Make it easy. Just move on. There's someone else out there waiting to close your deal. You just need to find them.

So be determined, and never give up on getting what you want. Be like Nike and, "Go for it!"

Another form of determination is getting up and going when you've been knocked down and think that you've "failed." You can call it perseverance. It's important for you to realize that not everything will work out as you've planned. Not everyone will do what they tell you they'll do. Not every deal will close when you want it to. You will fail in certain tasks due to your own mistakes, and then other times you'll fail due to something out of your control. But what's really important to remember is that you realize that failure is just part of your becoming a verified success.

Look at it from a positive perspective, learn from it, and then move on.

For example, if you went on 20 appointments and got a bunch of no's from the sellers on each appointment, you'd most likely get a little discouraged, right? But if you understood that it's all part of learning and you didn't give up, and then on your twenty-first appointment you got a deal that made you $50,000 dollars, would it be worth it?

Sure it would! All anyone can say is that you failed 20 times before you became a success, so learn how to fail fast. Some people will give up after 10 appointments. Some will give up after 5 appointments. The fact remains that all 20 times should be considered a learning curve, not a lot of failures. This is best described in the Thomas Edison quote below. I included two more quotes you should remember if you want to be super successful.

I HAVE NOT FAILED. I'VE JUST FOUND 10,000 WAYS THAT WON'T WORK.

—*Thomas A. Edison*

SUCCESS CONSISTS OF GOING FROM FAILURE TO FAILURE WITHOUT LOSS OF ENTHUSIASM.

—*Winston Churchill*

FAILURE IS SUCCESS IF WE LEARN FROM IT.

—*Malcolm Forbes*

3 – ELIMINATE NAYSAYERS

Here's something a lot of people never realize. Learning from your failures and getting to your successes becomes a lot harder when you're surrounded by naysayers. It affects your enthusiasm and your mindset. It affects your self-esteem, and it increases that self-doubt that most new investors have (i.e., *Is this for real? Does it work in my town? Will I be able to do this?*). Your success is jeopardized in such an environment.

In my life, I've had plenty of naysayers between my co-workers and friends, even my family, who repeatedly kept saying that I'd never succeed in real estate and I should stop dreaming.

At the end of the day, my negative co-workers are still out there swapping hours for dollars making their bosses (or stockholders) rich—if they're lucky enough to still have a job. On the other hand, my family is now very proud of me and even happier when I send them money.

My advice to you is this—Eliminate any and all naysayers, and you'll get ahead faster with your real estate investments. If these naysayers are too close to you and impossible to eliminate from your social environment, then find a way to neutralize them, so you don't have to listen to them.

This is one of the reasons that I encourage my students to bring their spouses or partners to my LIVE seminars. It helps get them on the same page with you, so you can show them the potential and the proof, so they can be supporters, instead of naysayers.

The story you should remember about naysayers is the story of George Foreman. I don't know if you remember, but George found himself broke when he was 40 years old. He had no money. So he decided to go back to boxing. *What do you think his friends and family told him?*

> "GEORGE, YOU'LL NEVER MAKE IT. YOU ARE TOO OLD FOR BOXING."

We all know what happened. George became the oldest heavyweight champion of the world at the age of 44 years young. He proved them all wrong. That boxing success launched his celebrity career and changed his life forever. You may recall, his George Foreman Grill was the brand that SOLD … for more than $100 Million.

Marko with George Foreman

So my point to you is this—If he had listened to all the media and naysayers, he probably wouldn't even be alive today. He didn't listen, and he did what he wanted to do. Even though the odds were against him, he proved them all wrong. You can and should do the same.

I learned a lot from George and consider him one of the most amazing people I've ever met.

> NEVER LISTEN TO THE CROWD,
> LISTEN TO YOUR CORNER!
>
> *—George Foreman*

Deal Case Study
– The Right Mindset Produces $47,000 in Profit

My coaching students and now friends, Brendan and Jamie, did a deal that required the right mindset. Many investors who were given the same type of deal would have given up when faced with the obstacles they had to overcome, but they didn't. **That perseverance and determination is what separates winners from the losers.** And it definitely pays off in the long run.

This deal was a referral from Brendan's son-in-law. His grandfather died and left his house in Seattle to his dad Bob and Aunt Jane, his dad's sister. Jane was living in the house with grandpa and had been taking care of him.

Unfortunately, Aunt Jane's boyfriend was living there too, and the both of them were jobless, drug and alcohol users that were siphoning off of grandpa's bank account. Bob lived in New York City and was the executor of the Seattle estate and the one who was making the mortgage payments. After grandpa passed away, Bob got tired of flying back and forth from New York to Seattle constantly trying to get Jane and her boyfriend out of the house, so he could sell it. At one point, he could not afford to pay his own mortgage, let alone his father's mortgage, plus try and fly back and forth.

Bob was very excited when he learned that my students, Brendan and Jamie, would buy the house together with "the problem"—as they affirmed that they would buy it "as is," including Jane and her boyfriend in it. Bob was relieved to be out of having to deal with the house, the boyfriend, and Jane. Needless to say, he was extremely motivated to sell.

This was a ranch/rambler style house, a 3-bedroom, 2 1/2 bath, attached single garage, and beautiful, big yard, in a nice neighborhood in a primo location in Burien, Washington.

After a short negotiation, the deal was on the table. Brendan and Jamie were buying the house for the balance of the $122,000 mortgage, paying back taxes of $4,875.00, and giving them $5,000 dollars.

As you're going to learn throughout this book, they did NOT need to go to a bank and qualify for a loan to buy this house. They used my Unlimited Funding Program strategies, where you bypass the lenders and that way you don't use your credit or your savings for the down payment.

Brendan and Jaime liked the deal and before they consummated it with Bob, they went and talked to Jane and her boyfriend. As you could imagine, they wouldn't just move out because they liked living there for free.

Brendan and Jaime soon realized that this was going to be a major hassle, getting these two people out of the house.

That was Obstacle #1—the possibility of the buyers (my students) getting stuck with the monthly payments while going through a legal process of getting Jane and her boyfriend out of the house. Since there was no official lease or any documents signed between Jane and her boyfriend and Bob, the eviction process could get complicated.

If you were Jamie and Brendan, would you take the risk?

As I said, I know for a fact that most investors would give up right there due to unforeseen complications and delays while being on the hook for making monthly payments. But not Brendan and Jaime. They persevered. They started thinking outside the box. This perseverance is what makes them different than most investors.

At the LIVE seminar training that Brendan and Jaime attended multiple times, they remembered my mentioning a document called "Cash for Keys." In essence, we sometimes pay occupants to leave when it is cheaper than evicting them. I call it an "ethical bribe." I have that special document and what it does is it guarantees the renters that they'll get paid—if they move out BEFORE or ON the agreed date. It's a win-win for everybody.

That is how Brendan and Jaime were able to get Jane and her boyfriend to move out. However, this took a few weeks, and Bob was running out of time. He had to have the house SOLD and the escrow closed.

Obstacle #2—when they finally solved the first obstacle and were ready to close, the title company said they couldn't close the deal <u>due to the unconventional deal structure</u> that Brendan and Jamie had presented them with. The thing was—time was running out.

At this point I will not go into all the details why this was a problem, but let me put it to you this way—considering the time crunch they were in and some other deal specifics, most investors would have called it quits, stopped negotiations, or just thrown up their hands and given up. Not Brendan and Jai-

xxxiii

me. They were going to make this deal work, and they were going to see it through until they made it work.

At the end, with the help of the closing agent at the same title company (but without officially doing it through the title company,) they were able to record the deed and acquire ownership of the house. Again, this required thinking outside the box.

Now, this was one of the most complicated deals I've seen in all my years as a real estate mentor—but don't get scared. Most deals are a lot simpler, and you'll see plenty of them throughout this book.

But here's my point. Was it worth it to Brendan and Jamie? You bet it was—Brendan and Jaime SOLD that house for $207,000—in just 2 days after their purchase of it. A month later the buyer closed the escrow, and they walked away with a **net profit of $47,795.00**. Not a bad deal if you ask me.

→ **Go ahead and watch the video Brendan and Jaime sent in where Brendan waves handcuffs – it's very funny. Go to www.MarkoRubel.com/book**

Here's part of the thank-you letter that Brendan and Jaime sent me. It talks about how much this deal meant to them. They asked me to share this letter with the readers of this book, so here it is:

> - Page 2 of 2 -
>
> At the time, wife had worked as a court bailiff, court clerk and in finance departments of local cities for over 30 years and was getting ready to retire. This deal made more money for us than she made Per Year! I am a police officer and have been for the past 31 years. This deal made us as much as 1/2 of my current annual salary with overtime. I believe that I will be retiring real soon because we are finding deals all of the time. When we increase our marketing budget the deals will come faster and more often. That is my driving force to retirement and we will make it happen - Soon!
>
> But, none of this could have or would have happened without the incredible opportunity presented to us by Marko Rubel! With his systems, mentoring program and willingness to teach and help us, we would have been lost. When he heard about this deal, he literally made my wife cry. Really, she hung up the phone, ran upstairs to me in our office, and tears were streaming down her cheeks. I asked her: "What's wrong!" "That was Marko, she said, he wanted to know if we had everything we needed for our closing today or if we needed his help." That's the way Marko is. He is very Passionate about ALL of his students becoming successful. He doesn't just focus on a few. We are all at different learning levels and have had different experiences in life. Marko's way is geared for anyone that has a dream, who believes in him and mostly in themselves. It just takes a little action and determination. That's what we did and it Really Works!
>
> Thank You and God Bless You Marko! Because of you our life has been changed for the better and is much more enriched. With our business, we are able to go out and help people that are in trouble with their house or need to get it sold fast. Then, we are able to provide a service to nice and good folks that had no hopes of buying a home and putting them into one. We get to help all kinds of really nice people that have been through some tough times and we get to help make their dreams come true. Just like Marko did with us and what he does with All of his students!
>
> We will Never be able to Thank You Enough.
>
> Brendan and Jaime

Table of Contents

SECTION I – My Unique Investing Niche (N2W) 1
The New Era Economy..3
Brutally Honest 5
My Story 7
My Discovery 11
Active vs. Passive Income 15
The 5 Wealth-Building Components of Real Estate 19
The Best Business Model—Your First Million......................25
3 Ways to Buy & Own Real Estate.................................35
Unlimited Funding Mechanism 39
Acquiring Ownership Using Unlimited Funding 43
Unlimited Funding —Can You Do It Too? 71
At the Seller's House 75
BIG 7 Structures of the Unlimited Funding Program...............81
Niche2Wealth Business Model.....................................93
10 Reasons for the Niche2Wealth Business Model 113
Final Thoughts —Important to Read 117

SECTION II – Deal Case Studies 121
Introduction to Deal Examples 125
Coaching Student Success #1 129
Coaching Student Success #2 153
Coaching Student Success #3 173

Coaching Student Success #4	187
Coaching Student Success #5	197
Coaching Student Success #6	209
Coaching Student Success #7	221
Coaching Student Success #8	233
Coaching Student Success #9	243
Coaching Student Success #10	255

SECTION III – Bonus Strategies for Deals that "Don't Fit In"	269
Bonus Strategy 1 – Sandwich Lease Options	273
Bonus Strategy 2 – Free & Clear Acquisitions	283
Bonus Strategy 3 – Wholesaling	291
The Next Step Determines Your Destiny …	305

– Section I –

My Unique Investing Niche (N2W)

You are in for an eye-opening discovery in this book …

I'm going to share with you the **most powerful business model** that has the potency to create an income beyond your wildest dreams and desires.

This business model is based on the **Unlimited Funding Program (UFP),** which is available to everyone and could make you a millionaire. It made me a millionaire and has made a lot of money—for a lot of people, some that you'll meet inside this book and in the video training provided for you at **www.MarkoRubel.com/book**.

As you learn about this unique investing model, you'll realize that it's possible to replace your current income in the next 3–6 months and semi-retire in the next 3–5 years.

I know … this may sound a bit hyperbolic.

However, all I ask is that you trust me enough and keep reading. I'm going to ask that you suspend any preconceived notions about real estate before you start. If you do, this book can be what I call a game changer.

This short book contains the tools necessary to transform your life. Your entire world is about to change if you can read this book, then apply it, and never stop until you reach your goals, no matter how high they are.

This book will answer questions like:
- How do you buy quality real estate deals at below market prices, without taking risks, regardless of your current situation or experience?

- How do you get favorable financing, with low interest rates, with low or no down payment, regardless of your credit, and without ever talking to any banks or lenders?
- Why is this type of financing virtually unlimited (thus the name *Unlimited Funding Program*)? And why is it available to <u>everyone</u> with the know-how?
- How do you profit <u>without</u> dealing with teants or having to get involved in rehabbing?

  How do you <u>profit hugely</u> even if the market stays flat, so you can amass millions when the market is going up?
- How do you <u>escape</u> the active income trap and STOP swapping hours for dollars at your job?
- How do you finally <u>LIVE</u> the good life that you deserve?

The New Era Economy

We are in a new economy.

The old ways of investing in real estate no longer apply. To not only survive, but thrive, you must learn and act on NEW but proven principles.

So what does it take to set you apart from the crowd and conquer today's unbelievable opportunities?

1. Working harder, working smarter. Hard work ... yes, that's a given, but plenty of people work their fingers to the bone day after day without getting results. Instead, I say, "Work **smarter**." Focus your attention on acquiring assets that will leverage your effort. It's the difference between *Active Income* vs. *Passive Income* as you will soon learn.

It's the difference between working IN your business vs. working ON your business.

2. Taking action FAST. Honestly, this should be number one. The world doesn't rest, and opportunity won't stand by. You have to grab every chance you can to make a difference in your life and your income, especially in today's competitive investing arena.

There are opportunities right there in your area, but you need to act now. Act fast.

Have you logged in the training area to access the additional resources that come as a part of this book? If you haven't yet, you're being too slow—go there now: www.MarkoRubel.com/book.

3. Using your time wisely by employing investing strategies that produce maximum profit in minimum time. The type of investing you will learn about in this book allows you to maximize your profits with only 2–3 hours per deal.

In addition, you will leverage your resources by using tested systems.

4. Learning from a mentor with proven success. I consider this the ultimate shortcut to reaching your goals. By simply modeling someone who is successful and following in their footsteps, you can accelerate your own path to success. This is the one thing I attribute most of my success to, and you'll hear the same from our coaching students when you read the deal examples in Section 2. Having a mentor is having everything.

I've always been able to hire coaches who have accomplished more than I have, were able to prove it, and were willing to show me the shortcuts. Towards the end of this book, I'll explain how to find and hire a coach that will make a difference and expedite your success.

Brutally Honest

I value my time but also respect yours.

Therefore, I'd like to get something off of my chest since it may save you time. It is not for everybody. Here's the truth, like it or not …

Getting wealthy takes work.

I'm tired of so-called "gurus" peddling their get rich quick promises that are just not true. These "dream ~~sellers~~ stealers" are getting you excited just to take your money.

The Internet is saturated with offers like "Get my system and you can flip houses all over the country with your cell phone without ever getting out of your pajamas" or "My money machine will show you how to get other people to do all the work, all you do is collect a fat check" and on and on … You get the idea.

Do you believe there's a "magic pill" that will make you instantly wealthy without having to work?

If you do, then you should stop reading right here because there's nothing like that in this book.

Folks, wake up! Stop believing everything you hear. Aren't you tired of all the hype out there? Don't you feel it's just too much? Get realistic.

How many people have you met who did nothing for 40 years and ended up wealthy? Not many.

I know a lot of wealthy people, and many of them got wealthy through investing in real estate. I can tell you that all of them put some effort in their financial well-being.

They planned and mapped their success. They invested in learning and consulting but didn't stop there. They weren't afraid of making mistakes and learning from them.

I believe that most people fail and never make any money in real estate because… **they take the path of least resistance.**

So you may be asking—Is the investing system that I'm about to share with you the "easy" path?

No, it takes work and energy up front to pay your dues to learn and master these techniques (like anything else worth doing in life).

But in the long run it is a thousand times <u>less work</u> than constantly trying the next so-called "easy" way to make money, buying another home-study course just to get disappointed again and again

Staying poor, being underpaid and dependent on that job that you may hate or don't have is <u>so much harder work</u> than mastering the techniques described in this book.

Look, I've been poor, I've been underpaid, and I've been wealthy—and I know which one I'd choose.

My Story

I grew up in Croatia (Southeast Europe—next to Italy and Austria). My hard-working parents raised me believing that if I finished school and worked hard that the rest would take care of itself and life would be good.

But looking at their life, I didn't see how their hard work was paying off. They worked long hours for a company and barely made ends meet. So I just didn't believe that school and work would get me far.

One day, back in September 1981, I was watching with my dad the world title fight between Sugar Ray Leonard and Tomas Hearns. I was only 13 years old. It was an exciting fight, and somehow I decided to try boxing. Long story short, over the next 10 years boxing was my love. With a lot of discipline, I managed to become the champion of my home country, Croatia, 3 times.

It was exhilarating, but in the end I realized that very few boxers make any money, and aside from being a hard way to earn a living, there was also a huge health risk in doing so.

Luckily for me, through all the years of boxing, my parents had been pushing me to study hard, and I was able to maintain good grades. I had something to fall on, at least I thought.

When I finally finished college, I started looking for a job. It was almost impossible to find a job, and even if I did find one, the pay would not allow me to move out of my parents' house for many years.

I was ready to work hard, and my boxing success didn't come without hard work, but I soon realized that hard work was not appreciated in Croatia. You got a job if you had connections or if you bribed someone—both against my ethics and how I was raised. It was a hard and disappointing fact to accept, but the inevitable conclusion was that I was living in the wrong country … work was not valued there.

So the lack of opportunity and the hunger for a better life made me look elsewhere. I traveled to Italy and Germany often, trying to find a job.

And one day I landed the opportunity to move to United States, the greatest country of all. It was definitely a dream come true.

I didn't have much savings, my parents couldn't help me, but I had a car, an old Yugo. I sold it and got myself a ticket to the USA

I still remember the huge excitement. I was sad leaving my parents and friends, but the excitement of going to the greatest country in the world was stronger.

As soon as I landed, I realized what my friends warned me of would actually pose a slight challenge for me … I didn't speak any English. So it was a culture shock. Imagine that!

Long story short, two years after going through school, I learned English and landed my first corporate job. Do you think I was excited? You bet I was! It was an opportunity to work hard and finally make some decent money.

Do you think that I stayed long hours working at the company? You bet I did. I wanted to impress my boss and do a good job. Do you think I may have come in on Saturdays?

Yes, not once, many times. I wanted to bring value to the company. My parents raised me with the notion that hard work pays off—so I didn't spare myself.

Until one day (7 months in the job) the company downsized. Two hundred and fifty of my colleagues and I were laid off, without a warning. I was devastated. It was like all my dreams were lost. I took it emotionally because I just couldn't get over the fact that I had worked so hard for them. What followed during the next few months was …

Stress. Worry.

I couldn't sleep at night, watching TV to late hours. One night I saw a "No Money Down" real estate infomercial. I had no money, so it sounded like something for me J. Out of desperation, I bought the course, and that's how it all started …

Now looking back, that first layoff was a real turning point in my life.

Sometimes things happen for a reason.

(Maybe you've had your own financial setbacks … and maybe it was for a reason too.)

I had to move to another side of the country to find another job, so I could pay my rent.

But I started reading about real estate and soon discovered…

My Discovery

I**ncome is _not_ freedom.** Actively working for income is not going to make me financially secure because that income can suddenly disappear.

I soon realized that even my managers and the senior co-workers who were making twice as much were not financially secure. They were in the same boat as I was. They had more income but also bigger mortgages and bigger car loans. If they were to get laid off, it would hurt them even more.

So making _more_ money was NOT the answer.

I wanted to be in control of my life, and what I learned from reading different books is that ASSETS create passive income. The more I read about it, the more it made sense.

I liked the idea of passive income generated by income-producing _assets_, the income that continuously comes in and pays my bills whether I work or not.

I would guess the same might be the reason why you got interested in real estate. You, like me, probably realize that one day you may not be able or want to show up for work, but your bills will still have to get paid. How are you going to do that?

So you need to own assets—I figured that much, but my problem was—_HOW_?

I realized that the only way to create PASSIVE income that comes in whether you work or not is to _OWN assets_, income-producing assets. Think about it … It IS the only way, isn't it?

But my big question was—_How do I buy assets if I have neither money nor credit?_

At that time, my savings were negative—I was in debt. My credit wasn't bad—it was non-existent (I'd just moved to US). So my question was …

HOW do I buy and own assets?

At the time I didn't know about Unlimited Funding "mechanisms," and I didn't know that it's possible to acquire assets without having credit or big savings.

So I decided to TRY to save as much of my income as possible … and then "one day" I'd be able to buy assets that would produce income.

How many of you have tried saving? And what's the problem with this approach?

It takes TOO LONG! It may take a whole life to save a half a million dollars, and by that time the half a million will not be worth much.

Just think about it—how much can YOU save every month? How soon will you have a few hundred thousand saved? … Life is too short for that, right?

My approach was the same WRONG approach as all my middle-income co-workers had. We all tried to build financial nests by saving "after-tax" dollars and then investing this *leftover* into stocks or mutual funds, which we had neither real understanding nor control of. This is a recipe for disaster.

I'll show you in one of the videos how my mutual fund investments have crashed and left me with loss … not gain. In 5 years, I lost $41,000. Not a good plan for retirement.

Side Note: If you've lost money in the stock market, don't feel alone. I did too and my students, Ivan and Judy, that you'll meet in the Deal Examples section lost $700,000 of their retirement money in the stock market. They were hurting when they implemented the methods you will soon learn. Then they got 20 houses using the method. They are making back their money—and you can too.

Back to our belief about saving and investing using financial planners and advisors …

We all believed our financial planners and advisors who were working for *their* company to make us independent of *our* company. Do you see a problem here? Think about it …

If the financial planners and advisors knew how to build financial freedom, they would have been working for themselves, instead of working for a company selling stocks. Right?

Let me ask you …

Wouldn't you want to be in control of your life instead of giving it to Wall Street?

I made little bit of money in the stock market and I lost a bunch, but I made millions in real estate.

Some of you may have seen the video where I show you $1,404,899.85 in pure profit generated within 12 consecutive months using what I write about here. That is one and a half million dollars in 12 months—a lot of money! I know real estate is the way to go. But it has to be done in a right way.

I taught the principles described in this book to beginner investors, and they were able to generate 6-figure checks on single transactions.

I coached many of my students and helped them build stable real estate businesses that enabled them to replace their jobs (you'll meet some of them in this book very soon). These businesses now generate more income in a single month than their previous annual incomes were. I have no doubt that this book has the power to completely change your financial situation. So keep reading.

When I started, I knew what I needed to have, and I know that you need this too …

You need **CASH FLOW**, **CAPITAL GAINS**, and consequently, you need **INCOME REPLACEMENT**. These are the **BIG 3s** that real estate gives you *(if done properly)*.

Think for a moment … How would your life look if you took care of the BIG 3s?

Would you feel less stressed if you had substantial cash flow coming in every month? Would you worry about retirement if you had big capital gains?

Would you stop thinking at night about your boss or co-workers once you have income replacement? I can tell you from my own experience that it's pretty cool when you "fire" your boss … or "fire" your difficult customers like some of the small business owners who are now my students have done.

You'll soon realize in this book how to utilize real estate and leverage it to its full potential to achieve the BIG 3s without taking any risk and staying in 100% control (unlike with stocks).

Active vs. Passive Income

Active income is the one that you EARN—that you work for, regardless if you work for yourself or someone else.

Active income comes in <u>only</u> when you work. As soon as you stop, the income stops.

Do you know that <u>most</u> real estate investors are earning <u>active</u> income and most stay broke?

They buy, fix, and sell properties. Or they flip properties. That is **active** income.

If you're not sure if that's active income, just ask yourself—will their income stop if they stop buying and fixing houses? The answer is yes—their income will stop.

I don't know if you noticed, but that approach is **not** much different than that of an employee working for a company. In both cases, the money is not working for you, rather you're swapping hours for dollars.

Let me tell you what I discovered …

Over the last few years I was invited to speak at more than 50 different real estate conferences and investment associations, in different cities, all over the country.

I even got nominated as the expert for pre-foreclosures and short-sale investing in front of the **National Real Estate Investor Association**, the organization that governs most real estate investing clubs, covering over 40,000 investors nationwide. Why am I telling you this?

I'm telling you this, so you'll realize that I got exposed to many, many investors out there and what I'm about to share with you has a lot of merit.

Most investors are working way too hard for the money they make. They all look tired and worried how they are going to find that next deal to pay their bills. That's not the "real estate dream" that you have, is it?

They work hard, but they are one setback away from being broke. If that one house or a few houses they may have for sale don't sell quickly, they are in trouble. **Is that the security YOU are looking for?** I don't think so… That is a headache, believe me, you don't want to have.

A wrong business model most investors have is really the primary cause of so much struggling and time-wasting, it's sad. It's the reason why the overwhelming majority of people new to real estate investing will fail in achieving their dreams even if they buy lots of courses, study them religiously, and work extremely hard. They will fail.

Problem #1: The issue is that their business model is based on earning ACTIVE income, and the PASSIVE income component is NOT present at all. In their minds they are waiting for that day when they'll have enough money saved to buy assets and have passive income. Again this is employee-thinking.

I want you to change that thinking and do what my students are doing. For example, you'll meet Rob in later chapters—he quickly put $50,000 in his pocket doing what I will teach you here, and at the same time got $1,762/mo. cash flow for 24 months—all in one deal.

Problem #2: They are monetizing only one component of the wealth-building ability real estate has. They are preoccupied making that first check, so they neglect the other benefits real estate offers, consequently making it even harder to earn that first check.

→ Your focus should be putting $10,000, $20,000, or $30,000 into your pocket ***as soon as possible*** (right?), but you need to REALIZE that it is harder to do that if you neglect the big picture. If you don't leverage ALL the benefits that real estate offers, not only will you never build real wealth, but getting that QUICK CASH will be a lot harder as well.

STOP HERE—Go to **www.MarkoRubel.com/book** and download the **Financial Freedom Matrix**. This is the foundation that I'm describing in the following section. There's also a video describing it—make sure you later watch it. Important information.

Here's my advice—once you download it, frame the Financial Freedom Matrix on your working desk and hang it somewhere where you'll look at it every single day, so you can eternalize the real benefits of investing in real estate. It will prevent you from getting sidetracked in the "guru offers" that will get you nowhere. It will keep you on the right path to profit and wealth.

The 5 Wealth-Building Components of Real Estate

WARNING: This chapter is the simplest to understand, but at the same time it's the most important chapter in this book. It describes the fundamental principle of building wealth with real estate. This chapter reveals the series of facts ignored by most investors and the consequent reason **why** most stay broke. It's simple, but most ignore it, so—pay attention.

Looking back, the title of this chapter should have been: "The Reason Why Most Real Estate Investors Struggle." Every time I teach a seminar or speak as a guest at a real estate conference, I am struck by how almost every attendee is approaching their investing business or starting their investing the wrong way.

Lack of understanding of the fundamental forces behind real estate investing is really the primary cause for so much struggling and time-wasting, it's sad. It's the reason why the majority of people getting into this business will fail. Please, for your own sake, try to understand the deeper meaning behind the fundamentals explained right in this chapter.

* * *

I know that all of you are bombarded daily with emails advertising another "new" moneymaking "secret" strategy or another way to make "big bucks with little work," and all of that is adding to your confusion. You probably don't know if you should focus on wholesaling or flipping houses; or one day you think rehabs are the way to go, another day it's land-lording, or should you do short sales or invest in tax liens? ... Confusing, isn't it?

Here's the good news—it will all be cleared up for you right here in this chapter. You'll have the litmus test for which strategy is worth your time and which isn't.

The 5 wealth-building components of real estate (that I also call leverage points) described here are the measure of the potency of a certain real estate investing strategy. It is how you figure out which investing strategy is the right way to go and which is not. So the next time you hear about that "new" strategy, you just need to run it against these 5 components, look if that strategy leverages all 5, and then you'll know if it's the right way or not.

That's why I advise you to read this chapter as many times as necessary to remember it.

Let's start ... You've heard many times the saying, *"More millionaires are made by real estate than by any other means,"* or *"Real estate is the fastest vehicle to wealth,"* etc. I've heard the same many times and just recently got reminded of the validity of it again when I was reading the Forbes list of the richest people in the world and their biographies. Can you believe that many of them made their first million in real estate? That's right.

So have you ever asked yourself—why is the potential of real estate so great? Why is investing in real estate so powerful?

Here's why—it's because real estate investing has the following 5 wealth-building components that no other investment has:

1. **CASH FLOW**—a properly structured real estate deal will provide monthly cash flow. If you have a tenant or a tenant/buyer or a "no-qual" buyer* in the property who is paying you, for example, $2,000 each month, and your financing obligation including taxes and insurance (PITI) is $1,500/mo., then your cash flow is $500. That cash flow is the type of income you desire—the passive income that comes in whether you work or not. SIDE NOTE: You will soon learn how to have cash flow without having tenants.

    A "no-qual" buyer is, as you will learn later, the buyer that you put in the house on a "seller-financed" arrangement where you act as a bank, and he/she is paying you.

2. **CAPITAL GAINS**—if you sell a property for more than you paid for it, you will realize capital gain. That gain is your profit. If the gain is realized within 12 months, in other words, if you purchased and sold a property within 12 months, your gain will be taxed as "ordinary income." If you kept the property for more than 12 months, then you would pay less in taxes because you would qualify for "capital gain" tax rates. Paying less in taxes means that you will keep more in your pocket, and that is what we all want, isn't it? In the end, it's not how much you make but rather how much you keep—remember that.

3. **EQUITY BUILD-UP DUE TO PRINCIPAL REDUCTION**—this is one of the wealth-building features of real estate that no other investment has. With real estate, you can have someone else paying down your loan and building equity for you. Your tenant or your "no-qual" buyer went to school for years and is now going to work every single day, just to give a big part of their paycheck to YOU, month after month. The more people you have doing that—giving you their money, in essence working for you, the faster you'll get wealthy.

4. **EQUITY BUILDUP DUE TO APPRECIATION**—unlike other assets, where most depreciate and lose value, real estate always goes up in value. Sure there are cycles that one has to pay attention to, but over the longer term, it always goes up in value. And this is where "leverage" comes to play. For example, if you are controlling a piece of property worth $200,000 using $1,000 as a down payment, when that property appreciates 10% a year, it means that your net worth increases by $20,000, which is a 2,000% increase in your investment—where else can you get that kind of return? You're right   nowhere.

SIDE NOTE: You will soon learn that it is possible with only a $1,000 down payment you can buy a $200,000 property and do it without qualifying for a bank loan. That's the most exciting part. Stay tuned! And by the way, using the strategy you will soon learn about, you don't need appreciation to get wealthy.

5. **TAX SAVINGS DUE TO DEPRECIATION**—IRS code 167 allows you to take a tax deduction annually for wear and tear, deterioration, or obsolescence of a property. So even though properties generally go up in value, the IRS allows you to take a paper loss, an income tax deduction each year. For residential properties, the depreciation schedule is 27.5 years. You can depreciate only the structure, not the land. For example, if the structure is worth $275,000, you will have $10,000 each year in paper loss that you can use to offset the income from that property. In other words, by owning an income-producing property, you are reducing your tax liability and saving money. The result is—you keep more—and that's our goal.

Now about the 5 components I've described, let me ask you the same question in two different ways to make sure you clearly understand this important point:

1. Do you think an investment strategy that leverages all 5 components described will make you more money faster than a strategy that leverages only one component? The answer is YES because your profit will come from 5 different sides.

*2. **How many of you would like to do work once and get paid five times?** How many of you feel that you'd get ahead faster if you get paid five times, but you do the work only once?*

That is the point here and the clue to why certain real estate strategies clear faster paths to your first million than other strategies. Which ones should you focus on? It will be very clear to you right here.

Let's compare the benefits of the *"buying-selling-flipping"* business model that is overwhelmingly preached to investors vs. the *"ownership"* business model.

Wealth Building Component of Real Estate	Wholesaling Flip, or Fix & Flip	Ownership
1. CASH FLOW	✗ Not Present	✓ YES
2. CAPITAL GAINS Buy Low - Sell for Profit	✓ YES, but... Taxed as Ordinary Income	✓ YES
3. EQUITY BUILD-UP Due to Loan Paydown	✗ Not Present	✓ YES
4. EQUITY BUILD-UP Due to Appreciation	✗ Not Present	✓ YES
5. TAX SAVINGS Depreciation - IRS 167	✗ Not Present	✓ YES

As you can see in the table above, when you Flip or Fix-&-Flip, you don't own the property, so you get <u>no</u> cash flow, no principal reduction, no appreciation and no tax savings. Who gets those benefits? The new owner gets them, **not you**.

It is clear that the only way to leverage ALL the wealth-building components is through OWNERSHIP, so obviously building wealth by <u>owning</u> real estate is a lot FASTER than buy-fix-sell or flipping properties.

You just need to learn how to OWN without taking risk or dealing with tenants.

NOTE: The "ownership" business model that you'll learn about here is not only a faster way to wealth, but it is ALSO a faster way to **quick CASH,** without risk or hassles.

In Section 3, we will dig deeper into exploring different investing strategies and how they compare against the above table. However, I decided not to do it here, so you can get to our discovery quicker. I know some of you might be impatient.

The Best Business Model— Your First Million

Let me first introduce you to the FASTEST and surest way to your first MILLION—the big picture; and then we'll address how to get to that quick cash in the next few weeks.

NOTE: You will meet Ivan and Judy, Lester, Bill and Elaine, and others in Section 2 who used the strategies explained in this book to create net worth in excess of a million dollars, without ever going to a bank and qualifying for a loan. And they did it over a few years, not over a decade. You will see some of their deals, and I suggest you go to **www.Markorubel.com/book** to watch the video interviews I conducted just for the readers of this book—for you.

KEEP IN MIND: This chapter is about the big picture, not the "how to." The "how to" will be discussed in subsequent chapters. You need to understand the big picture first in order to understand the ins and outs of the strategy. Don't rush through this chapter.

With this business model, the path to getting wealthy and the path to getting quick cash are the SAME.

In my initial three years in the business, I attended every possible seminar that was available at the time. I'd done over 20 deals and tried almost every strategy.

AND THEN … one deal made me more money within 30 days than all of the other deals I'd done up to that time. I'll tell you about it later on …

I also raked up my credit cards by buying get rich quick programs and seminars that never worked … Some of you may know the feeling. That's why you should pay attention here.

Here's what I discovered to be the BEST business model, the quickest and surest way not only to your first check but to build a million dollar net worth in real estate as well. I called it the **Niche-2Wealth** business model, and here's its ultimate goal.

Before I start, let me ask you to hold your questions until the next chapter. Try to focus on the end result here without thinking about HOW to do this. Please open your mind without thinking about how to do it. I'll answer that in the next chapter.

Imagine that there was a way for you to go out and acquire **25** properties in the next year. Let's say these are single-family houses worth **$200,000** each.

If the median home price in your area is $400,000, then you'll need only 12 properties to achieve the same goal. If the median is only $100,000, then you'll need twice as many, which again is very feasible since lower priced markets are easier to deal with.

If you wonder how you would buy that many houses without using your cash or credit … just know for now that it is possible using the Unlimited Funding methods I'll explain later—but please hold your questions until the next section. It's important that you get the big picture.

Now back to our plan… Let's own 25 houses worth $200,000 each …

Let's say you paid **$160,000** for each property. That's only a 20% discount, which is very realistic and achievable. By the way, after I train you, you will never again pay full-price for real estate like a rookie amateur investor. You'll know how to buy cheap.

Then let's say you put in each property someone who will pay you **$400** above your monthly payment. I'll explain later on how to do that without dealing with tenants (and problems).

And for now, keep in mind that this cash flow is achievable anywhere in the country—we are not talking about rental properties here. I'll explain later.

So this $400, in our example, is your **cash flow**—passive income from day one.

On a $160,000 loan, about **$200** from each mortgage payment will go towards the principal reduction or loan pay-down.

Let's summarize:

25 x $200,000 = $5,000,000 This is the value of your real estate portfolio.

25 x ($200K–160K) = $1,000,000 Your NET worth (your equity).

25 x 12 mo. x $200 principal reduction = $60,000 This is <u>additional</u> equity after 1y.

25 x 12 mo. x $400 cash flow = $120,000 Yearly passive income.

After one year, your NET WORTH (including cash flow) is $1,180,000.

Note: We didn't factor in any appreciation.

* * * * * **SIDE NOTE:** In the next section, you will meet students who achieved very close outcomes to the above numbers and in certain aspects exceeded them within 2–3 years, without ever qualifying for a bank loan or dealing with tenants.

How many of you would have less stress if you had … $120,000 every year coming in, whether you work or not, in PASSIVE income, <u>most</u> of which would be tax-free (staying in your pocket) due to depreciation (IRS code 167)?

Would you feel more secure if you had a net worth of over $1M?

Would it make you feel better knowing that someone else is paying down your loan and increasing your net worth by $60,000+ every year?

If you answered YES to the above questions AND if you desire to make some quick cash (in the next 30 days), then this book will change everything.

It will show you how to create wealth and how to get *"income replacement" money* quicker than using any other investing strategy.

Back to our example: You are making $120K in cash flow and $60K in loan pay-down every year. This is $180,000 without counting any appreciation.

What about appreciation?

Before we talk about appreciation, let me make sure that you understand that with this business model that I'm about to introduce, you do NOT need any appreciation in order to profit.

As you see from the above, we realized our profit by buying below market and selling for top price, all the while keeping control of the property and collecting a nice cash flow.

So we don't need appreciation to create wealth with this model, but when appreciation happens, we will profit even more.

Appreciation is something that comes and goes because real estate is cyclical. It goes up and goes down. Don't listen to gurus who make you think that real estate will never go up just to sell you their short-sale course. Or those who tell you to buy rentals making you believe that appreciation is here to stay for a longtime because it isn't.

Waiting for appreciation to kick in in your area is not a good reason for you to postpone implementing this strategy because as you are realizing, appreciation is not needed to profit. However, if you're lucky to be starting now in an area that is appreciating, you will make even more money.

Let's assume we'll never see appreciation at the double-digit rates as back in 2004–2006. Let's use the historic rate of 6.5% that can make you super wealthy. Let's look …

How much wealthier are you getting each year due to appreciation in the above example?

Let's take an average appreciation of 6.5% …

Your real estate portfolio value of $5M x 6.5% = $325,000 Wow!

This means that every year your net worth grows by $325,000 without your doing anything … without your having to save … without your working overtime!

So at the historic rate of 6.5% your net worth after **one year** is **$1,385,000**:

25 x ($200K–160K) = $1,000,000 plus
$60,000 of principal reduction, plus
$325,000 due to appreciation …

In addition, you made $120K in cash flow … all of it after 12 months of acquiring the properties.

After **2 years** your net worth is **$1,770,000** …

$1,385,000 from the first year, plus an additional $385,000 of appreciation and loan pay-down for the second year. That is a total of **$1,770,000** after the second year, and you've made so far $240,000 in <u>additional</u> cash flow.

These profits become even bigger if you continue to acquire properties beyond the initial 25. And there is not a single reason why you wouldn't.

After **3 years** … your net worth is **$2,155,000**, and you've made **$360,000** in additional cash flow, assuming you never bought any more properties.

Can you envision yourself with a net worth of over $2,000,000?

Imagine how great you would feel with a net worth of 2 million dollars.

Now for many of you this is unimaginable. I know how you feel reading this number.

I know what you may be thinking, "It's impossible, it can't happen to me."

I never thought it could happen to me either … Not long ago when I was moving, I found an old notebook listing my goals from 1998. I was just starting in real estate, and I wrote down my goal for the end of year 2000 as having 6 properties. This was a huge goal at the time.

What really happened? By the end of year 2000, I ended up having more than 20 properties and a nice cash flow. It feels great when you exceed your goals… so think big… you can do it too! It is absolutely possible.

And with the correct system and the right approach, it will be a lot easier than you may think now.

The hardest thing in this whole plan is getting that FIRST property, then the second one is a little easier, the third one a lot easier, and after that it is sooooo EASY.

Imagine that feeling of knowing that you're set and your family is secure, knowing that all of your bills are taken care of and your nest is growing on its own.

Knowing that you will NEVER again depend on getting a job, that your kid's college is paid for, that your retirement is on the horizon … and that you can finally start planning and fulfilling your desires *instead* of just dreaming about them …

It's hard to even describe in words how GREAT you'll feel … Freedom, excitement!

Life feels different when you are able to do whatever you want to do. If you noticed, I'm already getting excited for you.

As I said before … I've been poor, I've been underpaid, and I've been wealthy—and I know which one I'd choose every single time. Are you with me?

Within the next few months of reading this book and attending my webinars and live trainings, you will be on your way to replacing your current income. Reading this book is your first step, so make sure you read to its end.

When your real estate business is making you more money than your current job, you'll have the freedom of deciding if you still want to keep that job or not.

And in just a few short years, you will build a multimillion-dollar net worth, using my Niche2Wealth business model, giving you the ultimate freedom.

For now, let's focus on reading this book and understanding

the concept. We are still at the big picture moving towards an understanding of the strategy ... so be patient, you're just a few pages away. I'll explain what the Niche2Wealth business model is and how it works.

It's important to understand that with the Niche2Wealth business model, the paths to quick cash and to long-term wealth **coincide**, as I already mentioned.

Let's summarize the big picture (the long-term wealth picture) once again ...

Because you will be leveraging all the wealth-building components of real estate, your net worth will grow exponentially faster as described in this section.

This is called **power of leverage**. And real estate is the only investment vehicle that allows this kind of fast wealth-building, but only if done the right way.

Let's look at the numbers one more time.

Your yearly gain is $60K as loan pay-down, $120K in cash flow, and $385K in appreciation. That's a total of **$565,000** per year without doing any active work.

Here's something important to realize if you are a rehabber or thinking about getting into fix-and-flip investing.

My question for you is—how many properties do you need to REHAB to make this kind of income in one year? The answer is **too many**.

How many do you need to FLIP? The answer is **way too many**.

If an average profit per wholesaling transaction is $3,000 to $6,000, you would need to flip way over 100 properties EVERY year to catch up with the leverage described above.

The fact is you will never catch up with the leverage using active income activities. This is why most Investors stay poor. They can NEVER catch up.

Think about it—how are you going to catch up actively doing the business yourself (fixing, flipping, managing contractors, etc.) when in my business model in the previous example I have

25 people who are working their jobs and giving me a big part of their income every month? Catching up is impossible.

Would you feel you missed the boat if the prices doubled and you didn't own any real estate? This is exactly what will happen if you continue doing what you're doing, and that is either doing nothing or doing it the wrong way (wholesaling or fix-and-flip).

There's another IMPORTANT advantage of this business model ...

Here's <u>something important you need to keep in mind:</u>

What do you think? Is it easier to buy properties at 20% below their value (below market) or is it easier to buy them at 40% below their value?

Let me ask you the other way—Is it easier to get a seller to accept a small discount or to get them to take a big hit?

Obviously, it's a lot easier to buy 25 properties at a **20%** discount (which is all you need for our formula to work) than flip 100 properties that you have to put under contract at a **30–40%** discount or more in order for wholesaling to work.

Let me make sure you understand this. To get a seller to take a 20% discount, the seller doesn't need to be desperate.

If that same seller sold their house using a real estate agent, after paying a 6% real estate commission, 2–3% in closing costs, and a 2–3% holding cost, they would net only 5–10% more than what they would net by selling to you at a 20% discount. What does this mean?

It means that my approach will work with **more** sellers out there because the 20% discount, we need for our formula to work doesn't require very motivated or desperate sellers. So the more sellers you have to work with, the **easier** it gets and the faster you make your money.

This is not the case with other real estate formulas, like wholesaling, rehabbing, short-sale flips, etc. Those strategies require a lot bigger discounts at a minimum of 30–40% to create profits.

It should be obvious that not every seller will give you a 30–

40% discount, so you'll have to find a very motivated, if not a desperate, seller to make those strategies work. This means <u>more</u> marketing, <u>more</u> appointments, <u>more</u> work, and <u>fewer</u> opportunities.

Would you prefer to work smart instead of hard?

As with everything, there's a short way to get wealthy and a long way—which one do you prefer?

The above-mentioned Niche2Wealth business model is the shortest way, and it should be THE model if you truly want to get wealthy.

That's why I call it Niche2Wealth. I'll explain more about it later on.

I'm not saying you should never do any wholesaling or short sales. I do them till this day, and they make me money.

What I am saying is that those strategies should be only a part of your game, but NOT your main game because they represent a SLOW way to wealth, as they don't leverage all 5 of the wealth-building components of real estate from the previous chapter.

There are deals that will come your way as a result of your marketing or referrals that plainly do not meet our Niche2Wealth business model. In order to monetize those deals, we'll either wholesale them, sometimes short-sale them, or we'll pass.

For example, a motivated seller calls me and has a house that needs major repairs. Since I am not in the rehab business (and you shouldn't be either because it's too hard), I will attempt to contract the property with a goal to wholesale it. Why not make some money from the seller who already called, right?

So there's nothing wrong with wholesaling when you use it for the deals that fall in your lap but don't meet our criteria. That's why I developed the special tool called Money Finder that enables my students to find cash buyers and private lenders in their areas for deals that don't meet our criteria. You'll learn about that tool later.

However, the BIG mistake is trying to make wholesaling your main strategy or the strategy to start because it will not make you rich and it is not the easiest way to your first deal either. And that's why it should not be the first thing you focus on. As I said …

Those "side" strategies should definitely be part of your game, but **not** your main game.

Now before you go to the next page, please for your own sake … what we covered above is super important, so go back and review this section again if you don't understand the numbers and the power behind them.

You need to understand the above otherwise what's coming will confuse you even more. So go ahead and review this section one more time (if needed). This book is not intended to be just read; it needs to be studied if you want to get the most out of it.

For the remainder of this book I'll try to answer all of your questions and concerns, and give you extensive answers on these 3 important questions:

1. How do you buy quality real estate at below market prices, with favorable financing, without taking risk, regardless of your situation or experience?
2. How do you put $10,000 or more into your bank account in the next 30 days?
3. How do you put "residents" into your homes that will pay you a lot more per month than a tenant, take care of the repairs, and never ask for anything?

3 Ways to Buy & Own Real Estate

When I was planning to write this book, I realized that many of you got your mind polluted (for lack of better word) with all the marketing (emails, ads, etc.) that comes your way every day from so-called gurus, who are in fact the information marketers making money selling get rich programs.

They create, promote, and sell programs that will appeal to people and therefore, sell well but not necessarily make money for people. Many of the programs promote strategies that are plainly not feasible, may sound good, but don't work.

That pollution may distort or even block you from understanding this business and seeing where the real wealth is.

You now know that the only way to build real wealth with real estate is to OWN the property because OWNERSHIP is the only way to leverage all 5 wealth-building components of real estate.

So let me ask you a very basic question that determines EVERYTHING …

How can you buy and own real estate?

Take a moment and think about it … HOW?

Let me ask you the same question in a different way …

You understand and learned in the previous chapter that in order to build wealth you need to own real estate, but **how do you buy it** and how do you fund it? There are not that many options.

There are ONLY 3 ways to buy real estate:

1. Using Your CASH

You can use your savings to pay for property. Most people don't have hundreds of thousands of dollars in their bank accounts, but even if you do, how many properties can you buy? Not 10 or 20 … And why would you risk your savings anyway?

2. Using Your CREDIT

You can go to a bank and get a loan, but that requires good credit and a sizable down payment. Let's say that you have both … The required down payment will limit you to only a few deals, plus the high investor interest rates will make it impossible to cash flow.

On top of it, the banks will require a personal guarantee making this VERY risky. I don't know if you realize it, but by signing and personally guaranteeing the loan, you are putting in jeopardy everything you own … Do you realize that you are risking your position in life?

Why would you ever do that?

If something goes wrong and you can't cover those payments, the bank will foreclose and by doing so they'll most likely incur a loss. By your guaranteeing that loan, you gave them the right to go after you for recovering their loss, ultimately pushing <u>you</u> into bankruptcy!

Not only that, they can get a deficiency judgment against you, but the IRS considers "forgiveness of debt" as income to you and sends you the 1099. So not only have you lost the property and any money you used as a down payment, but you end up with a judgment against you and a big tax bill. I'm not sure you want to take that risk.

I can't even begin to describe how many people I've met in my 20-year real estate career that lost everything by personally guaranteeing loans.

Why would you ever do that if you don't have to?
REMEMBER—you should NEVER do this.

Side Note 1: Some of you may be thinking that the way to go is to use hard-money lenders. <u>Absolutely not.</u>

First of all, the financing terms make it impossible to buy and keep properties. It's short-term financing intended for rehabs. The interest rates are way too high to allow properties to cash flow.

Plus many will also require a personal guarantee. Watch out! These lenders are small companies and will be a lot more aggressive in going after you in case of default.

Side Note 2: Some of you may be thinking that you can get cash from private lenders. That is feasible for a few properties, but not for 20 and not over a <u>longer</u> term of 3 years or more, which you need in order to build massive wealth.

Private lenders are regular people like you and me, and most of them don't want to lock in and freeze their savings for many years. Plus, you will need to show them your <u>track record</u> in order to get their money, which is not possible if you're just starting.

Borrowing small amounts from private lenders is easy, but that's not what we are talking about here. We are talking about financing the whole purchase price and doing it for the long-term—a minimum 5 years. The problem, as said above, is that people don't want to give up their liquidity for that long. Short-term private loans yes, but the long-term is super hard.

In my long real estate career, I've met only a few who were able to put together multiple lenders and buy tens of properties. Unfortunately, one ended up in a jail for security violations, etc.

So if getting your own bank loan or using your cash is not an option, what do you do?

We are left with THE <u>ONLY WAY</u> TO BUY REAL ESTATE, and that is…

3. Using Other People's Credit

Dear reader, this is the ONLY smart way to buy properties without taking risk.

It is the foundation of our Unlimited Funding Program. I'll dedicate the next few chapters to explaining it.

But before we continue, think about it. **Do YOU know any other way to buy real estate except the above 3?**

- → *Is there ANY other way than explained above?* There is NO other way.
- → *Do you understand why using your cash is not an option?*
- → *Do you understand why signing for a bank loan is risky?*
- → *Do you understand why private lenders will not lock hundreds of thousands of their dollars in your property for many years?*

In every live seminar I do, and I do 5 every year, I ask the audience of 200–400 people these same questions—no one has ever come up with a fourth way. So obviously there's no other way, except the Unlimited Funding Program. Let's continue.

Unlimited Funding Mechanism

If I Can Show You How to Acquire Ownership and Build Wealth, <u>**WITHOUT Going to Banks and Using Your Credit, and WITHOUT Dealing With Tenants**</u>, How Many of You Would Follow My Advice?

From the previous chapter you realized that there are **only 3 ways** to buy properties, and out of those 3 ways, the first 2 (using cash and credit) are way <u>too risky</u> and have limitations that make it impossible to build real wealth.

You've also learned that ownership is the key to passive income and to real wealth. So the best way to acquire ownership is using other people's credit (3). We do that by using a set of strategies that I have named the Unlimited Funding Program.

It is a catchy name for a set of strategies where you basically buy the property "subject to" the existing loan originated by the seller. So in essence, we use the existing loan that was originated and guaranteed by the seller. We get the ownership via deed and simply continue making payments on that existing loan. This way we don't need to qualify for a loan, our credit doesn't matter, and we are **not** taking the risk by guaranteeing that loan.

Sounds confusing? Don't worry, the whole chapter is dedicated to explaining it.

There is an unlimited number of properties out there that already have loans on them, thus the name "unlimited." The reality is the number of properties you can buy this way is limited only to the number of motivated sellers you can find that have some equity. You are not limited by your credit, your employment, your tax returns, you debt-to-income ratio, etc.

You are not limited with your credit or your income because there's no bank qualifying and no one will ever ask you to provide that informtion.

You are also not limited by the cash you have because many of these deals are $0 down and don't require any down payment.

In addition, the seller's loan was originated as an "owner occupied" loan, and these loans in general have a lot <u>lower interest rates</u> than "investor" originated loans.

So even if you had the down payment and wanted to take the risk of getting the loan yourself *(the second way explained previously)*, you would <u>never</u> be able to get such low interest rates being an investor. Plus, you would not be able to get an <u>unlimited</u> number of loans.

This method doesn't require that the loan be assumable, as I'll explain.

In summary, here are the **advantages** of using the existing loan originated by the seller:

1. You don't need a down payment.
2. You don't need your credit.
3. You don't need to qualify.
4. You don't personally guarantee it.
5. There's NO risk to your credit/assets.
6. The interest rates are LOW.
7. The supply is UNLIMITED.

Once you learn how this works, you will realize that this is <u>THE ONLY WAY</u> to invest in real estate. *How else can you possibly buy without taking on the risk?*

It is the only way where you, or anyone, regardless of your situation, can buy an <u>unlimited</u> number of properties, thus the name unlimited funding. As a side note, you'll hear some gurus refer to "unlimited funding" when talking about hard-money lenders or private lenders, but don't get confused. This is different. It is about using the existing financing.

Now let me further explain how it works since using the existing loan is the important component of our Niche2Wealth business model.

Acquiring Ownership Using Unlimited Funding

I know you may be wondering how all this works. Let me tell you, it is so simple that you will be confused by how simple it is. Some people can't even understand it because they are looking for a more complex solution when, in fact, it is so simple that it can be explained in 10 sentences or less like here below.

All you do is get the DEED. When a title company (or an escrow company or a closing attorney) prepares the deed as part of the regular closing and once that deed is notarized by the seller and recorded in the county recorder's office, you are the OWNER.

So once that DEED lists you as the Grantee (the buyer on the deed) and the Grantor (seller) has signed it (and notarized it), you are the owner. When you take that deed to your local county recorder's office and record it, you tell the whole world that you are the new owner.

It does not matter how you paid for that ownership, what the consideration was, where the money came from, if any, none of it matters with respect to ownership... if the seller was willing to give you the deed, then you own it.

Now at this point, you really don't need to consider how all this is done because a closing attorney or a title company agent will do it all for you. But let me further explain this "subject to"-technique in a different way using a divorce example.

What Divorce Can Teach You About "Subject To"

Let's take this example: A young couple found a house they liked and wanted to buy. Since the wife was the only one working at the time, her credit was used to qualify for the loan and her name was the only name on the loan. The deed was recorded in her name only, and she was the one who signed the lien that got recorded to secure the lender. That lien is called Deed of Trust in some states, and Mortgage in the others. In many states, the property is a community property, so the other spouse "owns" half of it anyway.

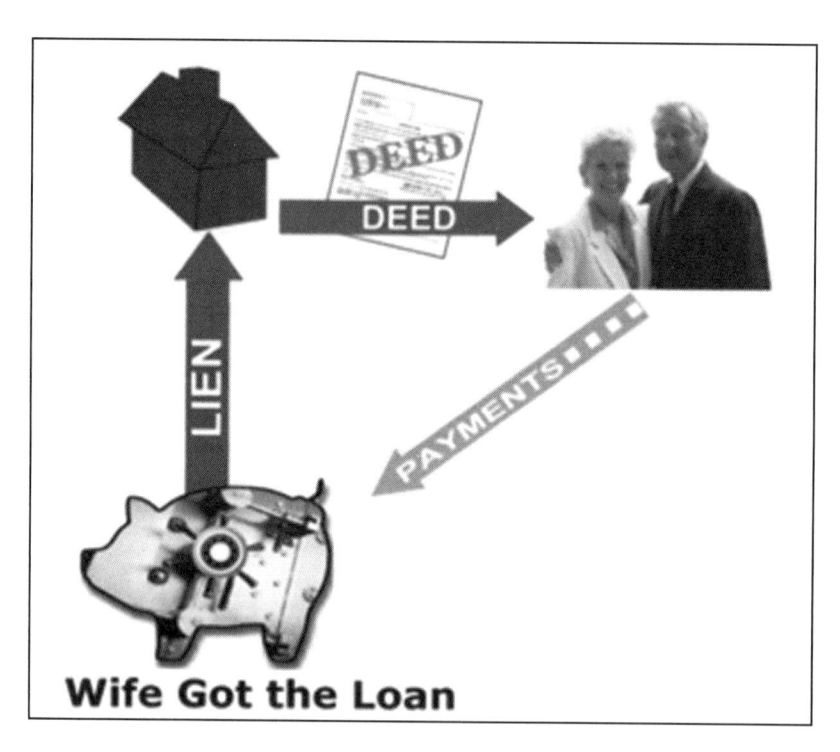

Wife Got the Loan

Now, some years later, unfortunately they are going through divorce. Let's say the wife didn't want to deal with the house, and after an amicable divorce, the husband John got the house. She signed over the deed and moved on, as shown in the diagram below:

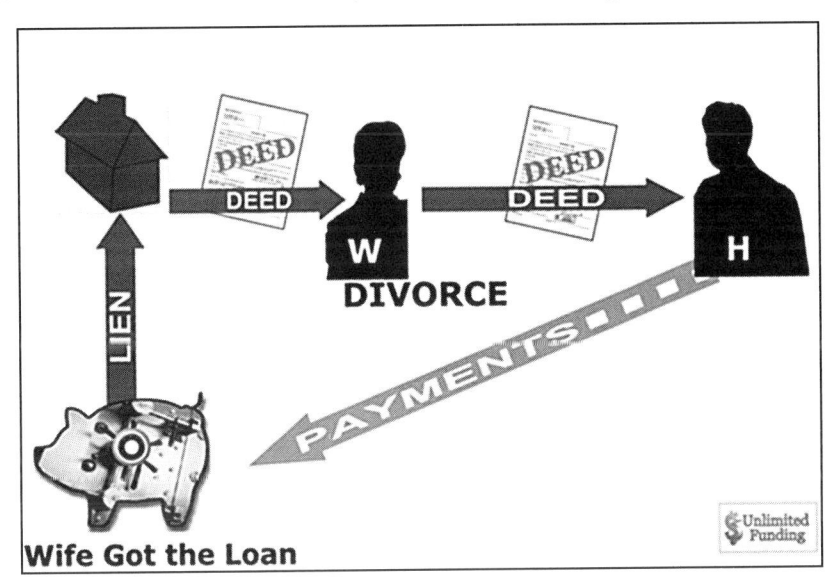

Wife Got the Loan

Simple and straightforward, right? So what about the loan? As you can see in the above diagram, the loan stays where it was. The bank is still secured and has the lien against the property in the same initial position, nothing changed.

NOTE: You didn't get the house free and clear because that first lien is still there. Believe it or not, I had some sellers ask me that—if they give me the deed, will I own the house free and clear with all the equity? The answer is no because I'd get the deed "subject to" any debt that's currently against it. By changing ownership, you can't eliminate the liens that are recorded against a property.

Back to this example: John owns the house while the wife's name is still on the loan. Of course, he is making the payments, but he does not have his credit at risk nor is he liable for the loan (while the wife still gets her loan paid with the bank). In essence, John owns the house without signing for a loan. How often does this happen? All the time.

Why would the wife agree to leaving her loan there? Maybe she doesn't want to deal with the house, but the husband doesn't have a good credit to refinance with his own loan. So lack of other choices makes her do it.

So now, let's apply the same principle to a seller in foreclosure (forget the divorce example). In this case you're the investor, and this is your first deal. You sent out some postcards or gave out a bunch of business cards and got a call from a seller in foreclosure. After visiting their house and explaining the process, they agreed to sell you their house "subject to" their existing loan. Here's how it works:

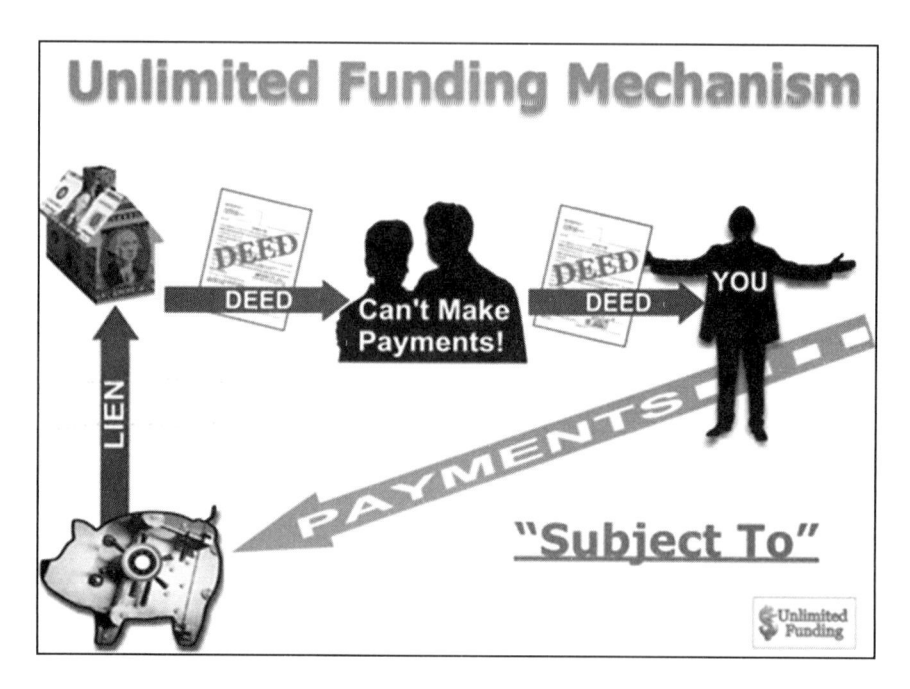

At the closing company, the closing agent or the closing attorney will prepare the deed with you or your company as a buyer. They will also prepare the closing statements and disclosures. After you and your seller sign all the paperwork, the deed gets recorded and you're the new owner. As you can see in the diagram above, the seller got the deed when they purchased the house, then got in financial trouble, and later on deeded the house to you. Now you can move in the house and continue to make the payments on that loan. Sure, you will have to first stop foreclosure by bringing the loan current, that is, by sending the back payments to the lender (also called "reinstating" the loan), and this can also be done as part of the closing by the closing company. *I included a real deal case study (Kevin's deal) at the end of this section that demonstrates the reinstatement process.*

If you don't want to move in yourself, then you will either sell the house to a buyer who gets a new loan, which pays off the existing loan and cashes you out, or you can put in the house a tenant who then makes payments to you and you make payments to the lender. Now, I do not suggest you have tenants—that's why I'll teach you a third way, which is the best way, in the Niche2Wealth section. You'll be able to have someone make those payments without your worrying about repairs and late night calls. All you do is collect the cash flow, and after a few nice deals your monthly cash flow replaces your monthly salary.

Now you probably have some questions, but hold them for later … For **now** just understand that I've purchased over a hundred houses this way, and this principle, this technique made me a millionaire. Some things you won't understand as of yet, which is normal. There will be more **specifics** later, but this is the starting point. What you do need to understand now is that this IS the only way to BYPASS THE LENDERS and get to financial freedom without qualifying and without dealing with hard-money lenders either.

To summarize, with unlimited funding, or call it "subject to," you get the deed, and the existing loan stays where it is. In other words, when you get the deed, you get it with any and all encumbrances (debt) that are owed against that property, including the first mortgage. That's why it's called getting the deed (or buying) "subject to" what's owed against it.

NOTE: Because of the fact that you're getting the deed "subject to" what's owed against the property, you need to always get the title search done by your closing company, so you know what it is that you're buying "subject to." The title search will list all the debt or liens of record, so you know if you want or don't want the property.

With this type of transaction, in many cases the seller does not get any proceeds from the sale, but they get relief from the payments. Sometimes there are payments that need to be caught up (like in the example above), and many times there's no money needed because the loan is current.

The sellers get the house sold, and they can move on with their lives. And you buy the property without using any money and without ever talking to a bank or a lender, or taking any risk.

Why would a seller do that? Why would they trust you?

Sure, if you don't make the payments after you get the deed, the seller is in trouble. The lender will report any late payments on the seller's credit, even though the house is yours now. Why? Because the seller is the one who originated the loan and the one who is personally guaranteeing it. That's why you should never promise that you'll make payments if you think you will not. We'll talk about that in later sections. Let's cover WHY sellers still agree to this type of sale even though it has some risk for them.

In the above example, they will do it to avoid losing the house to foreclosure. This is truly a win-win for you and for them. Here's why—if they end up in foreclosure, (1) their credit is damaged for 7 years; (2) they could be liable for lender's losses; (3) they could be taxed on that loss because the IRS calls it "forgiveness of debt"; (4) they may get evicted if they don't leave the house in time, etc. But if you buy their house, all 4 of these terrible consequences are eliminated. They will not be embarrassed in front of their neighbors, and they'll move without stress. Plus, when you catch up their payments and continue making them on time, not only is the foreclosure stopped, but the lender will report to their credit bureau that they caught the payments and are now making them on time, (5) which will in fact improve their credit.

So why do they trust you? They do because the risk of your not making payments is a lot smaller than the imminent risk of losing the house to foreclosure. And you will soon learn why it is easy to cover their payments and that smart investors never miss seller's payments. Let me tell you, in all these years of doing this business I have NEVER missed a seller's payment or been late on one. It is really a win-win when you keep your side of the bargain.

So you can see that by your getting involved, the seller wins too. As a matter of fact, the outcome for the seller is immensely better than without your getting involved. I feel good when I buy and profit with foreclosure deals because I really help those sellers along and they are very grateful for my doing it.

Now keep in mind, there are many other motivations the sellers out there have, besides foreclosure. When you, as an investor, can identify their problem (their pain) no matter what it is and if their selling the house to you solves that problem, they will do it. Why? Because **their need to get rid of that pain is greater than their fear of your not making those payments**, as simply stated as that.

Here's an example of an attorney who sold a house "subject to" for $10 to my coaching client. Why did the attorney trust my student? Read below to find out ...

x   x   x

Deal Case Study – Anto and the $10 Attorney House

Anto attended one of our live seminars, and during the break on first day, he came up to me asking to apply to our coaching program. After reviewing his application, I accepted him in our program a few days later.

And I was not wrong; he was an action taker, and he implemented my teachings right away.

The first step for him was to meet a few local real estate agents and obtain a list of expired listings (these are listings that didn't sell). Using the special positioning that I teach which creates a win-win relationship with agents, he was able to get a few agents who were willing to provide him with a fresh list of the listings that expired each week. By the way, any time when you're mailing to expired listings, it is important to mail to them the same week they expire, otherwise your response goes down due to the fact that the sellers end up relisting the house.

As a result of one of the mailings, a seller called. He was an attorney who'd purchased another house in a town 80 miles away and had been making payments on his old house for quite some time, which created a financial burden for him. The house was in nice condition too. Here's picture from the front.

This deal was signed in two meetings. At the first meeting the seller showed the house to Anto. The goal at that meeting was for Anto to figure out the seller's "pain." After analyzing the deal with his coach (one of my partners), he called the seller back and they met again. I suggest you watch the short 10-minute video where Anto talks about that seller and the process. Here is the relevant part of the purchase agreement:

> **2. PURCHASE PRICE.** Buyer to pay the purchase price as follows (check all that applies):
>
> ☑ **EARNEST DEPOSIT**, receipt of which is hereby acknowledged in the sum of .... $ 10.00
>
> ☐ **CASH DOWN PAYMENT** at closing in the amount .... $_____
>
> ☑ **TAKE TITLE SUBJECT TO AN EXISTING FIRST TRUST DEED NOTE**
> held by _Bank of America_ with an approximate unpaid amount of .... $ 101,000
> payable $ _963.00_ monthly until paid, including interest not exceeding _5.25_ %.
>
> ☐ **TAKE TITLE SUBJECT TO AN EXISTING SECOND TRUST DEED NOTE**
> held by _____ with an approximate unpaid amount of .... $_____
> payable $_____ monthly until paid, including interest not exceeding ____%.
>
> ☐ **A PROMISSORY NOTE** in the principal amount of .... $_____
> For the Terms of the Note, see paragraph 11 below.
>
> **TOTAL PURCHASE PRICE IS THE AMOUNT OF** .... $ 101,000

As you can see, this was a purchase "subject to" the first loan held by Bank of America with a principal balance remaining of $101,000. If you look carefully at the above cutout from the original purchase agreement, you will notice that Anto made a small mistake—the purchase price should have been $101,010. Obviously, this was a totally unimportant error.

Here's the closing statement from the title company, outlining the figures from the above agreement, showing that the purchase was done using the existing loan (line 203):

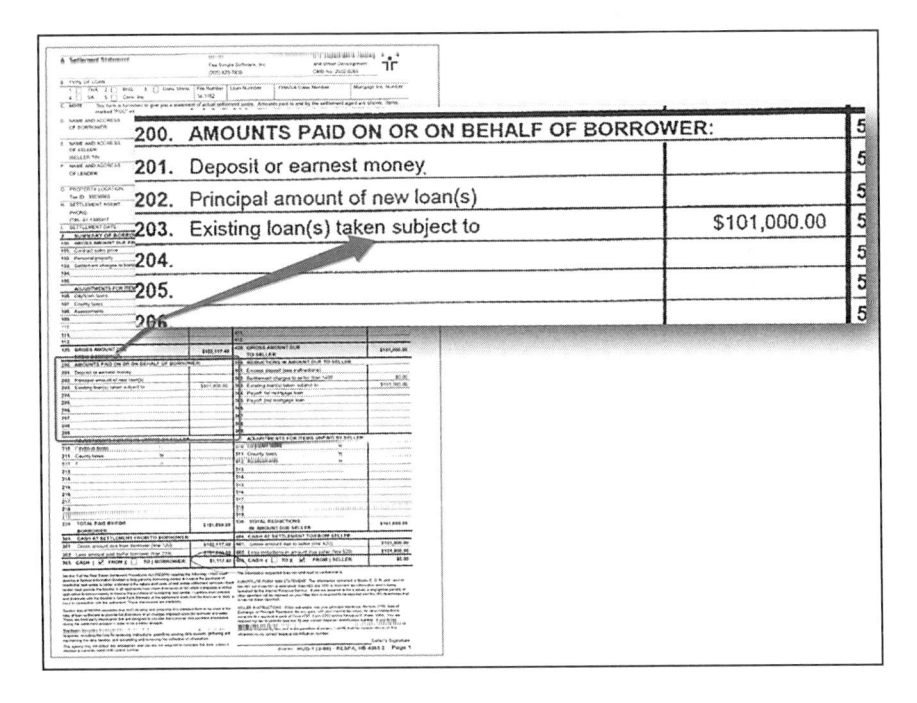

200. AMOUNTS PAID ON OR ON BEHALF OF BORROWER:	
201. Deposit or earnest money	
202. Principal amount of new loan(s)	
203. Existing loan(s) taken subject to	$101,000.00
204.	
205.	
206.	

51

This house needed absolutely no work. All Anto had to do was clean the carpet. My proposed exit strategy was to lease option the house out because this was the best way for Anto to make some immediate cash and also get the benefit of a loan pay-down, possible appreciation, and depreciation, all without dealing with tenants and toilets.

Side Note: *The lease option (also called "rent-to-own") is an arrangement whereby the tenant/buyer is renting the house from the investor and has an exclusive right to buy that house in the future. In exchange for getting that right, the tenant/buyer gives the investor a down payment (called "option consideration") usually in the amount of 3–5% of the purchase price, pays the premium rent, and takes care of all minor repairs. This is an excellent way to get all the benefits of having a rental, but without tenant hassles.*

Anto followed our process of advertising by using a few signs and a Craigslist ad. He soon got a potential candidate who brought in $10,000 in cash. Here is a picture of part of that cash that Anto took and sent me out of fun:

Here's the outline of the deposit agreement with that tenant/buyer:

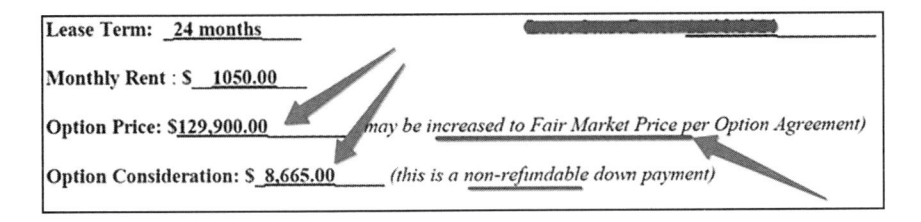

```
Lease Term:  24 months
Monthly Rent: $ 1050.00
Option Price: $129,900.00        may be increased to Fair Market Price per Option Agreement)
Option Consideration: $ 8,665.00   (this is a non-refundable down payment)
```

You can see above that the selling price was set to $129,000, and you can see the one line text next to it says that the price may be increased. Below is the cutout of the option agreement that shows the first part of the legal clause that refers to the variable option price.

```
3. OPTION PRICE: The OPTION price ("strike price") is: $ 129,900                    ;
provided, however, if OPTIONOR concludes at any time before OPTIONOR has received proper notice of
exercise of the OPTION from OPTIONEE that the fair market value of the property exceeds the foregoing strike
price, OPTIONOR may (but is not required to) propose to OPTIONEE that the Option Price be increased to the
fair market value of the property as determined by a professional fee appraiser selected by OPTIONOR.
```

Anto used my special one-page legal clause that allows the seller/investor to increase the buyer's option price to the fair market value in case the property appreciates in value. Depending on the market conditions, sometimes we set the tenant/buyer's option price to a fixed amount and sometimes to a variable amount, depending on the market.

If you wonder why the down payment (option consideration) came out as an uneven number, it is because all the buyer had was $10,000, so after subtracting the prorated first month's rent and the closing costs, the leftover was $8,665.00 which was used as a down payment.

→ **Watch the short interview with Anto. It's only 12 minutes long. Go to www.MarkoRubel.com/book/Anto**

Why didn't Anto sell the house to a conventional buyer with a new loan? Because the profit is much larger doing it this way due to the fact that now he is leveraging all 5 wealth-building components of real estate investing (if you forgot what I'm talking about here, go back and read that chapter—this is important).

Selling it this way, Anto's total profit will be between $30,000 and $40,000.

And one more important point for those of you who believe those "flipping gurus" and want to start your real estate career with wholesaling, which I know is the wrong way. You see the upfront profit here was over $8,000, which is more than the typical "assignment fee" you would get when wholesaling a property with ARV (after repaired value) of around $100K.

Plus, it's a lot easier to discount the seller down 15–20% like in this case, than 40–50% needed for the wholesaling formula. So not only do you make more cash right away, but you make a lot more money overall, and it is a natural transition to having properties that provide PASSIVE income, which should be your ultimate goal—income replacement.

Now, do not try to understand every little piece of this deal at this point. You will by the end of this book.

* * *

Now, let's go back to the reason why I introduced this example in first place, and that is the issue of TRUST.

As I already explained, the truth is that with this method sellers are at some risk of the buyer (you) not making the payments on their loan. You end up with full ownership. They lose all the control, but they are still liable for that loan, and you have no liability.

Sounds unfair? Not really because they would be in a lot worse shape if you didn't step in. So the sellers win as well.

Remember the universal rule—**No one gives up something in life unless they get something in return that they want more.**

In the above example—**Why did the seller, who is an attorney, trust Anto with his own credit?**

Why wasn't he worried that Anto would just walk away from the deal and let his loan go to foreclosure? At the end of the day, Anto didn't have any money in the deal except $10, so metaphorically speaking, he had no skin in the game, yet the attorney still went for it—why?

The answer is that the solution Anto was providing, which is relief from payments the attorney got tired of making, <u>outweighed the associated risk</u>. If he had a small doubt about Anto's not making the payments, that doubt was certainly a much smaller issue for him or otherwise he wouldn't have sold his house to him.

The solution you are providing to sellers by buying their houses outweighs the risk of your not making those payments. If they go with your proposal, then obviously they prefer taking that risk with you *(which, as I said, is very small if the investor understands the business)*, versus their risking getting behind on payments (like the attorney), losing the house to foreclosure, being separated from their family while waiting for the house to sell, and many other reasons.

The bottom line is—the only ingredient you need for this to work is a seller who is "slightly" motivated and therefore, ready to take the risk of letting someone else make the payments on the loan, and willing to sell their house for slightly less than they would net if agent sold their house.

Those "slightly" motivated sellers are all over the place, so **with this system you have an UNLIMITED opportunity to build wealth.**

And rest assured, if you keep your side of the bargain, which if you train with me you will, then you are providing a GREAT SERVICE to those people. Remember, you didn't put them in that position, but you are saving them.

For those of you who already own my advanced course and/or are using my foreclosure website in your business, you have seen all the great testimonials I've got from the **sellers** I've helped with their houses. They are raving about my service. And that makes me feel good. What's better than helping people and making a lot of money, right?

All that we've talked about over the last few pages comes down to the issue of TRUST—whether or not the seller trusts you—that's the issue here. Remember this saying:

→ **People do business with people they like and trust.** ←

Keep this in mind—Everything comes into play when trying to build trust, starting from the type of mailing you send out; how you handle the initial incoming call; how you position your services on that call; how you set up the appointment; how you dress; how you greet them and walk through their house; how you build up your company in their eyes; your professional affiliations like with the BBB (Better Business Bureau membership); the testimonials from past clients; the type of negotiation process; how you respond to objections; your overall tone of voice and choice of words; and this likely is not an all-inclusive list.

As you can imagine, it is impossible to put all that in a book, and many aspects require visuals to explain better. I give a lot of explanation in person at my live events. **However**, you do **not** need to know all of that to start. You can start with the information given in this book and the accompanying online training. Remember, the more the seller is motivated, the less everything else matters.

If you're willing to study, I'll equip you with what you need. You'll know how to present these type of deals and how to create credibility with the sellers, so they will not worry about your performing or not and you'll be able to earn their trust and get them to agree. After presenting this 1,000+ times, I've gotten really good at it, so I created a system for presenting it that works like a charm, and you will get the shortcut on how to do that when you attend our online trainings.

And don't worry, you will NOT need to go to 1,000 appointments to be get deals going—check Tara's case study—she got 2 deals on her first and second appointments. See Section 2 for an explanation of the paperwork, and watch her explain those deals in the online training at **www.MarkoRubel.com/book**.

The bottom line is—not every seller will do it, most will want the loan paid off at closing, but the "most" are not your prospects. Your (and my) prospects are sellers who are motivated and are willing to do it because the fast sale that you're providing solves some of their concerns that worry them a lot more.

Now you may be thinking—Is this legal?

Of course it is. My students are doing it in almost every state. In a few states I do not suggest you do it IF your seller is in foreclosure, but if they aren't, then you can use this method in those states as well.

I know you've never heard of something like this, so it's hard for some of you to believe it would be legal. Here's more proof that it is …

Every HUD-1 Settlement statement or form that is used as part of real estate closings throughout the US contains a line for *"buying subject to the existing loan."* It is a part of the HUD Settlement Form, which is a government-designed form. So if it were not legal, it wouldn't be preprinted on the government form, right?

Here's the part of the form where HUD is referring to this type of buying, and you'll find additional similar documents explained in Section 2—Deal Examples:

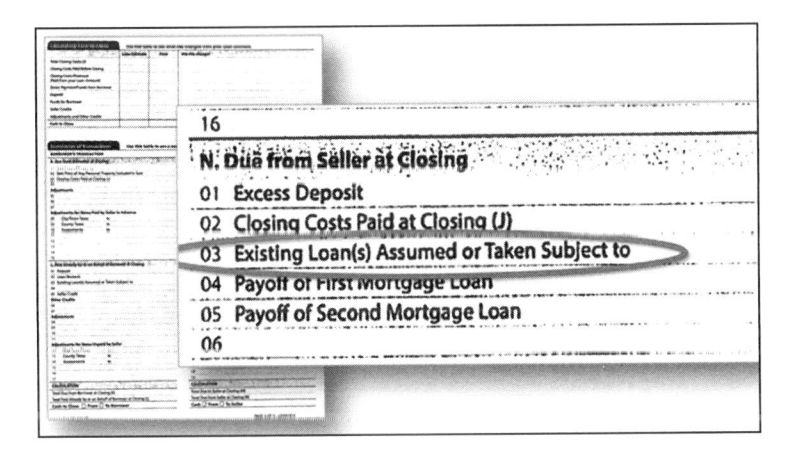

120. Gross Amount Due From Borrower	196,376.00
200. Amounts Paid By Or In Behalf Of Borrower	
201. Deposit or earnest money	0.00
202. Principal amount of new loan(s)	0.00
203. Existing loan(s) taken subject to	190,376.00
204. Promisory Note from Buyer to Seller	0.00
205. HOA Taken Subject Too	0.00

In the above document, the property was purchased "subject to" the existing loan with the loan balance at that time of $190,376.00 as you can see.

Here's the closing HUD Settlement Form from another deal, where the property was purchased by taking the existing loan "subject to" of $46,000.

120. Gross Amount Due from Borrower	49,664.91
200. Amounts Paid by or in Behalf of Borrower	
201. Deposit or earnest money	10.00
202. Principal amount of new loan(s)	
203. Existing loan(s) taken subject to	46,000.00
204.	
205.	

Now granted, some title companies will have no problem closing "subject to" purchases and some will refuse it. The most likely reason for some to refuse is because they don't understand it. No matter where you are, you will always be able to find title companies or closing attorneys who will close this type of deal.

Between literally hundreds of deals done by our coaching students, we've never had one who was not able to find a closing company and close on their purchase.

However, I can tell you this—if you have the wrong mindset and would accept "no," then you'd have a problem here. That's why one of the things I teach students in my live events and in my coaching program is to ask the proper questions and maintain a mindset that doesn't take no for an answer and moves forward. We've had students where their real estate agent or broker would tell them that this was illegal, but then the students proved them wrong. We even had one student whose attorney told him it was illegal and when I told the student to ask the attorney to print out the law that makes it illegal, the attorney couldn't find one.

To conclude, it's important to maintain a positive mindset and not to listen to naysayers who are ready to kill your dreams because they are incapable of realizing their own. This is an amazing opportunity that could change your life and the lives of those around you, so don't let someone discourage you.

SIDE NOTE: I am not the one who invented buying "subject to" the existing loan. I wish I could take the credit for inventing it, but I can't—it's been around for decades. What I can take the credit for is the creation of the extremely profitable investing business model based on it, streamlining it into a system, and then perfecting the related negotiation processes and legal structures/documents.

The only state that I know of that has a law that makes it more difficult is the state of Washington. There's apparently a law that says that you have to notify the lender when buying "subject to." Some investors in WA State are recording these deeds themselves, and some don't care if the lender is notified. I am not an attorney, so I advise my coaching students in that state to use a "sandwich" lease option structure that I'll explain later.

Does the loan need to be assumable?

Good thinking! The loan does NOT need to be assumable, and you will not be assuming any loans. Plus, assumable loans almost don't even exist anymore.

So the good news is ... it WORKS with ANY loan out there.

Let me ask you—do you know what makes a loan "non-assumable"?

Nowadays, every mortgage or deed of trust securing a property has a so-called "due-on-sale" clause in it. That clause or paragraph makes the loan non-assumable.

In essence, here's an excerpt from it …

"If all or any part of the Property or any interest in the property is sold or transferred without Lender's prior written consent, Lender may require immediate payment in full of all sums secured by this Security Instrument."

So to simplify, here's what it means:

It means that the bank can ask to be paid in full if they find out about the transfer.

But in REALITY, the lenders are happy to get paid. They have so many loans in default that they don't care who makes the monthly payment as long as the payment is made.

What happens if you violate the due-on-sale clause?

Nothing! Violating the due-on-sale provision is NOT a crime, and as said above, the lenders don't care. And if they did care, all they can do is call the loan.

The likelihood of a lender enforcing the due-on-sale provision on a house where the payments ARE getting made is VERY SMALL.

Remember, they are going broke with all the houses where the payments have not been made, so why would they ever touch a performing loan that's getting paid? They wouldn't. And there are other reasons why they wouldn't, even if the interest rates increase a lot higher than they are currently.

However, if it happens, you will not realize the back-end profit that you get when your buyer refinances. This is not the end of world because you already have made money from the down payment and cash flow.

As you can see, this is totally risk free for you because you never signed for that loan in the first place.

I've bought many, many properties this way, and I've taught a lot of people this method. Just between my coaches, who are practicing investors using the UFP methods, and myself, we've done hundreds and hundreds of such transactions, and we've never had a single lender even ask.

As I said, the lenders are happy to get paid. That's what they want.

Now, it is a smart business practice to protect yourself even in the case of an unlikely event like the bank demanding to be paid in full. All you need to do is disclose this possible risk to the seller and later on to your buyer in writing, and you're covered. I definitely advise you to do this every single time. We have a special disclosure for it, and your closing agent may have some they regularly use as well.

Here is an example of a disclosure used by a title company in Florida:

Here's the disclosure created by the San Diego Association of Realtors:

> **DISCLOSURES REGARDING "SUBJECT TO" AND "AITD" TRANSACTIONS**
>
> This is a form created by the San Diego Association of REALTORS® and as such is not covered by the C.A.R. User Protection Agreement. This form is intended for use primarily in the San Diego County area.
>
> Property Address: _____
>
> Buyer: _____
>
> Seller: _____
>
> A "Subject To" transaction is one in which the buyer purchases the property and the existing mortgage is not paid off at the time of closing. The lender does not consent to the transaction, the buyer does not assume the existing loan(s) and the seller remains as the borrower on the existing loan(s). The property, however, remains encumbered by the

Let me just say this—yes, you may still have many questions unanswered. Some of you don't understand the mechanics, some of you do but don't believe a seller would go for it, etc. I know it is impossible for me to answer or even guess all of your questions, so this is what I want you to consider—this has been done MANY, MANY, MANY times as you will see in Deal Section 2. If you are serious about making extra money, I advise you to attend our online trainings and learn more. The question is not "Does this work?" rather <u>the real question here is</u>—"Are you willing to make it work?" Got it?

And CONGRATULATIONS! You may not even be aware, but you have just discovered the most powerful method of buying real estate there is. It is simple, and it allows you to buy an unlimited number of properties without ever using your credit or talking to banks for that matter.

From this point on, **you do NOT need banks.**

Before we go forward, let's take a few minutes break to rest from the theory we covered and get excited with a deal case study from Kevin.

NOTE: Don't get worried that you need a lot of cash to start because you don't. You will see in the Section 2 plenty of deal case studies where my students "got paid to buy" and walked out of closing with $10,000 or more. There are plenty of truly $0 down deals out there (even in your area). Then there are deals that need between $1,000 to $5,000 to get some moving money to the seller in order to get them to commit; and there are deals that need more, like Kevin's deal below.

Deal Case Study – Kevin – The 6-Figure "Reinstatement" Deal:

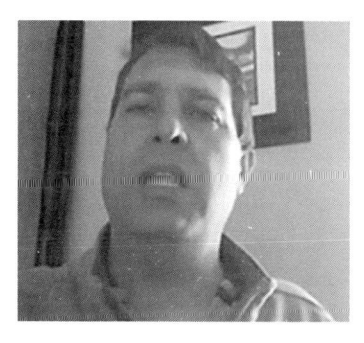

Kevin had never heard of me or my systems before. He came across a little online ad about the Unlimited Funding Program that my office put up and got really excited about the opportunity.

Like all achievers, Kevin was decisive and didn't wait. (By the way, you should not wait either). He started with our Foreclosure Training and Group Coaching. Soon thereafter he received a call from a seller in foreclosure. This seller was behind $20,000 in back payments, and the foreclosure auction date was in 2 weeks.

Here's the Purchase and Sale Agreement showing the purchase price of $256,126.00. As you can see from the attached part of the scanned agreement, Kevin was buying the house "subject to" the first loan (read under 2.D.):

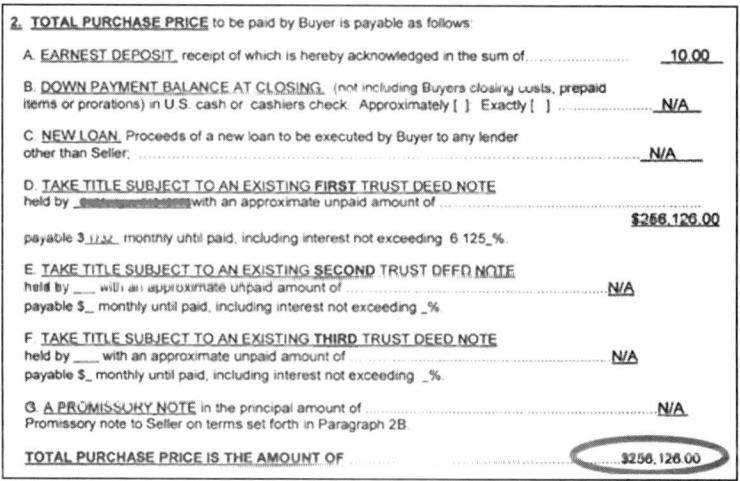

```
2. TOTAL PURCHASE PRICE to be paid by Buyer is payable as follows:
   A. EARNEST DEPOSIT, receipt of which is hereby acknowledged in the sum of............................  10.00
   B. DOWN PAYMENT BALANCE AT CLOSING. (not including Buyers closing costs, prepaid
      items or prorations) in U.S. cash or cashiers check. Approximately [ ] Exactly [ ] ...............  N/A
   C. NEW LOAN. Proceeds of a new loan to be executed by Buyer to any lender
      other than Seller; ..................................................................................  N/A
   D. TAKE TITLE SUBJECT TO AN EXISTING FIRST TRUST DEED NOTE
      held by _____with an approximate unpaid amount of .........................................
                                                                                                 $256,126.00
      payable $_____ monthly until paid, including interest not exceeding 6.125_%.
   E. TAKE TITLE SUBJECT TO AN EXISTING SECOND TRUST DEED NOTE
      held by ____ with an approximate unpaid amount of ..............................................  N/A
      payable $_ monthly until paid, including interest not exceeding _%.
   F. TAKE TITLE SUBJECT TO AN EXISTING THIRD TRUST DEED NOTE
      held by ____ with an approximate unpaid amount of ..............................................  N/A
      payable $_ monthly until paid, including interest not exceeding _%.
   G. A PROMISSORY NOTE in the principal amount of .................................................  N/A
      Promissory note to Seller on terms set forth in Paragraph 2B.
   TOTAL PURCHASE PRICE IS THE AMOUNT OF .........................................................  $256,126.00
```

The problem was that the house needed $20,266.04 to stop foreclosure. However, the value of the house was around $340,000+, the property was in immaculate condition, and Kevin knew that he'd very quickly recoup that money.

This was a beautiful house, with many upgrades (granite countertops being one of them), located in a nice middle-class neighborhood. The picture below is small, but you get an idea:

The title company prepared all the closing paperwork, including the deed which they recorded right after the closing. They also prepared the reinstatement letter to the foreclosing trustee which they used to reinstate the loan. You can see that letter below:

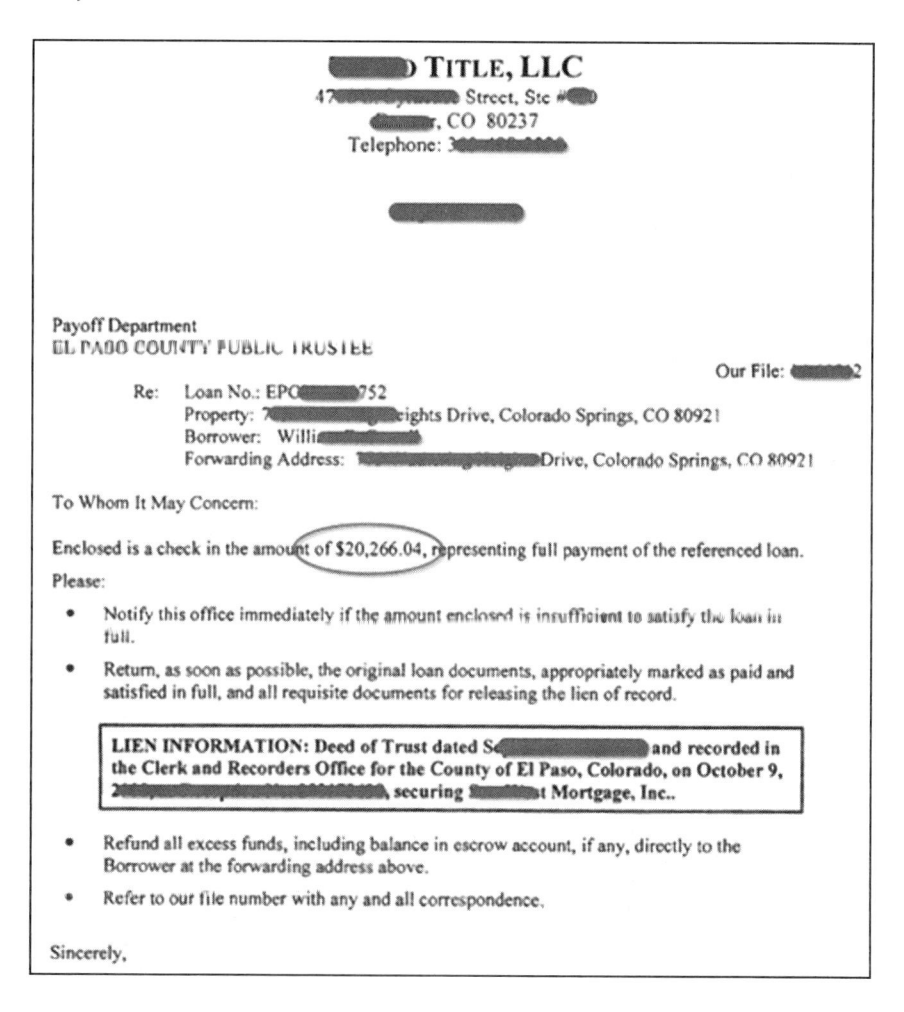

▇▇▇ TITLE, LLC
47▇▇▇▇▇▇ Street, Ste #▇▇
▇▇▇, CO 80237
Telephone: 3▇▇▇▇▇▇▇

Payoff Department
EL PASO COUNTY PUBLIC TRUSTEE

Our File: ▇▇▇▇2

Re: Loan No.: EPO▇▇▇752
Property: 7▇▇▇▇▇▇ Heights Drive, Colorado Springs, CO 80921
Borrower: Willi▇▇▇▇▇
Forwarding Address: ▇▇▇▇▇▇▇▇▇Drive, Colorado Springs, CO 80921

To Whom It May Concern:

Enclosed is a check in the amount of $20,266.04, representing full payment of the referenced loan.
Please:

- Notify this office immediately if the amount enclosed is insufficient to satisfy the loan in full.
- Return, as soon as possible, the original loan documents, appropriately marked as paid and satisfied in full, and all requisite documents for releasing the lien of record.

> **LIEN INFORMATION:** Deed of Trust dated S▇▇▇▇▇▇▇ and recorded in the Clerk and Recorders Office for the County of El Paso, Colorado, on October 9, 2▇▇▇▇▇▇▇▇▇▇▇▇▇▇▇, securing ▇▇▇▇t Mortgage, Inc..

- Refund all excess funds, including balance in escrow account, if any, directly to the Borrower at the forwarding address above.
- Refer to our file number with any and all correspondence.

Sincerely,

The process was straightforward as described in the previous section. The title company prepared the deed that the seller signed, they notarized it, and then they recorded it. The existing loan was not paid off, it was taken "subject to" as you're learning here. The title company sent the above letter with the cashier's check to the public trustee who was handling the foreclosure process on that house.

NOTE: When you're doing this type of deal where you're reinstating a loan, you should always get a confirmation or a receipt from the Foreclosing Company <u>acknowledging</u> that the foreclosure process is stopped. If you don't verify it, the check may get lost, and then the property gets auctioned off, so both you and the seller lose.

Here's the receipt Kevin received the same day the reinstatement cashier's check was given to the foreclosing trustee, as the acknowledgment:

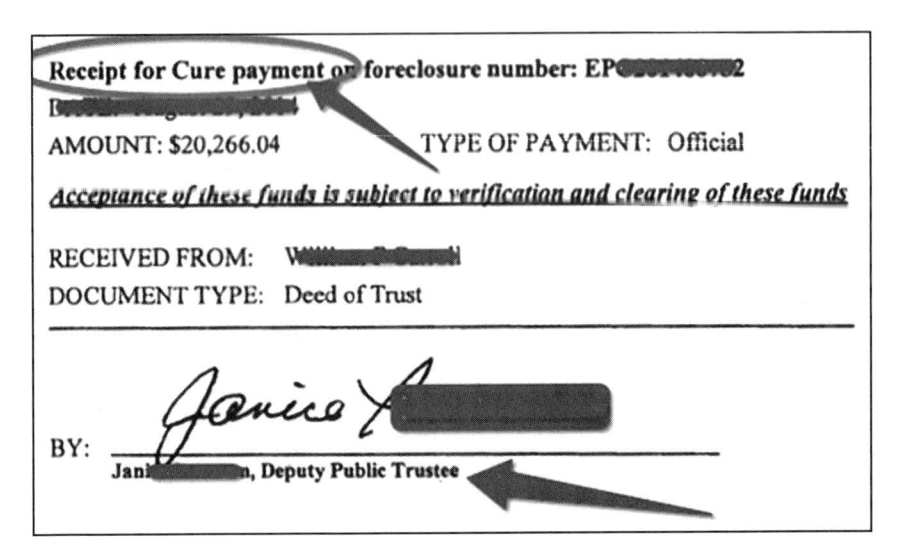

```
Receipt for Cure payment on foreclosure number: EP███████2
████████████████
AMOUNT: $20,266.04          TYPE OF PAYMENT: Official

Acceptance of these funds is subject to verification and clearing of these funds

RECEIVED FROM:    W██████████
DOCUMENT TYPE:    Deed of Trust
_____

         Janice X████████████
BY:  _____
     Jan████████n, Deputy Public Trustee
```

Kevin was stressed out a little, which is normal when you're doing your first deal. It is a little stressful when you're doing it the first time because you're worried if all of it is going to get done in time, but it always does if you're on top of it. Once he got the above receipt from the public trustee, he could now breathe. The seller was ecstatic when he called and informed them that the foreclosure was stopped.

At this point Kevin had to think about selling the house. Since the market was very stable in his area, I suggested not to sell the house outright to a buyer who would get a new loan and pay Kevin off. Rather, I suggested to offer a lease option arrangement to someone who was not ready to buy due to their employment or credit issues. The condition was that they must have at least $20,000 to put down, so Kevin could get his money out of the deal. Another important criteria for that person, which under lease option we call a tenant/buyer, was to be able to afford the payments. You should never take a down payment from someone who has it but can't afford the payments—that's why we do check their credit and ask for pay stubs.

Using our selling marketing, he found that person in 21 days. They were excited about the house and had $20,000 to put towards securing the house as a down payment (in this arrangement, this is called an "option consideration"). They also committed to an additional $15,000 towards the downpayment within 2 months.

Kevin gave them a 2 year option term, which meant that they could get their own loan and cash him out at any time during the 2-year term. The selling price, in this case the "option" price was $355,000 if they exercised their right to buy within the first year, and $385,000 if they purchased within the second year.

Here's the part of the lease option selling agreement outlining the selling price:

> **Purchase Option.** It is agreed that Lessee shall have the option to purchase real estate known as: ~~~~~~~~~~~~~~~~~~rado Springs, CO 80921 for the purchase price of Three hundred fifty five thousand Dollars ($355,000) with a non-refundable down payment of Thirty five thousand five hun~~~~~~~~rs ($35,500) payable upon exercise of said purchase option, and with a closing date no l~~~~~~~an 365 days thereafter. This purchase option must be exercised in writing~~~~~~~~~~~~~~~~~~~~~~~~~~~, but shall not be effective should the Lessee be in default under any terms of this lease or upon any termination of this lease. Down payment shall be used to reduce the purchase price of the house.
>
> **Other Terms:** This Purchase Option shall extend to September 30th 2016 except␣at the purchase price shall increase to Three hundred eighty five thousand dollars ($385,000.00) if

All in all, including cash flow, this will be a six-figure profit when the tenant/buyer exercises their option and gets the new refinancing loan. There is a small chance they may never buy and walk away—if that happens, Kevin can celebrate because he will keep their $35,000 down payment and resell the house, most likely for a higher price.

As you can see, this was an amazing deal that required no communication with the lender, no one asked Kevin about his credit score, his W2, or his tax return. It was a lot easier than that, and it was all done in less than 30 days from meeting the seller. And when counting the resale, it ended up being close to a $0 down deal because he got his (or his private lender's) money out; and then the $15K additional down payment tendered 2 months from closing made this a profitable deal from the start.

Now, compare this to standard fix-and-flip deals where you need to secure funding from either a hard-money lender or a private lender, spend months dealing with contractors, and then spend another month or two until you find a buyer who can actually get approved for a conventional loan and close the purchase. And most of the rehab deals don't net a profit of $35,000 even after 6 months of work, an amount that Kevin got in less than 30 days, with probably not more than 5 hours of his time. Plus, he has a back-end profit coming when the buyer refinances, making it a 6-figure deal. Beautiful!

And one more point, if you wanted to generate a 6-figure check on a rehab deal, you'd need to get into a more expensive house, with a lot of work needed, and that means you'd be taking on a major risk. Kevin's risk in this deal was very small. Plus, a profit on a rehab deal like that would be highly taxed as ordinary income while Kevin will be paying a lower capital gains tax rate on his profit when the buyer purchases after 12 months of Kevin's ownership, which is stipulated in the agreement.

NOTE: There are two more tax advantages on a deal like this. Kevin still owns this property during the option term, so he can depreciate the property and shelter his other income. Also, the $35,000 of option money that he received is not taxable until the option is exercised or forfeited. Wow!

Let me ask you ... **How would your partner or spouse feel if you did a deal like this?**

I know how Kevin's wife felt because she was with Kevin in my next seminar. Folks, this is a family business that when you follow my teachings, becomes not only financially rewarding but emotionally rewarding as well. As a result, you become a much happier person overall, and isn't that the ultimate outcome you desire anyway?

I think all this business is not about money in the end—it's about the happiness.

Here's Kevin's son helping to address the envelopes. Nothing wrong involving kids in the family business from early on.

*Results presented are not typical—read the Earning Disclaimer

UNLIMITED FUNDING
—CAN YOU DO IT TOO?

You may be wondering ... If this is so simple, why isn't everybody doing it?

The answer is—most people have never heard of it, and most investors don't fully understand it, so they are scared of complications that do NOT exist.

And the truth is—it is simple, but ONLY when someone who has done it shows you. There are steps that you could mess up ... like everything else in life.

It took me years to figure it out, but when I teach it to my students, they can go out and do it right away. They use my experience, and you can do it too.

You have probably seen the videos from Nate, a young California surfer, who used the Unlimited Funding Method #5 to generate a $101,000 check. You probably remember Judy's video where she used the existing loan at 3.6%. Or Monica, who got $30,000 in three weeks.

You will meet many more students in Section 2 that's coming up and online at **www.MarkoRubel.com/book**. I prepared a lot for you there. Just make it a point to watch one short video every day.

Some of you have purchased the *4 Real-Life Case Study Training* where I flew to four students' cities and got it all on the video. This is four hours of real-life, in the trenches training you can get for less than a hundred bucks, so all of you should have it. It shows you real-world scenarios of students making money in the field. No hype, just learning.

If you've come this far in this book, then you should get this training. Here's the secret link:

www.MarkoRubel.com/book

The fact is—ALL OF YOU reading this book can do this. The beauty is that your situation doesn't matter.

The only ingredient you need is a seller who is "slightly" motivated, and those sellers are all over the place. I don't know if you realize it, but with this system, you have an UNLIMITED opportunity to build wealth.

It is the only way that ALL OF YOU reading this book can start because YOUR personal situation simply does NOT matter.

I hope you're getting excited! Because once you learn how to do this, you will realize that there is no reason for you to ever again worry about money.

Let me tell you—this was the biggest discovery of my life.

My first deal using this method made me more money in 30 days than all the wholesaling and rehab deals combined that I had done up to that point.

This very same method made me a multimillionaire because I could acquire and OWN a large number of properties through the up-cycle.

And let me reiterate—your situation does NOT matter.

It really DOES NOT matter, so please don't create excuses and obstacles for your success. If you want to find excuses, you will find them all over this book or in life. If you want success, you will not see any.

If you simply have a desire to make some extra money, pay some bills, or give yourself an extra vacation or two, you can do it.

If your goal is to create massive wealth and completely improve your life, you can do it as well, using this method.

When I started, I didn't have much money, plus my credit wasn't bad … it was non-existent. Looking back now, this was a great circumstance because it kept me from making a mistake by going and getting a loan myself.

COMMON QUESTION: *How come no one else is teaching this besides you, Marko?* I'm sure there are plenty of people teaching it. The US is a big country, so I'm sure I'm not the only expert on this subject out there. However, you don't hear of many so-called gurus teaching it because they don't understand it. The truth is, most gurus are good at Internet marketing or TV informercials, so they teach wholesaling because it can be taught without having actual experience. I will teach you later on in this book how wholesaling works, even though wholesaling is the least effective method there is and shouldn't be your main game, as I'll explain.

At the Seller's House

Here's an example of a typical Unlimited Funding deal that can quickly put $25,000.00 into your pocket, give you anywhere between $300–$700 in monthly cash flow, and result in a minimum of $70,000.00 in overall profit with no more than a few hours of your time invested. And no risk. Would that work for you?

3 Bedroom – 2 Bath House

Condition – Perfect

Seller is motivated – purchased another house and can't continue to make double payments. Needs to sell! Not desperate but motivated.

FMV (fair market value) = $250,000

Owed on the loan = $200,000 (only one loan @ 5% interest rate)

PITI (principal, interest, taxes, & insurance) payment = $1,400/mo.

As a result of the direct response marketing that I'll teach you, the seller called you and asked you for help. After asking a few simple key qualifying questions using my **Phone Prescreening Form**, you determined that there was enough motivation to go and visit the seller.

Go ahead and download my Phone Prescreening orm from www.MarkoRubel.com/book and don't change it. It has been tweaked over thousands of phone calls, so the questions are strategically worded and positioned.

While on the phone, you asked:

Mr. Seller, if an agent brought you a buyer today and the buyer was willing to pay you $230,000, would you consider that offer?

After briefly considering his situation and his months of hard effort in trying to sell that resulted in hassles and still an "unsold" house, the seller willingly replied, "Yes."

At the house, after you built the necessary rapport and credibility, you asked the seller again the same question, now in person:

Mr. Seller, if an agent brought you a buyer today and the buyer was willing to offer you $230,000, would you consider that offer?

The seller again answered, "Yes." And **then** you asked this follow-up question:

Mr. Seller, we learned from helping a lot of sellers that the sellers are usually very happy if we can get them close to what they would net if they sold it through an agent.

If you could net close to what you'd net by selling through an agent, would that work for you?

The seller has already confirmed that in the previous question, but here you asked again in order to set up what follows … (this is part of the strategy).

After the seller replied "Yes," you went together <u>with the seller</u> to calculate what that **net** would be.

I give my students my proprietary tool that streamlines that calculation. It's called the **Net-Equity-Worksheet**, and it "educates" the seller on the cost of sale and the net.

SIDE NOTE: I talk more about this great tool on the free webinar, and every attendee is given a download link, so make sure you go to **www.MarkoRubel.com/book**. If we're doing the webinar, sign up for the first one and attend it *(we do them usually at least once a month)*.

Here's the essence of the process.

You will deduct the cost of sale from the $230,000 that the seller indicated would be his acceptable price. The cost of sale will amount to between 10% and 15% depending on what you and the seller agreed to include in it.

At a minimum, it will include a 6% real estate commission, 3% of the closing cost, and 3–4% of the holding cost. The holding costs are monthly payments the seller needs to make until he finds the buyer and the buyer buys it.

Let's use 12%, which is a pretty typical number in this type of scenario.

Twelve percent of $230,000 is $27,600, so after subtracting this amount and the seller's loan balance, the NET to the seller is $2,400.

$230,000.00 – Price the seller indicated would be acceptable

minus $27,600.00 – The cost of sale you got the seller to agree to

minus $200,000.00 – The remaining balance on the seller's loan

$2,400.00 – NET in the best-case scenario

After the seller realized that there would not be much profit to realize from the sale, you would ask the seller the following question:

Mr. Seller, in a perfect scenario you would net $2,400. We know that we don't live in a perfect world, so what if we can buy your property for the balance of your loan, would that work for you?

In most cases like this where the seller is **motivated** and assuming you have built rapport and credibility properly, the answer will be: **YES**. Think about it, why wouldn't they? They are getting close to what they wanted without waiting for it. Remember, he indicated that he'd accept $230K. What we calculated above is his net, so he's getting very close to what he indicated he'd accept.

Plus, don't forget he is a MOTIVATED seller.

After the seller agreed to the purchase price, you would discuss other terms that are "easy" to agree on, like the closing date, the move-out date if the seller lives in the house, what personal property would stay or go (like fridge, washer, dryer, etc.), and any other point that needed to be agreed on.

You would do that in order to build a momentum of a lot of yeses, before you introduce the "loan staying in their name" concept. This is very important to remember. I see a lot of experienced investors make the fundamental mistake of introducing the "loan staying in their name" way too early, even before they agree on the selling price. Think about it logically—what's the point of introducing the "loan staying in their name" if they haven't even agreed on the selling price? It makes no sense. All you would be doing is giving them one more reason to say no. All of this is very simple when it's done in a logical sequence.

Remember—the sequence is the key here.

Obviously, I'm giving you here a short explanation, but I hope you're getting the idea how the presentation works. I call it the **P-E-N** process, which stands for Presentation-Education-Negotiation. I created a system for presenting this kind of deal that makes it very logical for the seller to agree. Sure, it took me a lot of wasted appointments to perfect it, but now if they even have a slight motivation, they're going with me. I'm getting that deal.

What's also very cool about it is that when I'm able to teach someone the process, they are able to quickly get successful with it. Why do you think that is? It is because the P-E-N process is in fact a system. A system is a series of steps, a proven pattern, which brings you to a desired outcome. This is the system for getting sellers to sell us their house subject to their existing loan. So if you use the proven pattern, you get the proven outcome.

This is the part that you need to be trained on, and it goes way beyond this book. It requires specific training, which explains the psychology and the system for getting them to accept the "loan staying in their name" and to feel good about it. 't took me over a decade to perfect it, but I can teach it to you in 4 hours when in person, and then you own powerful, worth millions in potential revenue.

IMPORTANT: You don't need to worry about now. Finishing this book is a lot more important for this point. There is a lot more I need to teach you here you make money. So please for your own sake persist in reading.

Back to the seller's house. Once you agreed to everything on your notepad with the seller, then you move to getting the Purchase and Sale Agreement signed, which will serve as guidance to your closing attorney or the title company to close this transaction.

At this point it is important for you to realize that this seller is NOT desperate, and this concept doesn't require very motivated or desperate sellers, which opens the door to more business.

Also note, we didn't pressure the seller with *"What's the least you would take?"* and *"Is this the best you can do?"*—typical guru-crap that will kill your deals.

This education process, using the Net-Equity-Worksheet, helps the sellers keep their pride, and it doesn't make them feel like they've been taken advantage of.

The overall process solved their problem of double payments in this example and made you money, a lot of it, as you'll see below.

It is also pretty typical that you <u>get the seller to make</u> the next one or two payments in this type of situation.

What I described above is the **Unlimited Funding Method #1** called:

$0 Down – Instant Ownership

There are total of **7 Unlimited Funding Methods** that make the Unlimited Funding Program fit different seller scenarios. We'll cover them in the next chapter, and keep in mind, I will also cover them in the upcoming webinars.

Let me answer a few side questions you may have…

How much can I pay for the property-what's the maximum purchase price I can pay in order to profit? This is something you to determine (calculate) even before you get to the seller's house, and it is the question many of you have now. You want to know how much you can pay for the property to profit. Unfortunately, I still cannot answer it. Here's why—the maximum purchase price that you can pay depends on how you're going to sell it, and that will be discussed in the chapter following the next.

In essence, you'll learn that your maximum purchase price **cannot exceed 75%** of the fair market value (FMV) **if you're selling outright** to a buyer with perfect credit who will get their own loan. However, if you sell using one of our Niche2Wealth strategies, you can pay **up to 80%** of the FMV and sometimes more.

I have to say, some of you may be confused by this, so it's best is if you read the whole book first and then go back and reread some of the chapters.

This is a million-dollar business that I'm describing here, so it is normal if you are confused with some parts of it.

In Section 2 you will meet my students who started like you now, who were confused, and many of whom have now accumulated a million dollars plus in net worth. You'll meet them soon. And as we are going through their deal examples, this will become clear.

What is Equity? This is another question some of you who are new to real estate may have.

Most sellers consider Equity to be the difference between the fair market value (FMV) of the property and the amount they still owe on the mortgage.

As investors, we consider the seller's Real Equity to be the 'net' amount that the owner would receive after selling a property, paying all the costs associated with the sale (closing costs, commission, etc.) and paying off the mortgage.

BIG 7 STRUCTURES OF THE UNLIMITED FUNDING PROGRAM

Once you start receiving calls from motivated sellers, you will realize that equity positions are different from seller to seller. Some have a lot of equity, and you can't buy their house for the balance of their loan because there's just too much equity to expect them to give it all up. Some will have no equity. And some will have negative equity, and the only way to make money with those deals that have no equity is to get the seller to pay you or to do a short sale.

The sellers' needs are also important factors to consider when structuring these deals. Some will need to have cash from the sale because that is the only reason they are selling—maybe they have medical or other bills they need to pay off, etc. So unless they get cash for their equity, they won't sell.

Some will want to get cash but don't need it right away, so they will still want to sell even if they have to wait for their equity. Then some sellers will be behind on payments as you've already learned.

My point is—there are different situations out there. Over the course of doing this business for many years, I've been able to fit all the possible deal scenarios that have an existing loan into 7 deal structures. I call them the BIG 7 Unlimited Funding Methods.

SIDE NOTE: If the property is owned free and clear and there's no loan against it, then these 7 structures won't apply. I'll give you a review of a few very powerful moneymaking strategies for properties that don't meet our Unlimited Funding criteria in Section 3.

1. UFP METHOD #1: $0 Down – Instant Ownership

This is the scenario where you got the seller to agree to sell you the property for the balance of their loan(s). That means that your purchase price is equal to what's owed on the property. In most cases, the seller is current on his payments.

I love this type of deal because you don't need any money to do it.

The key is to find motivated sellers with a loan-to-value (LTV) of around 80% and then get them to agree to sell it to you for what's owed on the property. We do that by educating the seller on the cost of selling. If you recall the deal example in the previous chapter, I mentioned the P-E-N process and the Net Equity Worksheet that we use to outline all the costs involved in selling their property.

Usually, using that strategy of showing them the cost of sale if they sold it with a real estate agent, you can get the discount of 15–20%. If their loan is at 80% of LTV or close to it, you can get a $0 down deal.

This is a truly no-money-down deal where you don't need credit and you're not taking on any risk. Are those deals available? ALL THE TIME.

How do you find them? One way is to get a list of properties that have an approximate equity of 20% and mail them a postcard offering your services that provide a quick sale for them.

2. UFP METHOD #2: Paid2Buy – Seller Pays You

Let me ask you, what if there was a method where you can get paid by the seller to take over their beautiful house, would you be excited?

Imagine a seller giving you the ownership of their immaculate house at a below market price, together with a nice low interest rate loan that's on their credit, and on top of it they write you a check. *This is almost unbelievable, isn't it?* Get a beautiful house and get paid to take it.

If I told the above scenario to most people outside of the readers of this book, they would think I'm lying—but this is what happens more often than you would think. And I'll PROVE it to you because I am a guy who is not easy to convince, so I know that if I were you, I wouldn't believe it either. That's why …

→ In **Section 2** we'll cover a few deals where our students got paid to buy. You will see the closing statements, and you'll hear in videos why the sellers agreed to pay them.

Pay attention to the first deal in Section 2 where Lester got paid at closing $12,500 to buy and got full ownership of a beautiful house with a nice 4% fixed loan. Then in a week he had a buyer who gave him $17,000 down and $475/mo. in cash flow. You'll see the documents and hear Lester explain why the seller did that.

As I stated at the beginning of this book, I will give you the proof for everything I'm showing you here. You should have no doubt that these strategies work exactly as I'm describing them.

In this scenario, the seller has very small equity, so once you run them through the education phase of your P-E-N process, they will realize that they need to bring money to the closing if they want to sell their house.

For example, if a house is worth $100,000 and they owe $90,000 on it, then once you go through the cost of sale of 15–20% and subtract the loan balance, the number you get will be a NEGATIVE number.

$97,000 Conservative sales price for a quick sale, minus
$6,000 Real estate commission
$3,000 Closing costs
$4,000 Holding costs (payments, utilities, etc. until the house sells)
$90,000 Loan balance on the first
- $6,000 Net (negative)

This is the process you do together with the seller's participation. When done properly, the seller will immediately understand that it will cost them to sell their house. Many times they know it even before you go through this process of showing it to them.

Then you will present the benefit of their needing to bring less money to the closing if they sold it to you or your company. Like in the example above, you would tell them that in the perfect scenario they would need to bring <u>at least</u> $6,000 to the closing to sell their house.

If their buyer didn't get the final loan approval and the house "fell out of escrow," they would end up losing even more.

Then you propose that if your company buys it, they will need to bring "only" $5,000 and all the uncertainty will be removed. If the seller is not broke, they will go for it.

Remember, this will work with motivated sellers that are not broke—but are motivated.

Here's something interesting—even when the sellers are not in the negative as in the example above, we would ask the seller to make the next few payments, which if they agree to do, they would in fact be "paying you to buy." Don't you love creative real estate?

3. UFP METHOD #3: Note4Equity – Seller Carries

Now, this is an opposite scenario to the previous. In this case, the seller has a lot more equity and their loan is below 80% of the property value.

So even when you discount them down 15–20%, they still have equity. In other words, your discounted purchase price is still substantially above the existing loan balance. For example, if the property FMV is $100,000 and the loan is $70,000:

$97,000 Conservative sales price for a quick sale
$6,000 Real estate commission

$3,000 Closing costs

$4,000 Holding costs (payments, utilities, etc. until the house sells)

$70,000 Loan balance on the 1st

$14,000 Net

After explaining to the seller that their net when selling with a real estate agent would be $14,000 in the best-case scenario, then you'd get them to agree that in order for your company to buy it quickly the most you can give them is $10,000. This would probably be a very generous offer in my world, but let's say that's what you offered and the seller agreed. How would that deal be structured?

If the seller was willing to wait for that equity, you would be buying the house "subject to" the $70,000 loan, and the seller would carry back a promissory note in the amount of $10,000. That means that you would sign an "I owe you," which is documented in a promissory note. The terms of that note and its maturity date would depend on the seller's needs and your negotiation skills. Sometimes that note will be secured by the lien against the house, making the seller feel comfortable that they'll in fact get that money.

This way you buy the house by taking over their loan, and the remaining equity will be paid at a later date. I teach my students to never mention the interest rate when talking about the seller carrying back their equity. My students can talk about monthly installments and the balloon payment, but not the interest rate. As a result, all of them are getting interest-free carryback financing by the seller. This is "cheap" money, plus it provides more opportunity to profit on later by discounting that note. I will cover more on this point in my live event. By the way, it's a great strategy. As I said, I love creative real estate and you will too!

4. UFP METHOD #4: Cash4Deed – Tiny Down = Deed

In this scenario, the seller needs some money to move and will not let you buy for the balance of their loan without their getting cash. For example, the house is worth $100K, the loan is at $75K, and the seller agrees to sell it to you for $78K. In this case you will write them a check for $3K at closing, and you will still receive a great deal with the long-term financing in place that allows you to sell any way you want.

In the previous example from method #3, where they agreed to carry back a note for $10,000, we could offer them $5,000 cash instead of the note. Then at that point they can decide which offer they would like more. If you have access to cash, then the $5,000 may be a better deal for you; if you don't, then the $10,000 note is definitely a better option because it gives you a $0 down deal—you don't need any cash to buy (except for the closing costs).

NOTE: Some deals are a combination of methods #3 and #4. For example, instead of a $10,000 note, you may need to give them $2,000 cash at closing because they need it to pay for the moving truck, and then you will give them an $8,000 note in addition.

5. UFP METHOD #5: Reinstatement – Foreclosure Reversal

This is in essence the same as any of the methods explained previously, but in addition the seller is late on payments and the lender has started the foreclosure process. When you receive the deed on the property in this scenario, your ownership is subject to that foreclosure action, so if you don't stop foreclosure, you will lose the property.

If you remember **Kevin's deal** that we covered earlier, in order to reverse the foreclosure, you need to send the lender the back payments owed by the seller. You need to bring the loan current in order for the foreclosure process to stop.

This is a very powerful method because the sellers in this scenario don't have a lot of options and **are very motivated**. That results in great deals.

Here's an example of a great deal that I purchased using this method:

Worth: $470,000 (fair market value)

First Loan Balance: $220,000 + $25,000 to reinstate

Purchase Price: $335,000

NOTE: The purchase price of $335,000 was comprised of the first loan, the reinstatement amount, and the seller carryback note for the remaining equity in the amount of $90,000.

Selling Price: $445,000

Cost to Sell: $24,000

Note Discount: $10,000

TOTAL PROFIT: $96,000 (sold to an outright buyer who got a new loan)

As you can see, this was a great deal, but it needed $25,000 to reinstate. After you do a few deals using the first 4 methods explained here previously, you'll make enough money, so you can tackle deals like this that need more money to do.

Remember, I mentioned that I have a tool called **Money Finder** that offers a list of cash buyers and private lenders in your area, updated twice per month. Once you have a few private lenders to work with, you can get a small loan from them to provide that reinstatement money.

Now, as you can imagine, getting a seller to agree to a $130,000 discount requires *some* skill. Negotiating a deal like that requires a special negotiation approach that will result in a huge discount but still have the seller understand that it's good for them. We call this a "partnership approach" method, and it's one of the most powerful and brilliant strategies I've invented. It took me literally millions of dollars in lost opportunities before I was finally able to tweak it and make the method work. Since this is a very proprietary strategy, I teach it only in my live events. In 3 hours you will learn something that took 10 years to develop.

6. UFP METHOD #6: P-J-L – Junior Liens Discounted

The Payoff-Junior Liens (P-J-L) is the only short-sale strategy that I suggest you do.

To start, most of you know what a short sale is—a sale of a property with consent of the lender for less than it's owed. The lender agrees to take a loss in order for the property to be sold. They do that to avoid having the property repossessed and possibly losing more.

Now, when there's only one loan, the short sale doesn't make sense because once the short sale is approved you'd need to use all cash or get a own loan to pay the lender of the short sale. In this case there's no possibility of buying "subject to" because the loan is getting paid off at a discount.

Doing this type of transaction is for investors who don't know better. It makes no sense to do because there's a high risk in doing it and the profit is small—because you would be leveraging only one of the 5 wealth-building components of real estate investing.

At one time I had 3 loss mitigators working for me, negotiating short sales for us in our office. This was back in the days when short-sale flips using simultaneous closings were allowed. And after doing many short sales, I accidentally stumbled upon a little niche that is a lot more profitable. I call that niche P-J-L. It really is the new generation of strategies, Short Sales 2.0.

Here's how it works.

P-J-L stands for "paying off junior loans," so it is a strategy that you use when there's more than one loan on a property. The criterion is that the first loan is below 80% of the FMV. Your strategy is to short sale or discount the second loan and then get the deed "subject to" the first loan in foreclosure, which you will reinstate.

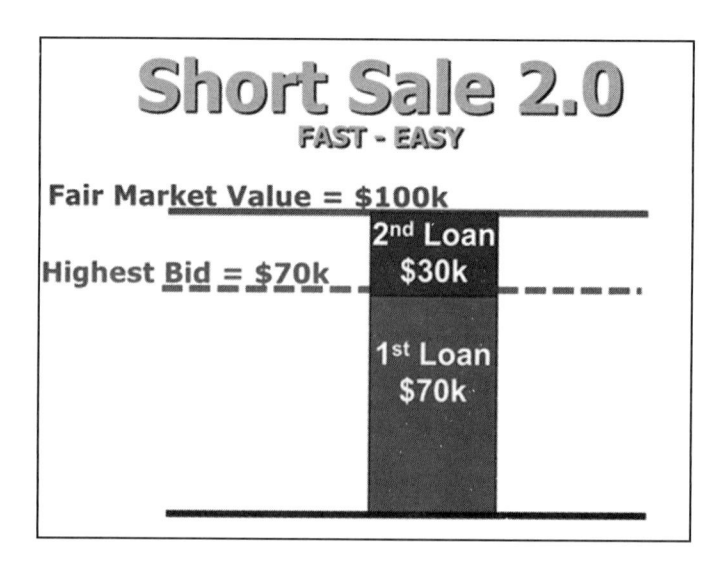

Short Sale 2.0
FAST - EASY

Fair Market Value = $100k

Highest Bid = $70k

2nd Loan $30k

1st Loan $70k

It's important to note that second loans are a lot easier to discount because they are under threat of being wiped out by the first loan. For example, you have a $100,000 house with a first loan of $70,000 (including the reinstatement) and a second of $30,000. At the foreclosure auctions, investors usually bid up to 65–70% of the property value.

So if the $70,000 loan is foreclosing, most likely no one will bid above $70,000 and the second will get nothing. That's why in this scenario, the second lender is motivated to take a substantial discount. So let's say they agreed to take $3,000, which is more than they would get otherwise.

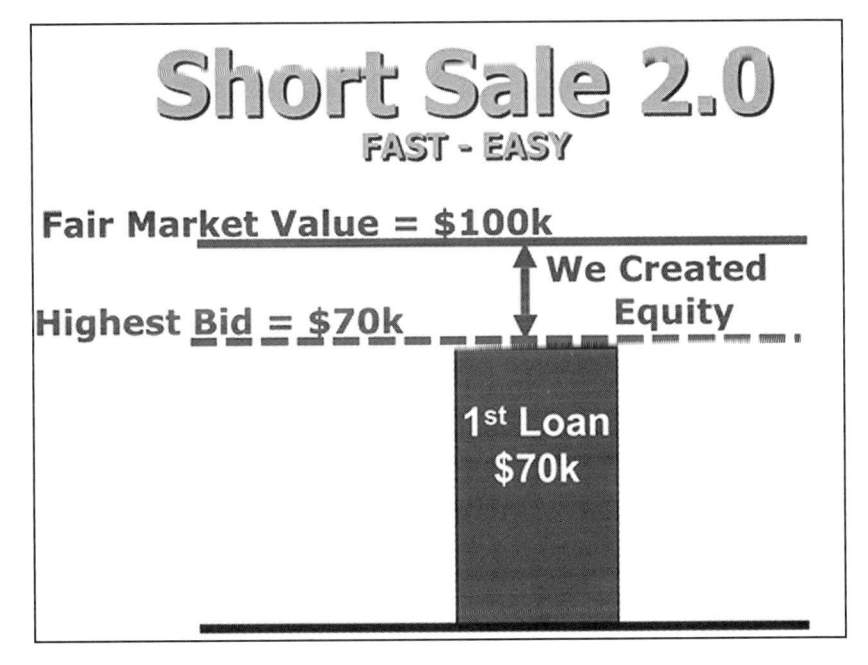

Short Sale 2.0
FAST - EASY

Fair Market Value = $100k
Highest Bid = $70k
We Created Equity
1st Loan $70k

In essence, you discounted the second loan to create equity. At the closing that second gets paid off completely, and the first gets reinstated. This way you have long-term financing on the property that allows you to sell the house any way you want and capture all 5 wealth-building components real estate offers.

In that example, the investor has purchased the house for $73,000. These types of deals are super easy to negotiate with the seller because the seller has no choice to stop the foreclosure—she owes more than the house is worth. What choice does he have?

Like in everything we do, you created a win-win solution here. The seller saved her credit and avoided deficiency judgment, tax consequences, etc.

→ **There will be an example of this deal as well in Section 2, with a video.**

---

7. UFP METHOD #7: Assign2Buyer – Wholesale "Subject to" Deal

This is a simple assignment of a "subject to" deal that you put under contract and get the seller to give you the right to assign.

If the house doesn't have enough equity for you to buy it, you can just find someone who would like to get that house without qualifying for a loan. You can take a small assignment fee and let the buyer close directly with the seller.

This method is used as a last resort with deals that are not as attractive. It allows you to make some money from deals you would otherwise pass. The disadvantage is that the profit potential is very limited.

*   *   *

The truth is that a lot of the deals out there **do not require any money to do**, so you can start doing them. All you need is a little bit of knowledge, and you'll have that from this book and through my webinars and live trainings.

I have made A LOT of people successful and helped them change their lives for the better. You'll meet 10 of them in Section 2. If you decide to believe in me and attend my trainings, you will be one of them. Then you'll know that this book is in fact as life-changing as I promised at the beginning. But for your own sake, please continue reading because there's a new moneymaking discovery in the next chapter.

So to summarize, there are plenty of deals you can do without having any money or credit using the Unlimited Funding Methods that we covered. So you have no excuses, my friend.

There are also deals that are very profitable and may require a little bit of money to do. One example was the "Foreclosure Reversal" UFP method #5 described previously.

The bottom line is—4 out of 7 UFP methods require NO money to buy property, except a $10 earnest deposit. The three other methods require a few thousand dollars, which you will soon have after a few deals.

At this point, you may not understand all of it, but since I know the ins and outs of it all, please believe the following:

You can do this.

It doesn't matter what your situation is, it doesn't matter if you have money or credit, it doesn't matter if you know what a "mortgage" is or what a "deed" is—you can do it.

You can use the Unlimited Funding Program to make a lot of money and ultimately become a millionaire. All you really need is the right mindset and determination to do it.

Niche2Wealth Business Model

You can have everything in life you want, if you will just help other people get what they want.

—Zig Ziglar

The above quote is the premise of our Niche2Wealth (N2W) business model, which will allow you to profit without the headaches of dealing with tenants, contractors, etc.

Before I give you the essence of it, please answer the following question:

Do most people out there have perfect credit or bad to average?

Do most people out there have the 20% down payment required to get a loan?

The answer is NO—to both.

As you realize from these two questions, MOST people out there don't have perfect credit and don't have the 20% in cash for a down payment.

The rocky economy has left a lot of people with damaged credit ratings. Plus the tight lending guidelines make it very hard if not impossible to get a bank loan for many.

What does that mean?

It means that if you're selling your houses the same way **everybody** else is selling them, then you'll get what **everybody** else is getting—and that's an **unsold** house. Or a house that takes too long to sell.

By the way, this is in a way a definition of "insanity"—doing the same thing over and over and expecting a different result.

If you're in a hot market where properties do sell fast, using our N2W approach still makes more sense because you'll get at least 5–10% more for your property.

The bottom line is—if you are looking for a buyer who CAN get a bank loan, you are selling to a <u>minority</u> of people out there, thus increasing your holding time/cost and ultimately <u>reducing</u> your selling price and profit.

What if you can sell to the <u>majority</u> of people out there with <u>any</u> kind of credit?

What if you can double your profits by doing that?

The result will be an <u>expedited</u> way not only to sell your properties but to build wealth as well.

Here's the premise of my N2W business model:

When you can sell properties that most people want to live in and when you can sell them in a way that most people can afford to buy them, then you are fulfilling the need of the majority and consequently, you end up making a lot of money.

This goes with the old saying—Fulfill other people's needs, and you'll fulfill yours by doing it.

Let's go in the opposite direction from the majority of sellers out there …

Think about the famous quote from Mark Twain: *"Whenever you find yourself on the side of the majority, it is time to pause and reflect."*

This is exactly what I'm telling you here to do. So while all the homeowners and all the <u>other investors</u> out there are competing for those few "picky" buyers with perfect credit and down payments, we'll focus on the totally <u>opposite</u> direction … an untapped opportunity.

We'll act as a "bank" (provide the financing) and sell to people with ANY credit. Yes, you'll be the bank—don't worry, it's possible even if you have no credit and no money, as you'll learn in a minute.

Since people with ANY kind of credit make the majority of people out there, our pool of potential buyers will be hundreds of times <u>bigger</u> than our competition's.

This is something totally NEW to you, and again it will make more sense once you learn how simple it really is … but try to understand how powerful it really is when you can sell properties to the <u>majority</u> of the people out there.

Those buyers cannot even consider most other houses for sale because they need a bank loan to buy those other houses, which they can't qualify for.

This makes your house stand out from all the other houses for sale. You literally have no competition to sell your house. Your house comes with financing while all the others don't. Your buyers cannot look at those other houses because they require getting a loan.

In most cases, our houses for sale are the ONLY houses in those neighborhoods that are available without a need for bank financing. Because of that …

Our houses sell <u>faster</u> and for <u>top prices</u> because we have multiple buyers interested in them, instead of the other way around. This results in <u>faster</u> sales and <u>greater</u> profits.

In addition, due to the higher demand for "no-banks-required" financing like this than the supply available, you can get a 5–10% higher sale price. Yes, you heard me right—you can sell property for 5–10% more than it is worth. Wow!

I know you are probably totally confused right now, but this is really simple. Here are the basics of how this works …

We will act as a "bank" and provide financing on our own by passing on the existing financing from the previous seller.

In the deal-example given in the previous section, if you remember, we purchased the $250,000.00 house for the balance of the existing loan at $200,000.00.

Now, if we were to sell that house "outright" using conventional methods, we would net around $25,000.00 or less, after paying the real estate commission, closing costs, and making a few payments until we found the buyer and that buyer got the new loan approved. This is not bad considering that with the Unlimited Funding Method #1 we had no money or work involved in this deal.

However, wouldn't you want to double or triple that profit? Why not?

We will double or triple that profit by selling to the MAJORITY of people out there with ANY kind of credit and a little down payment. Here's how:

We will advertise the house as "No Banks Required—Any Credit Welcome." This will attract hundreds of buyers to call us in a single weekend.

Most people out there realize that owning their own home is a smart decision, and they want to buy but can't get a loan.

When they see an ad where their credit doesn't matter, they jump on it right away. So rest assured, you'll get more calls than you can handle.

Using my automated prescreening system, you will easily select the buyer with the largest down payment ("automated system" means no work on your side!).

Then you will act as a bank and finance that buyer. You will use a "wrap" concept that has been used for decades, so you'll have plenty of title companies willing to escrow this type of transaction.

This is the typical outcome for the above deal:

$250,000.00 – Selling price

$25,000.00 – Down-payment received from the buyer (10% is typical for this type of transaction)

$225,000.00 is the balance owed to you from the buyer. You will simply have the buyer pay you monthly based on the terms of that loan that you two agreed on. In essence, you will finance the buyer. It is similar to the seller carryback note where you owe money to the seller. In this case the buyer owes money to you and you are charging them interest on that money. From each monthly payment you receive, you will be making the payment on the loan you took over "subject to" from the seller. The difference is your cash flow.

Because the buyer has less than perfect credit, you are entitled to charge a higher interest rate. So it is very reasonable to ask for a 6.95% interest rate or higher.

Here's your PROFIT based on the existing $200K loan at 5% and the new $225K loan owed to you at 6.95%.

Upfront profit = **$25,000.00** – From the buyer's down payment

Monthly cash flow = **$415.74** – Due to the difference in the loan amounts and interest rate spread

Back-end profit = **$33,631.10** – Cash you will get if the buyer refinances you after 3 years.

Your **total profit,** taking into consideration the whole deal, is **$73,597.32** within a 3-year term. Not bad for a few hours of work.

I don't know if you realize it, but you just TRIPLED your profit.

NOTE: The above numbers I pulled using my amortization tables, so don't try to calculate them in your head.

And it gets BETTER. The above example is very conservative in many aspects. It is very common that we sell those properties for 5–10% above their fair market value (FMV). It is as common if not mandatory that we charge higher interest rates of 9–11% which doubles our cash flow. All that together creates a lot more profit than depicted in the above example.

Plus, there's one more benefit in this structure—if the buyer defaults, you get the house back (most likely worth more) and keep the down payment. Then you can do it all over again and make even more money. Beautiful, isn't it?

This strategy can get you $30,000 in months or $50,000 month after month. Once you do enough deals, you start having months where you get some back-end profits due to some buyers refinancing and in the same month you get new down payments, some from the houses you got back due to default and some from houses that you just acquired. When you add all of it up, you'll have some strong months, month after month.

What I described above is called selling on a "wrap." I'll give you an example below of a real deal case study that illustrates how powerful a moneymaking concept this really is. Then we'll cover our second Niche2Wealth selling-strategy, the N2W Lease Option method.

Wrap sales are EXTREMELY profitable because you profit 5 times with:

1. **The ABOVE Market Sales Price**—People pay more when the financing package is included with it. This profit is realized through the down payment you receive at the onset of the transaction and through the back-end profit at the end when the buyer refinances you out, using a new bank loan.
2. **The Interest Rate SPREAD**—You are generating cash-flow profit by charging interest that's higher than the interest you're paying on the seller's loan you took "subject to."
3. **Interest on the Equity you created**—You are charging a higher interest on the difference between the buyer's loan with you and your loan with the bank.
4. **The Loan Paydown**—The loan that you took "subject to" is paying down every month, creating more equity for you; and that loan is paying down a lot faster than the loan that your buyer is paying to you.
5. **Defaulting Buyer and Appreciation**—If the buyer moves out or defaults and you get the house back, you can resell it again and hopefully for a higher price. You keep the down payment and all the cash flow you collected thus far.

And there are more profit centers, like charging financing points, etc. As I've said many times, with creative real estate investing the N2W way, it always gets better.

The following case study illustrates how a house with NO equity can still make you plenty of money when you use our N2W Wrap method.

Deal Case Study – Rob—How a <u>Dead</u> Deal Was Resurrected to Make $109,000

This is by far one of my favorite case studies, and I am so glad I can share it with you. Not only did we help Rob to make a huge profit on what Rob thought was a dead deal, but we got to save his own house from going into foreclosure and ruining his personal credit.

→ **Create an action item right now to listen to Rob tell you about this in our interview that you can find in our online resource center at www.MarkoRubel.com/book/Rob.**

Rob was one of our Inner Circle coaching students who called me using one of his emergency phone calls *(it's an arrangement where students get my personal cell phone for emergencies)* early one morning, all stressed out. I remember the call because I was taking a little mini-vacation with the family at a nice resort in Las Vegas, and I was by the pool. When my phone rang and I didn't recognize the number, I knew it was probably one of my coaching students with an emergency.

The house he had been trying to sell for many months had become a burden such that he could no longer afford. It was a house where he'd personally lived, so it was bought conventionally before we met and there is no paperwork to show you on that. Rob had taken out a second loan a while back, and the debt on the property was too high and there was no equity.

The many months that the house was listed for sale and sat on the market put Rob in a position where he could no longer afford the payments. He was facing foreclosure. I know you are probably asking, "Why didn't the house sell?" The answer is very simple—it was overpriced. Why? Because a real estate agent friend recommended the higher price in order to cover the cost of sale since there was almost no equity in the property. By the way this is typical from what I see with houses with low or no equity—agents list them too high.

It was a beautiful house in one of the upper middle-class neighborhoods in San Diego.

Here is the summary of the numbers.

Loan balance at that time: $830,000 ($750,000 1st loan & $80,000 2nd loan), which grew to $850,000 because of the late payments Rob could not afford.

Loan Interest Rate: 6.25%

FMV: Approximately $870,000

Selling Price: $899,900 – 2% = $881,900 (the buyer was a realtor and wanted a 2% commission that was advertised by Rob)

Down Payment Received: $50,000

Interest Rate Charged: 7.9%

Selling Terms: Sold on N2W Wrap (in California called "AITD"—all inclusive trust deed with owner financing to realtor buyer who had good credit but didn't want to put down the 20% needed for a conventional purchase)

Monthly Cash Flow: $1,724 per month; the owner paid the property tax

Gross Profits: $109,000—a lot better than a loss to foreclosure, isn't it?

I still remember Rob's emergency call. Rob was in a panic and all stressed out; he was facing foreclosure. His realtor had overpriced the house to cover the cost of selling. First it was listed at $1,099,000. Then it was reduced to $999,900, and then to $899,900.

When Rob called, the first thing that came to my mind was, "Why didn't you tell me about the house sooner?" At this point, he was already behind on payments and his agent suggested that Rob do a short sale because there was no equity in the house.

The first thing I told him to do was relax and look at the power of our Niche2Wealth system. Rob was so stressed out he couldn't see clearly what I was trying to share with him, so it took me a little longer to get him on the same page with me. I told him to hold off on the short sale and the agent's idea, and to apply our Niche2Wealth strategy to his house. Rob could always do a short sale with the agent if this didn't work. There's always plenty of time for a losing proposition like that.

Marko's Money Tip: Don't always think that the first solution is the best, especially if it comes from someone who doesn't know creative real estate or does not have a vested interest in your success. There is usually a creative answer that allows you to save your cash and your credit. Rob used me as his coach to help him analyze this deal with a different set of eyes, and with my experience we turned this upside-down deal into a huge profit.

After getting Rob to calm down and to agree to hold off on the short sale, he followed the steps to advertise the house using the signs, listing techniques, recorded messages, and window flyers, as I teach.

If you want to hear Rob explain how stressful this was, listen to our live video interview.

Rob knew that if my suggestions didn't work, he would lose the house for sure whether by short sale or foreclosure, so he made the change in strategy and the tweaks to his marketing of the house that I suggested on our calls. Within two months, Rob found a buyer with a **$50,000 down payment**. Rob sold the house for $899,900 less 2% commission for the buyer because the buyer was a realtor. The buyer gave Rob $50,000. $5,000 was paid into escrow when Rob and the buyer signed the agreement as an earnest money deposit and then another $45,000 at closing.

Stop and think for a moment ... *Imagine the feeling of getting $50,000 in your hands out of nowhere when you were happy to get nothing just to avoid foreclosure. It is a tremendous feeling, isn't it?*

The buyer didn't even have bad credit. His entire motivation was to use his savings to grow his real estate business (the buyer was a real estate agent) rather than put a 20% down payment the bank would require in a conventional purchase.

Here's a cutout from the purchase and sale agreement with the buyer showing the earnest money deposit and remaining $45,000 of the down payment Rob received:

1.	Total Purchase Price to be paid by Buyer is payable as follows:	
A.	Earnest Money (non-refundable) received from Buyer:	$ 5,000
B.	Additional Earnest Money due from Buyer on _____ (date):	$
C.	Purchase money loan to Seller on terms set forth in Paragraph 2a: (including discount points)	$ 831,900
D.	Proceeds of a new loan to be executed by Buyer to any lender other than Seller as set forth in Paragraph 2b. Name of Lender: _____	$
E.	Balance due at closing (not including Buyers closing costs, prepaid items or prorations) in U.S. cash or locally drawn certified or cashiers check. approximately [ ] exactly [X]	$ 45,000
F.	Total Purchase Price. approximately [ ] exactly [X]	$ 881,900

When the agreement was signed, the seller gave an earnest money deposit of $5,000. The earnest money deposit is a non-refundable portion of the total down payment to ensure the buyer goes through with the deal. The larger the value of the property, the higher the amount you should ask for the earnest money deposit. The thought process here is that the higher amount will prevent the buyer from backing out of the deal at the last minute if their earnest money deposit is at risk. While not foolproof, the higher earnest money deposit is common when values are in this range.

Here are photos of the initial earnest money deposit check and the balance of the down payment paid by the buyer. You will note that the checks are made out to the title company for the buyer's protection.

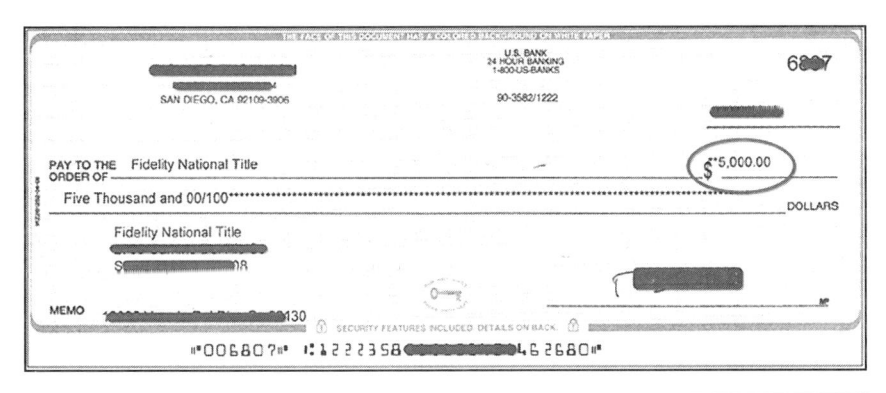

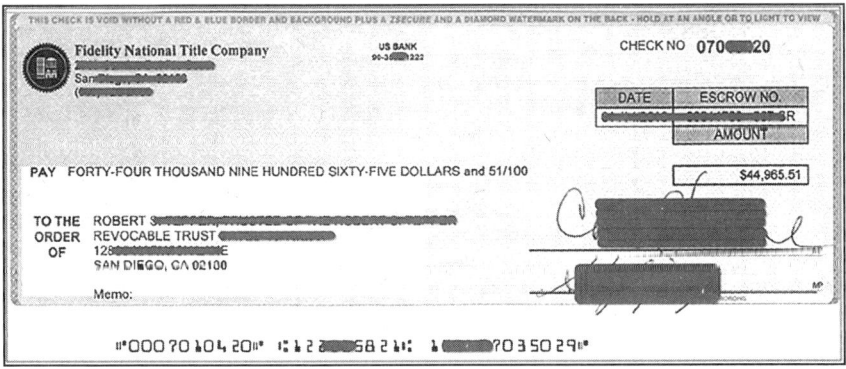

The checks went from the buyer to the title company, in this case Fidelity National Title Co. It is common for the earnest money deposit and the down payment to be handled this way. The money doesn't go directly to the seller, so if there is something wrong and the seller can't perform, the buyer is protected, and vice versa, if the buyer cannot complete the transaction, the seller will receive the earnest money deposit allowed by the signed purchase and sale agreement.

> **Marko's Money Tip:** Use a reliable escrow company, title company, or closing attorney to handle your transactions whenever possible. While there are situations when you need to close privately, using the closing method most common in your state will legitimize the closing in the mind of your seller when you buy and your buyer when you sell. It's worth it.

Let's take a look at the final closing statement when it was all said and done:

FIDELITY NATIONAL TITLE COMPANY

Sellers Closing Statement
Estimated

Description	Debit	Credit
TOTAL CONSIDERATION:		
Total Consideration		881,900.00
NEW AND EXISTING ENCUMBRANCES:		
Seller Carryback from Rob... Trust	831,900.00	
PRORATIONS AND ADJUSTMENTS:		
County Taxes from ... sed on the Semi-Annual amount of $4,356.78	193.63	
ADDITIONAL CHARGES:		
Property Taxes to San Diego County Tax Collector	4,792.45	
Sub Totals	836,886.08	881,900.00
Proceeds Due Seller	45,013.92	
Totals	881,900.00	881,900.00

Do you see the closing statement was done by a reputable title company? These deals have been around for a long time. Now this may sound new or even strange to some of you reading this book; however, it's been done by smart folks other than just me.

I wish I could take the credit, as I said before, but I can't. All I can take credit for is for streamlining it, systematizing it, and creating a business out of it.

By creating a step-by-step process to get started, the special marketing materials, the buyer and seller deal conversion credibility websites, the unique Niche2Wealth negotiation method found in our Inner Circle coaching program, and the one-on-one coaching with emergency calls to me, I created a repeatable and sustainable business that anyone with a dream can use and succeed with.

Rob's closing itself was really pretty simple, with just one extra thing that Rob needed to have prepared to be legally compliant, and that was the **Truth in Lending Disclosure**. After all, Rob was now the bank, so he had to comply with this simple requirement. I gave Rob some simple instructions that you can learn by watching the video interview that allowed Rob to find a **licensed loan originator** who prepared all the disclosures. It really is simple when you know the steps.

→ **Watch as I tell Rob the simple steps, and listen to our live interview by going to www.MarkoRubel.com/book/Rob.**

SIDE NOTE: If you do many of these type of deals every year, then you need to comply with the Dodd-Frank regulations, which is not hard to do. Warning—don't let some uninformed people scare you with Dodd-Frank—it's just another rule to follow, and you'll continue to profit.

In the end, Rob really had only two options.

Option 1: Short Sale / Foreclosure

Option 2: The Niche2Wealth Wrap Strategy, which resulted in $109,000 when all was said and done.

1 – Down payment of $50,000

2 – Monthly cash flow of $1,724.61 X 23 months = $39,666

3 – Back-end profit when the buyer refinanced the house = $17,307

Plus, there was a refund of $3,651.20 for taxes paid that belonged to Rob, which brings his total profit to over $109,000 from a dead deal that would have resulted in a foreclosure being reported on Rob's credit, plus possible deficiency judgment and a 1099 for the amount of the loss to the bank which would be taxable income to Rob.

So I ask you to decide—Is this a better outcome? It sure was for Rob, and I hope this helps you realize the power of our Niche2Wealth business model.

And if the buyer had walked away and not closed and refinanced Rob on his note, then Rob could have repeated the process again and again and made even more money.

When watching Rob's interview, pay attention when he explains how he attended Fix-and-Flip seminars and the outcome of his first deal. Learn from his mistakes.

Tip from Rob he wanted me to share with you:

"Of all of the systems we have ever seen out there and we've seen a lot, Marko's Niche2Wealth system is simply the best. We went to see his live event and joined the Inner Circle coaching. It's all there for you. It's by far the most profitable system for the time you invest, and most investors have no clue how this niche works. It's been here for over 25 years and took Marko over 10 years to make it a real business.

"I found Marko when I wasn't looking. If you are reading this, then you are looking. Marko should be your mentor. His system works, and he cares about his students."

Lease Option as Niche2Wealth Strategy

Would you agree that the N2W Wrap strategy is a super powerful way to profit?

Let me surprise you—even though it is a super profitable strategy, I advise you to use it only at the start of your career when you're in the "cash accumulation" phase. Why? Because when you sell on "wrap" and receive a high down payment, it is very likely that the buyer will refinance and cash you out. This is not a bad thing, but you lose an asset that can later provide passive income.

Therefore I suggest that unless you live in Texas, the majority of your deals should be sold using our N2W Lease Option strategy vs. our N2W Wrap strategy.

In Texas, some misled legislators made lease options illegal, so since you can't do them there, you should continue doing wraps. If you're in Texas, don't get discouraged by this because Texas is an excellent state for my business model and I have a lot of successful students there.

The N2W Lease Option strategy is, as you've already learned from Anto's Deal Case Study, where you find a tenant/buyer who will rent the house from you with an exclusive right to buy it during the given term.

The tenant/buyer signs the lease and option agreement, which gives them the right to possession and defines the rent amount, the term, and other conditions. The option agreement gives the tenant/buyer the exclusive right to buy at a price that could be fixed for the term of the option or that could be adjusted to the FMV. I have a special legal clause for that. Keep in mind if the tenant/buyer wants to buy, then you have to sell.

> **Marko's Money Tip:** Always keep lease and option agreements as <u>separate</u> agreements. This lowers any potential problems of the transaction being classified as equitable mortgage and preventing you from evicting a defaulting tenant/buyer, pushing you to go through a lengthy judicial foreclosure.

The typical down payment, which is called "option consideration" is between 3% and 5% and is non-refundable if the buyer defaults or the option expires.

The typical rent is set to fair market rent or even up to 20% above that. Part of the rent could be, but doesn't need to be, credited towards the purchase price as rent credit.

So as you may realize, when you "sell" using lease options, you remain the owner—the deed doesn't change. That's why I put "sell" in quotations because you don't really sell, but it's not renting either.

We usually offer a 12- or a 24-month term to the tenant/buyer. The reason that you don't want to offer a longer term is to be able to raise the price, rent, or change the terms to maximize your profit. And also to be able to eliminate a pain-in-the-neck tenant/buyer if you happen to get one. I've had hundreds of tenant/buyers, and only 3 were pains. So your odds are good.

The Advantage of "Selling" on Lease Option vs. Wrap:

You keep depreciation—Since you keep the ownership, you can depreciate the property on your tax return, which allows you to shelter your other income and keep more money in your pocket.

It's more likely you'll get the house back and make more money with it—The lease option (LO) down payment is generally a lot lower than in wraps, so tenant/buyers are more likely to walk away from the deal leaving you with the house that's then worth more; plus you have the down payment and cash flow they've been paying you. Now, don't get me wrong here—you do not want to set people up for failure—you need to do everything possible to put people in the house who will benefit from the arrangement, so everyone wins. Plus, you need to comply with what you promised in your agreements to stay out of legal trouble. However, statistically I can tell you that most tenant/buyers do not buy, so you'll likely get the property back.

> **Marko's Money Tip:** Always use an attorney to explain lease option documents to tenant/buyers. It establishes proper positioning which lowers the chances of tenant/buyers damaging the house. Due to the setup I've been using, I don't remember getting any but one house back in all these years that had more damage than the normal wear and tear.

The Disadvantage of "Selling" on Lease Option vs. Wrap:

As said above, with the LO you will get less money upfront—3% to 5% versus 10%+ with wraps. Plus, your monthly cash flow will be lower because the wrap buyer gets to deduct the mortgage interest paid to you, so they can afford the higher payment.

→ **In Section 2** you will learn more about N2W Lease Options since it is the preferred exit strategy for my coaching students after they go through the "capital accumulation" phase.

Quick Review of All Available Exit Strategies

Here are all the available selling strategies we use and my guess-percentage of how often we use them:

1. **N2W Lease Option** – The only strategy that leverages all 5 wealth-building components of investing in real estate. It is the fastest way to long-term wealth because even when the property is purchased you end up getting the top price without the cost of commission, etc.

    At the start of your career, you use it after the first few deals, putting a minimum of $30,000–$50,000 in your bank account. After that, you use it as often as you can.

2. **N2W Wrap Sale** – As you learned, this strategy highly maximizes profits. It leverages 3 wealth-building components, plus the fourth—appreciation if the buyer defaults. It doesn't leverage the fifth—depreciation since the ownership passes.

    It is more often used at the beginning of your career. Later on it transitions to 50-50 wrap vs. option and then down to 30% wraps and 60–70% LOs.

3. **Outright Sale** – This is when you sell conventionally where the buyer gets a new bank loan and cashes you out. The seller's "subject to" loan gets paid of as well.

This is **the least profitable** way to sell. It leverages only one wealth-building point and that is—buy low, sell high. If you had ownership for less than a year, you will pay more in taxes since the profit will be taxed as ordinary income. You should avoid selling outright whenever possible because of the above. You can't build wealth selling outright.

Here are a few scenarios when selling outright is the way to go. If the property has a loan that has or will soon have a very high interest rate, you sell outright because the high interest rate would cause negative cash flow. Another reason would be if you purchased the property "subject to" but had to put more money in the deal than you were able to get out using a wrap sale. For example, you had to reinstate the loan and give some money to the seller, so you'd want to free up that money quickly.

4. **Wholesaling – Flipping** – As you already know, you buy only "pretty" houses that don't need more repairs beyond carpet and paint. However, sometimes as part of the regular course of business, you will get a call about an "ugly" house. When those houses fall in your lap, you should not get tempted to rehab them because the risk and time investment is not worth it. So you wholesale a deal like that to a rehabber.

   The percentage of these sales will be very small in your business because your advertising is targeted to pretty houses. I'd say it would be no more than 1 deal in 10 or 20 N2W deals. Flipping leverages only one wealth-building component and will not get you far. There's no money there (despite what you hear in your emails).

5. **Rent** – Once you get a minimum of 10 properties sold on wrap or LO, you can keep some houses as rentals. I do NOT advise you to have any rentals in the first few years of your business because the LOs will accomplish the same with a lot less hassles. Remember—LO tenant/buyers are responsible for most repairs.

IMPORTANT: As said earlier, these exit strategies determine how much you can pay for the property. So if you have a deal that you could buy without using much cash and the loan has a good interest rate, your exit strategy will be the N2W Wrap or LO. In that case you can pay the seller up to 80% of the FMV (minus repairs if any). However, if you have to sell outright, then you can't pay more than 75% of FMV (minus repairs if any) because your cost of sale is higher when selling outright and you can't get an "above" market price as you could with N2W Wrap/LO strategies.

10 Reasons for the Niche2Wealth Business Model

Here are <u>10 Strong REASONS</u> why this is **the best way** to profit **today**:

1. You buy without using your credit or money (in most cases), using the Unlimited Funding Methods. Therefore, you don't depend on banks or lenders.

2. The financing you "inherit" with the property is at a low interest rate, allowing you to get cash flow from day one.

3. You are leveraging on the current economic conditions. There are plenty of sellers, who are slightly motivated, just about to be behind on payments, or already in foreclosure and really motivated.

    → We'll cover "Winning Foreclosure Strategies" in one of the **webinars**.

4. Your product, "the house with financing," appeals to the **majority** of people in this economy. You are solving a need and getting paid a lot for doing it.

5. You get **top price** and a **fast sale** because most people out there want the "product" you have for sale.

6. You **PROFIT** is **double** or even **triple** compared to other investors because you are leveraging <u>multiple</u> profit centers. In addition to a difference in price, you are profiting by charging higher interest rates, financing points, etc. (there are a few more profit centers that I don't want to confuse you with here).

7. You are working SMART, **not hard**. You're not rehabbing houses and then hoping to find a buyer who will qualify for the loan (minority). The typical N2W transaction takes 2–3 hours to do.
8. It is easy to delegate. After the few first deals, your entire selling process will be delegated. Your entire marketing will be automated, leaving you with a high six- or even seven-figure business that you can run part-time.

    → *If you want to work SMART not hard, take a lot of notes during our trainings.*

9. If the buyer defaults, you get the house back, keep the down payment, and do it all over again … getting more down payments and additional cash flow. If the house has appreciated, you are the one who benefits from it.
10. You are providing a great service by helping sellers and buyers.

If you are confused by some of it, it may get clarified as we go through deals in the next section. It is normal not to pick up every little detail the first time you're reading this book. I don't expect you to understand it all. This is a new concept for most of you, and that's why I have created webinars and provide you more training on it.

All I want to do with this book is to show you what 99% of investors are missing. And I feel great that I accomplished that if you are with me reading at this point.

We'll take the learning in two steps. First you will learn how **Unlimited Funding** works, so you can quickly buy some properties and make some quick cash.

Then our second step will be to learn how to sell it the **Niche-2Wealth** way and double or triple your profits. At that point you'll be on the way to big money.

My feeling is—if you got this far, you have what it takes to succeed. You have the desire to learn and change your life, and I commend you for that.

I suggest you attend all of our webinars, join our monthly coaching, and learn as much as you can from my team and me.

We will show you how all this works and show you the proof, a lot of proof, so you will know without any doubt that these strategies are proven to make you wealthy, as they did for our coaching students you'll meet in Section 2.

Final Thoughts
—Important to Read

Before I get to Section 2 and show you millions of dollars generated by strategies we've just covered, **I want to thank you for reading this book so far**, and I sincerely hope you'll take action and educate yourself more on this very lucrative real estate niche. I'll tell you later on how I can help you do that.

Don't put this book down and fail to take your next step.

As I've said many times, it is completely normal if you don't understand everything that I've covered. Making millions takes some learning and 100 or so pages cannot possibly give you every little detail. It's normal that you still have many questions unanswered.

But here's a BIGGER POINT ...

Most people don't act when they see something that requires some learning. They see it as an effort ... and do nothing.

Instead, they simply let the days just pass them by as they go through life half-awake.

Leading many to a life like this ...

They had dreams when they were young, replaced by responsibilities as they matured, and were left with <u>nothing but regrets</u> when they were old.

Sure they'd hoped to be happier. They wanted to be more successful. But every day was the same, nothing ever changed. They didn't feel like they had the time, the discipline, or the resources to take the necessary steps.

My whole goal in writing this book is to wake you up and show you that it is possible. So you realize that you don't need money to profit, that you don't need good credit or a lot of time—all you need is a desire to step out of your daily routine, and then you take that next step.

Learn and implement.

And by doing so, you'll put yourself and your family on the path to a more enjoyable and fulfilling life, a life without stress and worry about money.

This way, instead of letting life pass you by, you _slam on the brakes_ and stop the routine. You stop wishing and waiting, and take a different and more fulfilling alternative than everyone else. _All it requires is for you to make an_ effort.

Will it be easy? Not at first. But each day it will get easier. And shortly after your first few Unlimited Funding deals, it will get as easy as you wish it were right now.

Besides, even if it was difficult at first and even if it took you 6 months to get your first big check (which it won't), **what choice do you have?** Just settle and resign to living an unfulfilling life? Of course not.

Because once you realize that 6 months will go by anyway, it really becomes not a choice but an IQ test. And you either "get it" or you don't.

I hope I've woken you up to reality, and you realize your dreams aren't going to happen on their own. A better financial situation isn't going to magically appear out of nowhere, nor are you going to wake up one day and suddenly be living your dream life. The fact is … **_You either get serious and make an effort, or live with the regret that you never did._**

Obvious, right?

Even as obvious as it is, many don't get it and continue living in mediocrity. They continue _dealing with people they can't stand, settling with a reality they'd rather not, preparing to do the same thing day after day._

They want things to be better, without a doubt, but are unwilling to take the simple steps to make it happen.

YOU have to be your source of change. If you want to change the outcome, you need to change what you're doing. If things are going to improve, you have to improve them. And it all starts today, right now.

So repeat frequently, and let your unconsciousness mind absorb it:

If things are going to change, I have to change. If I want my life to be better, I must stop looking for a magic pill and get to work. I will take action today.

A Personal Thought

As I end the first part of this book, let me share with you one final and personal thought concerning my view on the information age we live in and why I felt I needed to write this book for you.

We are continually being bombarded with promises of immediate gratification, instant success, overnight riches, one-click solutions, and fast temporary relief, all of which lead us to believe things that are untrue and even worse … harmful.

That's why you need to start screening the information and emails coming your way because if you don't, you'll certainly head in the wrong direction.

I've tried in this book to give you a real sense of the real estate business that has changed my life and the lives of my students. I want to show you and explain to you that there are not that many choices when it comes to making money in this business.

It tears me up talking to so many beginner (and even seasoned) investors who are on the wrong path and don't ever realize it.

Now that you're here you've got a choice …

You can put it aside and go on living your life as if nothing ever happened and nothing really needs to change. If you do, then I owe you an apology. Because it means my words weren't strong enough, my thoughts weren't presented clearly enough, and all I did was waste both of our time.

Or …

You can decide right now that starting today you're going to start learning and implementing the system that I shared with you, the system supported by nothing but proof. Realize you're doing it for yourself, for your family, for your friends, and for your life. If so, then all the time and effort I put into writing this and all the time and effort you put into reading it have been the highest and best uses of our time.

Only you can decide.

If you don't mind, I'd really appreciate knowing what you decided and the actions you plan on taking next. Shoot me an email at: MR@MarkoRubel.com

To your better future,

Marko Rubel
MR@MarkoRubel.com

PS: We're NOT done yet. The next section is even more exciting because it's the proof. However, this is the time for you to **go to the online resources at www.MarkoRubel.com/book** and start learning more.

> YOU WERE BORN TO WIN, BUT TO BE A WINNER,
> YOU MUST PLAN TO WIN,
> PREPARE TO WIN, AND EXPECT TO WIN.
>
> *—Zig Ziglar*

— SECTION II —

Deal Case Studies

You're About to Discover How You Can Finally Create $1,000,000 in Net Worth over the Next Few Years ... Plus, How to Earn a 6-Figure Income While Doing It.

In Addition, You'll Learn How to Quickly & Easily Create Passive Income to Replace Your Current Salary/Hourly Wage ... Plus, Start Fulfilling All Your Dreams!

You are about to learn what it takes to make some serious money from a few of my students who have used the strategies explained in this book to improve their lives and their incomes. I want you to know that you can do this as well, so I've picked 10 people of various backgrounds and locations.

<u>All of them are my coaching students.</u>

Some have just completed their first deals and are excited about the opportunities ahead of them while some have done 10, 15, even 20+ deals and have built in short order a net worth of over $1,000,000 and are going for more.

You'll get to hear from all of them, and you'll finally realize this is something you can do.

I asked each one of them to tell you, in their own words

about their background, how they met me, to randomly pick one or more of their deals to describe, and then finally to give you advice from their perspective—from where they are now, looking back. Enjoy!

> HAPPINESS LIES IN THE JOY OF ACHIEVEMENT AND THE THRILL OF CREATIVE EFFORT.
>
> —*Franklin D. Roosevelt*

VERY IMPORTANT—WATCH THE VIDEOS AS YOU READ THEIR EXPLANATION OF THEIR PARTICULAR DEAL

This is a <u>very important</u> section of the book. It's proof positive that there are <u>3 important things to pay attention to</u>:

1. **The Niche2Wealth Business Model is the FASTEST way there is to get you into big profits and wealth.** It is the only real estate investing strategy that will get you into the big profit arena fast—even if your credit is lousy and you don't have a lot of money to get started.

2. **Your Background Is NOT the Deciding Factor.** The investors mentioned in these examples are from various backgrounds from a stay-at-home mom, to a police officer, to a software engineer. There's even an example from a CPA. So your background or a current situation does not determine your success.

    SIDE NOTE: I coached a high school dropout who was more successful than a Harvard graduate. I found that the Harvard graduate had a terrible time making a single appointment. Why? I don't know, but with that said, I feel that education is never a guarantee that someone is going to become a success in this business, or in any other business for that matter.

3. **Your Location Does Not Matter**. In the 10 examples I've given you, I do not and cannot cover all 50 states, but I do have students using these methods in almost every state. Going through these examples, a lot of things will be obvious to you. One is that our Niche2Wealth business model works from the East to West Coasts and anywhere in between. That means it'll work in your area as well.

Do you know what all these investors have in common?

They all share a stronger, deeper, relentless <u>commitment</u> to becoming successful.

This commitment is far beyond what most ever think about deploying.

That's one of the big reasons why I consider these ordinary people "EXTRAORDINARY."

They didn't give up when they encountered obstacles, hurtles, and big challenges!

They kept their head down, dusted themselves off when things didn't work out, and continued to work harder than they previously did, all the while staying focused on their end game plan.

That's why their results are not typical.

Again, they are ordinary people just like you and me that are making themselves extraordinary. These types of people always go the extra mile, no matter what. They know even though they stub their toes, they're not going to quit … ever.

I hope you're ready to be extraordinary as well and leave the mediocrity you may be experiencing now … behind—once and for all!

HISTORY HAS DEMONSTRATED THAT THE MOST
NOTABLE WINNERS USUALLY ENCOUNTERED
HEARTBREAKING OBSTACLES BEFORE THEY
TRIUMPHED.
THEY WON BECAUSE THEY REFUSED TO BECOME
DISCOURAGED BY THEIR DEFEATS.

—B. C. Forbes

How Important Is Your Success to You?

The first 5 video interviews review **the hidden secrets to success** in real estate. Watching all 10 interviews will give you a deeper understanding of what it takes to become a millionaire using real estate as your business!

If you want to make money, live a better lifestyle, provide a better environment for your family, now's the time to invest a few hours in your future.

You need to watch the first 5 interviews THIS WEEK.

NOTE: Student Advice to You (referred to as "Message to Reader") has NOT been edited. It is printed in this book in its original form and format, exactly how they were emailed to me.

Since we live in a world of social media and virtually no privacy, their last names and cities have been omitted. This was done in order to protect these individuals and their families.

Introduction to Deal Examples

My advice if you want the biggest bang for your buck is to read every single deal example I've provided you with (by the 10 investors you'll hear from) in this section.

Once you've done that, you'll have a very good understanding of the business by the time you're done reading this section. Then just follow the advice given in the last chapter called "Your Next Step".

Even though I say it is "mandatory" that you read about every deal and look through the documents I've provided to give you a much better understanding, I want to bring your attention to something else to let you know the real power of these strategies.

Here's what you're about to find out—As you go through each deal, you'll notice that these deals, even though they're in separate parts of the country, they're all pretty similar. Sure, there are some great learning points from each of them, but conceptually they are very similar.

What does that tell you?

It means that these types of deals are all "cookie-cutter," and therefore easy to structure.

As we're going from student to student, from one side of the country to the other, from deal example to deal example, the deals are pretty similar.

What do you think—is this good or bad?

Is It good or bad that your second deal is the same as your first, your third as your second, etc.?

It is actually GOOD because it was meant to improve your efficiency. I do things by design, not by default. A few moving parts is always better in this business than a bunch of moving parts. Why? Because it's easier, and what you'll find out is that fewer things can go wrong when fewer parts are moving all the time.

When fewer parts move, this helps you organize your business and hone it down to a science. When you get the system down, you'll find yourself working smarter, not harder, and isn't that what everyone wants?

Here's what I generally ask people—Do you want to have more time to enjoy life and be with your family more, or do you want a business that you have to micro manage, so you're stressed out all the time?

You can never get wealthy if some of your deals are rehabs, some wholesaling, some rentals, some "subject to," etc. Why? Because you will never be able to optimize the process and make it efficient.

For example, a rehabber who does less than 10 deals a year can't have her own crew, so by hiring different contractors all the time, she'll have a lot more hassles managing them.

Another example is a Niche2Wealth investor who is building an "any credit" buyers list, but then going and trying wholesaling and building an "investor" buyers list too—two different lists and two different businesses not only doubles the effort, but also results in half the efficiency.

It is true for many areas in life, but especially for real estate investing that if you want to be a "jack of all trades," then you'll end up being a "master of none."

SIDE NOTE: I know the above goes contrary to what some of you have heard—that you have to become a "transaction engineer," and as such, you need to learn all the different investing strategies, from wholesaling, to fixing, to renting, to notes, etc. This is NOT true, and that term was invented to sell you more seminars because to be a "transaction engineer," you need this seminar, then you need that seminar, and on and on, until you spend all your money.

The beauty of our Niche2Wealth business is—it is actually SIMPLE.

I know what some of you're saying … It's not simple. This is complicated stuff.

No, it's not. It seems to be complicated when I dump a million-dollar business on you over 200 pages or so, in an hour or two. That is complicated, but the business in itself is not.

I can go on and on … but let's turn to the students in this section and watch the videos, so you'll understand that it is, in fact, simple and—you can do it.

Coaching Student Success #1

Learn How a High School Teacher Applied Niche2Wealth Investing and Went from One House to $1,200,000.00 Net Worth & $13,500.00 per Month in <u>Passive</u> Income

Watch the video interview where Lester reveals how he got to 24 houses and plans to get 50 more. Learn how he overcame the initial fears and self-doubt that prevent many from succeeding. The advice he gives is invaluable – take notes!

Go to www.MarkoRubel.com/book/Lester

Lester Shares 3 Deals: UFP Methods #2, #3, and #4

Lester has been my coaching student for a few years now, so I've had the opportunity to see the type of houses he buys, and I've even had the opportunity to be at one of his closings. In the picture below we are on the way out from the title company after he picked up a nice check—you'll notice the happy smile on his face …

He has displayed that happy smile quite often over the last 3 years. At the time of writing this book, Lester controls **24 houses** that he purchased without ever qualifying for a loan using the exact techniques described in this book. Those houses have now over **$1,200,000 in equity**—yes, that is **over ONE MILLION DOLLARS**. Imagine the feeling if that were your portfolio we were describing…

On top of it, he has already made close to $300,000 cash from the down payments he received from those houses. In addition, the people who live in his houses are paying down his loans and growing his equity by $60,000–70,000 every year.

Do you think Lester has to stress out about his bills?

Not anymore because **he has over $13,500 in positive cash flow** coming in every month, regardless if he works or decides to be on vacation. That is the power of PASSIVE INCOME—exactly what I've been telling you about throughout the book.

→ **Please pay attention at 13:00 minutes in the video interview when he starts talking about the great feeling of having passive income.**

By the way, it would take you 20 years to get to this kind of passive income using a conventional investing approach, where you save for a down payment, go to the bank and qualify for a loan, and then hassle with tenants and toilets. And it is highly unlikely you'd ever get there wholesaling or rehabbing houses.

Now, I'm not saying never; however, you do the math and draw your own conclusion on how many houses you'd need to wholesale or rehab to get to Lester's earnings and passive income.

Some of you may be thinking, "Lester had a lot of money and has a real estate or financing background, so it's easy for him." None of that is true. He used to be a high school teacher. AND like many of you, myself included, he had inner obstacles that were stopping him from getting ahead and thinking BIG.

→ **Watch the online video interview and listen carefully as Lester confesses his self-doubts and how he overcame obstacles to reach success.**

---

* * *

I asked all the students you'll meet in this section to email me a short paragraph about their background, how they met me, and what advice they have for a person reading this book—for you. So before we "dissect" Lester's 3 deals, let me share with you what he emailed me, in his own words:

Your Background: *(Lester writing here ...)*

I have an education degree and taught high school for a num-

131

ber of years. I wanted to have more freedom in my life/schedule, so I started my own screen-printing and embroidery business. The business was good, but I kept thinking I needed to find a way to generate some passive income sources. I purchased one single family home and then realized I needed more options in purchasing.

How you met Marko:

Just by chance, I saw Marko speak at another investing event. This was the first speaking event I had ever attended. I was trying to find ways to get more working capital. Marko spoke and I thought his ProfitGrabber software was something that I needed to keep organized. Marko didn't speak about the ways to use other people's money and credit. A year later, I decided to go to one of Marko's seminars. I attended in San Diego, joined his Inner Circle (coaching), and started the great journey I'm on now.

Your Message to Reader:

Marko's program works. At the first seminar I attended with Marko, the same one when I joined the Inner Circle coaching, I really felt like I understood what he was teaching and I could do it. I feel very fortunate that I decided to get the coaching. My coach pushed me to get over the fear that I had at the time. I'm pretty sure I would still be coming up with reasons why I couldn't do this, but my coach pushed and I quit procrastinating. It has been one of the most rewarding things I have ever done. It's taken work, but this has improved my family's financial situation by many factors. My wife no longer works, and we have much more time to do the things we want.

The program is not get-rich-quick, but if you take what Marko teaches and start talking with potential sellers, you will be amazed at the simplicity and the rewards.

* * *

Like many of you reading this book, Lester knew that he should own some real estate for his retirement, so he took all of his savings and purchased his first house for cash. Then he realized that he couldn't make enough cash flow by renting out that house and that he couldn't buy enough houses to make a difference for his retirement without a ton more cash. That is what initially had him look at our "Unlimited Funding Program".

As he says above, Lester met me at the first investor seminar he ever attended. He purchased my ProfitGrabber Pro software program because he knew that he wanted to have a big business and believed it would help him get organized. It took him a year to attend my seminar, which he did in San Diego. He joined my Inner Circle coaching program and got started working with me and with one of my guys as his coach. He went from owning one house purchased with all his own cash and seeing the limitations of that method, to owning over 24 houses in a few short years, and he even can't believe what he's achieved. Here I am with Lester at my training.

Over time, Lester's vision for what is possible has grown along with his portfolio. Now Lester, has a goal to go from owning 24 houses to owning over 75 houses, and he totally can see how it will happen.

> **Marko's Money Tip:** It's so important to have a vision for your business and your future. When I was interviewing Lester over Skype to gather his thoughts for this book, I noticed that he had precise Excel spreadsheets about the equity in all of his properties, and you can see the enthusiasm on his face when he is reviewing that spreadsheet. This is a clue about his success—he is excited about growing his net worth and that is why he's so successful. Be excited about your future, envision it daily, and it will help you move towards your goal.

Now I don't want you to think that Lester or me or others in this book didn't have obstacles and it was always just clear sailing. It was not like that. We had obstacles, and you'll have them as well. However, it's easier to overcome obstacles when you are focused on the ultimate goal because those obstacles look less important in comparison to your goal. So my advice is to always, always keep your goals in front of you.

Lester had many months where he made $20,000–30,000, and he has even had $50,000 and $60,000 months. What would it take in a job or investing the traditional way where you bought the houses all cash (if you had the cash) or by putting down 20% and getting a loan (if you could qualify for enough loans) for you to have those kind of monthly paydays? How many of you would like to be like Lester and "retire your wife" from her job? How many wives reading this would like to retire your husbands? It's all possible.

Let's look at some of Lester's deals.

Deal Example #1:
Unlimited Funding Method #2 – Get Paid to Buy

Here is a deal where Lester got paid $12,500 from the seller to buy their house. The house was in a middle-class neighborhood and in perfect condition. Lester paid the seller around 85% of the fair market value (FMV) of the house. The criteria I teach my students is to not exceed 80% of the FMV. However, this was a nice house that "came with" a cash payment, so it was a still good deal. Here are pictures of the house and a summary of the numbers:

Purchase Price: $205,700

Down Payment: - $12,500 SELLER PAID THAT TO LESTER

Purchase Terms: take over existing loan "subject to" and seller paid Lester to buy because the purchase price was lower than the loan balance

Loan Balance at that time: $218,288 @ 4.25%

Selling Price: $238,000

Down Payment Received: $17,000

Amount financed by Lester: $221,000 @ 8.25%

Selling Terms: N2W AITD sold on owner financing in one week

Cash Flow Amount: $475/mo.

As I mentioned to you at the start of this book, the general population has no clue that this business even exists, and the investor community and most of those in the real estate industry (attorneys, agents, and title companies) are completely unfamiliar with these strategies.

→ Watch the online video interview to learn how even Lester was surprised he got paid to buy, and when he told his wife about the deal, she was too.

However, just remember, because you are reading this book, now you're an "insider," so you know WHY the sellers are willing to do that and why it's still a win-win transaction.

These sellers called and made an appointment with Lester after they received a small postcard Lester mailed to houses in the targeted zip code describing his services. As Lester learned when he went to meet the sellers, there were several generations and families living in the house together, and there was some conflict amongst the family members. So for the sellers, their motivation and what was attractive about Lester's offer was the ability to close quickly and move on with their lives.

The house was in absolutely perfect condition. It had 5 bedrooms, granite countertops, and hardwood floors with lots of upgrades and great square footage, as you can kind of see from this picture:

Here is the purchase agreement that Lester walked away with. Look at the minus sign (-) in front of the $14,290.00. That's because the seller is paying Lester to buy the house because the purchase price is less than the loan balance.

2. PURCHASE PRICE. Buyer to pay the purchase price as follows (check all that applies):	
☑ EARNEST DEPOSIT, receipt of which is hereby acknowledged in the sum of.............	$ 10.00
☑ CASH DOWN PAYMENT at closing in the amount of...	$ -14290
☑ TAKE TITLE SUBJECT TO AN EXISTING FIRST TRUST DEED NOTE held by Wells Fargo with an approximate unpaid amount of .... payable $ 1863.00 monthly until paid, including interest not exceeding 5.0 %.	$ 220,000
☐ TAKE TITLE SUBJECT TO AN EXISTING SECOND TRUST DEED NOTE held by _____ with an approximate unpaid amount of .... payable $_____ monthly until paid, including interest not exceeding ___%.	$ —
☐ A PROMISSORY NOTE in the principal amount of .... See the Attached Addendum for the terms of the note.	$ —
TOTAL PURCHASE PRICE IS THE AMOUNT OF	$ 205,700

You'll notice that the purchase and sales agreement states $14,000 when actually it was $12,578.12, as you can see on the HUD form below. Why was the loan balance actually $1,500 different from what the seller had told Lester at the meeting? Because they didn't have the latest mortgage statement at the time Lester wrote up the agreement. See line 203 where the loan was taken "subject to" in the amount of $218,288.12.

J. SUMMARY OF BORROWER'S TRANSACTION	
100. GROSS AMOUNT DUE FROM BORROWER:	
101. Contract Sales Price	205,700.00
102. Personal Property	
103. Settlement Charges to Borrower (Line 1400)	1,215.25
104.	
105.	
Adjustments For Items Paid By Seller in advance	
106. City/Town Taxes to	
107. County Taxes to	
108. HOA ASSMTS.	532.46
109.	
110.	
111. EQUITY PD. BY SELLER TO BUYER	12,578.12
112.	
120. GROSS AMOUNT DUE FROM BORROWER	220,025.83
200. AMOUNTS PAID BY OR IN BEHALF OF BORROWER:	
201. Deposit or earnest money	10.00
202. Principal Amount of New Loan(s)	
203. Existing loan(s) taken subject to	218,288.12
204.	
205.	
206.	

The house was in such good shape and the sellers had cleaned it so nicely that Lester didn't need to do a single thing more in order to show it. In fact, Lester used the techniques we teach our Inner Circle coaching students and began marketing the property as soon as he had the signed agreement.

So literally Lester closed with the sellers on a Thursday, showed the house to a potential buyer the following day, a Friday. The buyer signed the paperwork to buy that day, and Lester closed the following Friday, getting another $17,000 from the buyer, all within 8 days.

How would you like to sell your houses that quickly? You will if you listen to me and sell to people who are in the majority out there—people with ANY kind of credit history. There were no delays due to bank loan-qualifying or any of that. As you can see, our business is simpler than that.

Below in the picture of the selling HUD statement you can see that the total down payment was tendered to closing in one deposit of $12,000, 2 deposits for $2,000, and an earnest deposit of $1,000, totaling $17,000:

120. GROSS AMOUNT DUE FROM BORROWER	244,568.56
200. AMOUNTS PAID BY OR IN BEHALF OF BORROWER:	
201. Deposit or earnest money	1,000.00
202. Principal Amount of New Loan(s)	221,000.00
203. Existing loan(s) taken subject to	
204.	
205.	
206.	
207. **DOWN PAYMENT + $1K EARNEST DEPOSIT**	
208.	
209. PORTION OF DOWN PAYMENT	12,000.00
Adjustments For Items Unpaid By Seller	
210. City/Town Taxes to	
211. County Taxes to	
212. HOA ASSMTS to	
213. LEASE DEPOSIT	2,000.00
214. BAL OF DOWNPAYMENT BY 1-31-13	2,000.00
215.	
216.	
217.	

The underlying loan is a 30-year loan at 4.25%, and Lester sold it the next day at 8.25%, thus giving him a **$475/month cash flow** on a house he never had to do any work on at all.

To recap this deal, it gave a profit of $29,500 between the seller's payment to Lester of $12,500 and the buyer's down payment of $17,000 when the buyer purchased it, all for 5–6 hours of work, plus $475 per month cash flow. So in a total of less than 3 weeks, Lester met a seller, bought their house, closed, sold it the next day, closed with the buyer a week later, and made $29,500, plus monthly cash flow.

Now compare this to a fix-up deal that takes months to complete and then months to find a buyer who can close, all while stressing out about the high interest hard money that you had to borrow and the payments you have to make.

In addition to the monthly cash flow, this deal still has a nice backend because of points and differences between the seller's note Lester is paying and the buyer's note Lester made with his buyer. Plus there is always a possibility of the buyer's defaulting and Lester's getting the house back and making more profit all by doing it all over again.

As you can see from this deal, and especially if you watch the video interview with Lester, the opportunities in this business are amazing. This is not about getting rich overnight. It takes learning and it takes work, **but the returns are huge.** Where else can you make $30,000 with 5–6 hours of your work (obviously not including the learning)?

→ **Why would people sell and leave their loan in place? When you watch the video interview, pay attention to the important tip that Lester shares about discovering the real seller motivation.**

In summary, there are people out there that have problems and needs we can solve and get paid handsomely for.

Can you imagine getting full ownership of a beautiful house at below market price, with a long-term loan in place that you never qualified for, and in addition, you get paid thousands of dollars to take it? I hope, <u>now you can</u>!

As they say, you can't win if you don't play, so you won't get deals like this if you never get into the business. You need to expose yourself to opportunities. That's the first step.

You miss 100% of the shots you don't take.

—*Wayne Gretzky*

→ **Advice: Pay attention to Lester's advice at the end of the video. <u>It's important advice you should not miss</u>. He talks about something more important than know-how.**

Deal Example #2:
Unlimited Funding Methods #3 & 4 – Cash + Note

In his short real estate career, Lester "got paid to buy" in about 20% of his deals, varying from a seller making a payment or two, to having them write him a check for $15,000.

The following deal is even more typical. Most of the deals out there are where we pay sellers a few thousand dollars for their equity (or as moving money) and take their loan over (UFP Method #3); or have them carry back part of the purchase price in terms of a seller carryback note (UFP Method #4); or combination of both.

As you've already learned, we work with "pretty" houses only. The most I usually do on my deals and the most I teach students to do on their deals are cosmetic repairs. For example, paint and carpet is common and sometimes fixing the yard. More often than not, all we need to do is get the carpet professionally cleaned and have our handyman do some touch-up painting. This way we don't waste time on fixing the house, but rather we make money fixing the financing, as you've learned in this book.

I asked Lester to share with you one of his deals <u>where the buyer refinanced</u> the house, paid Lester, and completed the transaction. This way you get an understanding of the whole process **from start to finish**.

Here's Lester in front of the house, just a typical middle-class neighborhood house:

The seller had a lot of equity, so Lester was worried about being able buy it because he didn't have that much cash to pay the seller.

SIDE NOTE: Even if he had, it would make no sense to put $60,000+ in one deal. In this biz, our goal is to get houses using the least cash possible, and if we use any, we should be able to get most of it back right away when we get the buyer's down payment. So putting tens of thousands of dollars in a single deal is not a good business practice because that much cash can buy 10 or more houses.

So despite being concerned if he could do the deal or not, Lester still went for it because he maintained the right mindset. Remember, having the correct mindset is the key to success in anything—that's why I talked about mindset right at the start of this book and showed you a deal our student who is a police officer did. I talk about mindset very often in all of my trainings because it is so important.

After seeing the house, Lester followed our P-E-N process to build credibility in front of the seller, educate the seller on the costs of sale, and position his offer as a good solution. As mentioned already, presenting offers and solutions to motivated sellers is **not** a random process; rather, it is a strategically designed process that ensures a high probability of getting the deal.

Lester's proposal to the seller was to buy his house at 80% of its FMV, which was $120,000. The seller's loan balance was $51,000. Do you see a problem here? Even with a nice 20% discount, at the price of $120,000, the seller still had $69,000 in equity.

Lester proposed to give the seller $3,000 cash at closing and to pay him the remaining $66,000 at a later date when Lester's buyer refinanced the house. During that part of their conversation, Lester presented the benefits of the quick and easy sale to entice the seller to go for it.

The seller was determined to get this house sold ASAP, so **he agreed** to Lester's proposal. You better believe that Lester got excited! Here's the part of the purchase and sale agreement outlining the above:

2. **PURCHASE PRICE.** Buyer to pay the purchase price as follows (check all that applies):

☑ EARNEST DEPOSIT, receipt of which is hereby acknowledged in the sum of...	$ 5.00
☑ CASH DOWN PAYMENT at closing in the amount of...	$ 2995.00
☑ TAKE TITLE SUBJECT TO AN EXISTING FIRST TRUST DEED NOTE held by _Chase_ with an approximate unpaid amount of... payable $ _773.56_ monthly until paid, including interest not exceeding ___%.	$ 51,000
☐ TAKE TITLE SUBJECT TO AN EXISTING SECOND TRUST DEED NOTE held by ___ with an approximate unpaid amount of ___ payable $ ___ monthly until paid, including interest not exceeding ___%.	$ —
☑ A PROMISSORY NOTE in the principal amount of... See the Attached Addendum for the terms of the note.	$ 66,000
TOTAL PURCHASE PRICE IS THE AMOUNT OF...	$ 120,000

As you realize, this is a screaming deal because the seller carryback note had **no interest—a no payment** note. That means that Lester will pay no interest on the $66,000 and will have no payments until his buyer refinances and at that point the seller will get paid off. **It really is free money.**

And get this … the whole deal was negotiated over the phone, so Lester never met the seller in person. The seller's daughter showed him the house.

It is not typical to never meet a seller, but it is possible to get a deal done on the phone when you need to if you use a professional buying website that is strategically designed to build credibility and create urgency. That's why Lester and my students use the exact same website I use, with my seller testimonials, just modified with their contact information. I knew from the start if I wanted to make the students I coach successful, I would have to give them all my tools, starting with a website for buying, a website for selling, my credibility presentation portfolio I use for appointments, my marketing materials, etc.

I have to give them what it is I use to make myself successful. I believe success is easy if you duplicate what other successful people do in the field you want to be in.

Back to this deal. Here's the Buying HUD, outlining what was agreed on in the purchase agreement:

200. AMOUNTS PAID BY OR IN BEHALF OF BORROWER:	
201. Deposit or earnest money	5.00
202. Principal Amount of New Loan(s)	
203. Existing loan(s) taken subject to	50,840.55
204.	
205.	
206.	
207.	
208. DOWNPAYMENT DIRECT TO SELLER	2,995.00
209. NOTE BACK TO SELLER	66,000.00

You can see above how the closing company incorporated everything that was agreed on in the purchase agreement into the closing. Note that the loan balance was updated here because what the seller had given to Lester over the phone differed from what it actually was (perhaps the seller was looking at the last monthly statement).

> **Marko's Money Tip:** Always use a specific clause in your purchase agreement that specifies what happens if the actual loan balance is higher or lower than initially stated by the seller. Our agreements are written in our favor, so they say that the purchase price is lowered if the actual loan balance is lower. If the actual loan balance is higher, the purchase price stays the same and the down payment is reduced.
> *Can you see how that would benefit you?*

This house was in a great shape, so after cleaning it, Lester quickly sold the house for $153,000. The buyer put down $13,500 and agreed to pay 8.25% interest on the remaining $139,500 financed by Lester. Here's the Selling HUD-1 Settlement statement:

120. GROSS AMOUNT DUE FROM BORROWER	158,726.75
200. AMOUNTS PAID BY OR IN BEHALF OF BORROWER:	
201. Deposit or earnest money	7,500.00
202. Principal Amount of New Loan(s)	139,500.00
203. Existing loan(s) taken subject to	
204.	
205.	
206.	
207.	
208.	
209. BALANCE DUE OF DOWN PAYMENT	6,000.00

Now note this: Lester is making the payment on the $51,000 loan at a 4.75% interest rate, amortized over 15 years, and the buyer is making payments on the $140,000 loan at 8.25% interest and amortized over 30 years.

The result is $600/mo. cash flow.

Another great thing is that the first loan was a 15-year loan in its seventh year of paying, so a huge part of Lester's monthly payment is going towards paying off the principal.

As you can see from the cutout of the monthly statement below, $570.06 each month goes towards Lester's equity:

Activity Since Your Last Statement				
TOTAL RECEIVED	PRINCIPAL	INTEREST	ESCROW	OPTION PRODUC
$773.56	$570.06	$203.50		

rtant Messages About Your Account

The principal reduction is an important component in building wealth with real estate, and you will never benefit from it <u>unless</u> you have ownership and you get someone paying you each month. I can't stress enough how powerful the strategies are that you're learning in this book.

Here below is the December loan statement, showing that the principal reduction in the last 12 months was $6,694.31:

Loan Information:
Principal Balance	$50,840.55
Total Principal Balance	$50,840.55
Escrow Balance	$0.00

Payment Factors:
Principal & Interest	$773.56
Escrow Payment	$0.00
Monthly Payment Due	$773.56
Past Due Payment	$0.00
Unpaid Late Charges	$0.00
Fees/Advances/Other Bal	$0.00
Total	$773.56

Year-to-Date:
Interest Paid	$2,588.41
Taxes Paid	$0.00
Principal Paid	$6,694.31

Now, **imagine** having 20 houses like that where someone else is paying down your loan. Following the above, you would hypothetically have 20 x $6,694.31 = $80,329.56. You would be doing nothing and your net worth would grow by $80K every year, in addition to your houses appreciating and your collecting the cash flow.

145

How else in the world can you save $80,000 every year? I guarantee you that even people who make $250,000 a year in salary, like doctors, are not able to save $80,000 after they pay taxes on their income and living expenses. So no matter what kind of great job or career they have, they can never catch up with you.

If you take the proper steps to build <u>this</u> type of business, you will be leveraging all 5 wealth-building components of real estate, and a few years from now, you could be living your dream life. How do I know? Because I've been there and I have taken many other people from where they were to where they wanted to go, many of whom you'll meet here in this section, just keep reading …

Back to the deal. About 2 years later, the buyer refinanced the loan with an initial balance of $139,500 that was extended by Lester at the time of the sale and paid Lester off.

Here's a bank statement showing an incoming wire for $136,898.32 when the buyer refinanced:

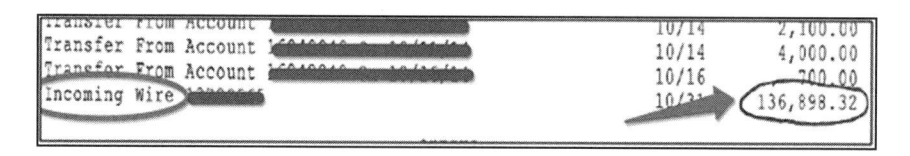

```
Transfer From Account                    10/14      2,100.00
Transfer From Account                    10/14      4,000.00
Transfer From Account                    10/16        700.00
Incoming Wire                            10/         136,898.32
```

The above amount was exactly the principal balance left on the loan extended by Lester that the buyer was paying on. This is how much the buyer owed at the time of refinancing.

From that amount, Lester had to pay off the first loan and the seller's note. The first loan in the original amount of $51,000 was paid down a lot due to the $570+ going towards the principal every month, so the remaining balance at the time was only $35,000.

On the seller's note, Lester still owed $66,000 because he was not required to make any payments on it. However, he asked the original seller if he was willing to take a discount to get paid even before closing. Lester offered $55,000 as a payment in full, and the seller took it. The seller agreed to accept $11,000 less because he didn't want to take the risk and wait. Again, this is the beauty of creative real estate done the N2W way—it always gets better!

Here are the two parts of the Lester's bank statement showing the two payments going out of his account. One for $25,000 and another for $35,000, which is a total of $55,000 that the seller agreed to accept.

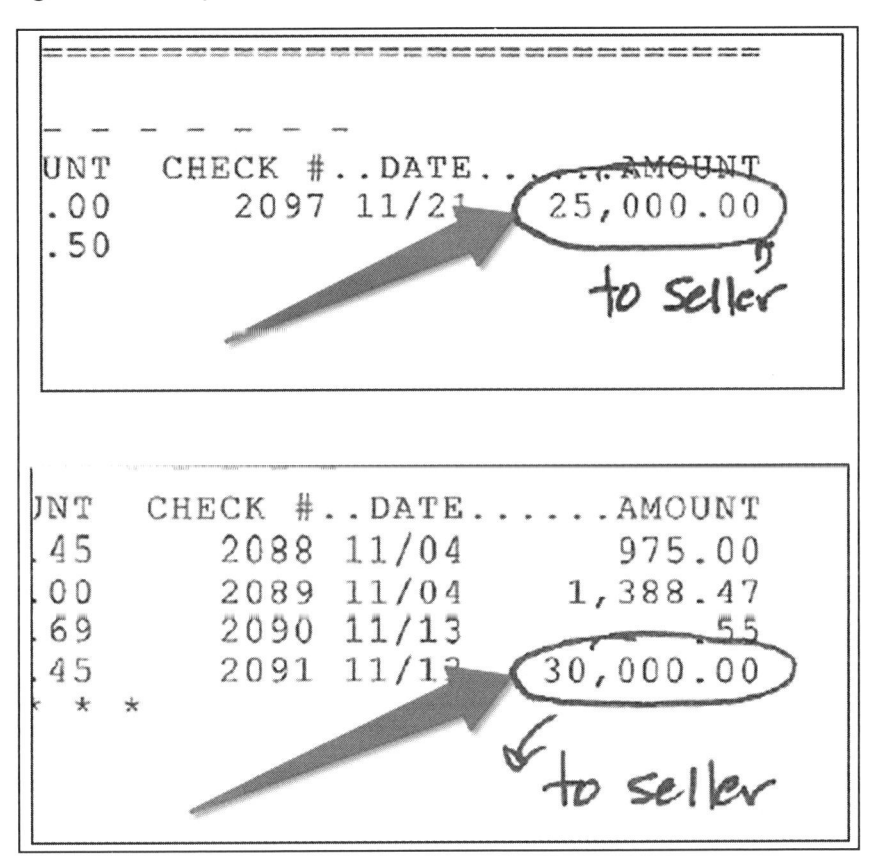

```
UNT     CHECK #..DATE...    AMOUNT
.00        2097   11/21    25,000.00    to seller
.50
```

```
JNT     CHECK #..DATE......AMOUNT
 45        2088   11/04       975.00
 00        2089   11/04     1,388.47
 69        2090   11/13          .55
 45        2091   11/13    30,000.00    to seller
  *  *
```

The total **back-end profit was $46,898.32**, which is $136,898.32 minus $35,000 (first payoff) and minus $55,000 (seller's note at discount).

The total profit was over $70,000 when you add the $13,500 down payment received at the sale and $600/mo. cash flow over 26 months.

In retrospect, a house purchased for $120K and sold for $150K, if sold outright conventionally, would have produced less than $20,000 in profit. However, the same house quick-turned the

147

Niche2Wealth way generated over $70K in profit. *Powerful, isn't it?* I hope you realize that making $1,000,000 is not so unrealistic when you use these strategies.

→ **Do you want to get ahead financially? Do you want to use the Niche2Wealth business as your vehicle?** If so, then go online and get involved with our organization. You can get support on a few different levels, depending if you are a beginner investor or a seasoned investor. We also offer everything from home-study courses to one-on-one coaching to expedite your success.

Go to **www.MarkoRubel.com** and click on "coaching" if that's what you need. Once you fill out the application, my director of coaching program will contact you to explain the various options we offer. In my opinion, this is the best way for you to start in this business because it expedites the process.

Let me give you one short example of another variation of the Unlimited Funding Method #4.

Deal Example #3:
Unlimited Funding Method #4 – Cash from a Private Lender

We call the Unlimited Funding Method #4—Cash4Deed.

This usually involves a small down payment that we pay to the seller, so they can use it to move, and then we take over their loan "subject to."

However, sometimes the sellers have a lot more equity and will not want to wait to get paid at the later date like the seller in the previous example. They will want cash for their equity right at the time of sale.

For us investors, it makes no sense to leave huge amounts of cash in properties, so the only way we take advantage of those deals is by using private lenders.

This deal was for another "pretty" house as you can see below, that Lester purchased below FMV:

This seller had a lot of equity and was not willing to take a note for it because he was moving to Australia. He wanted to be cashed out. He didn't care about his loan staying in his name, as you probably already heard from the video interview. If you have not, then you need to watch the video by going to the online resource center that I specifically designed for the readers of this book. The web address is at the top of this chapter.

After Lester and the seller agreed on the selling price, there was still $27,300 left in the seller's equity. Lester used a private lender to get that amount and secured the lender in the second position. Here's the buying closing statement:

112.		
120. GROSS AMOUNT DUE FROM BORROWER		194,922.36
200. AMOUNTS PAID BY OR IN BEHALF OF BORROWER:		
201. Deposit or earnest money		20.00
202. Principal Amount of New Loan(s)		
203. Existing loan(s) taken subject to		166,328.87
204.		
205.		
206.		
207. PRIVATE PARTY LOAN		
208.		
209. CASH DOWN PAYMENT TO SELLER		27,300.00
Adjustments For Items Unpaid By Seller		
210. City/Town Taxes	to	
211. County Taxes	to	
212. HOA ASSESSMENTS	to	
213. PRORATED HOA DUES		218.74

*I will teach you how to find private lenders in your area. As you already know, I have the tool called—**Money Finder**—it is based on the recorded documents in your county and identifies the private parties who lend money in YOUR area.*

Using a private loan, this was still a $0 down deal for Lester, which he quickly sold and received $18,000 as a down payment. So within a few weeks from meeting the seller, he already had nice profit in his bank. Here's the selling statement:

120. GROSS AMOUNT DUE FROM BORROWER	241,328.54
200. AMOUNTS PAID BY OR IN BEHALF OF BORROWER:	
201. Deposit or earnest money	1,000.00
202. Principal Amount of New Loan(s)	217,400.00
203. Existing loan(s) taken subject to	
204.	
205.	
206.	
207.	
208.	
209. BALANCE OF DOWNPAYMENT	17,000.00
Adjustments For Items Unpaid By Seller	
210. City/Town Taxes to	

As per Lester, this deal will be over $100,000 profit when all is taken into consideration.

In summary, as stated many times throughout this book, there are plenty of deals in which you can buy $0 down or the seller pays you to buy. **So if you don't have a lot of money saved, you can still start and succeed in this business.** The situation of not having money is only a temporary situation and can be quickly changed. So no whining—I've been there!

Then once you have $1,000 to $5,000 available, you can buy even more houses. Between $0 down deals, getting paid to buy, and these, you won't ever need anything else.

However, there are also deals, like the one above, where unless you have access to more cash, you will not be able to do them. Finding private lenders is not the first thing you need to do because there are plenty of other deals where you don't need a lot of money as I've explained. However, our Money Finder tool will help with that.

NOTE: The above deals were done in Texas. However, I've coached investors in almost every state, and as I've mentioned before, these deals work the same way anywhere—even in your area. Also, it really doesn't matter if you're in a hot or slow market—with slight adjustments this works in both.

And my final message, the one I give to everyone I teach, including you in this book ... **IF you want to succeed, you need to focus on your next step, not on excuses and reasons why this would not work for you.** I hear people say, "Yeah, but my town is different" or "My market is different ..." and then at the same time I have a student in that very same market who is doing extremely well. Then when I tell them that, they say, "Oh yeah, but she is my competition, so how can I do it?" ... and on and on. The point is—there are plenty of houses out there, so competition is almost irrelevant. People should stop making excuses or resolve to stay where they are. Make sense?

Marko & Lester on stage at our workshop...

→ **For more on the Lester's deals and his success using Niche2Wealth system, go online and watch the video interview. He shares some invaluable tips during that video.**

---

*Results presented are not typical—Read the Earning Disclaimer

Coaching Student Success #2

Find Out How an MBA Graduate Left Conventional Real Estate and Banking and Is Now Building Her Family's Empire Using Marko's System and His Coaching ... Currently at $751,000 in Gross Profit & Equity ... After Only 8 Houses

Watch this video and watch Sara reveal exactly what it takes to succeed in real estate using my systems. She also shares how she got her first 6-figure check ($115,393.52) after an emergency call to my cell... she was scared...

Go to **www.MarkoRubel.com/book/Sara**

Sara Shares Two Deal Examples:
(1) Got Paid $9K to buy   (2) $10 Down to a 6-Figure Check

Since joining our Inner Circle coaching program, Sara and Rick have completed eight highly profitable real estate deals worth over **$751,000 in gross profits and equity**. The best part of Sara and Rick's deals is that for most of them, they have only used $10–100 of their own cash and none of their credit to buy their houses.

In the first deal that I'm going to explain, they **got paid $9,000.00** to buy a pretty house, not an ugly one. Before the seller sold them the house, he gave it a new coat of paint and put in all new appliances; and on top of all of that, he paid all the closing costs. Now that's what you'd call a beautiful deal. And again, it's one of those deals that most people who are unfamiliar with the techniques explained in this book would think was impossible. They just wouldn't or couldn't believe these strategies work, yet these kinds of deal do exist, so both you and I have less competition.

In the second example, the happy couple walked away with a **$115,393.52 check** for a house they only paid $100 for.

Some people might say, "This business doesn't work in California," and to that I reply, "Yeah right—It works anywhere where there are people!"

As you watch the video, you'll get excited as Sara shares with you all the excitement she had walking out of that particular closing. **You'll also enjoy hearing her say it as much as I did.**

Sara and Rick at our live seminar for their second time ...

→ **If you're an agent,** you'll get to hear Sara explain why she is not looking for listings anymore. As a matter of fact, she is now passing on all potential listings to her friends. Why does she do this? Find out when you watch the video. She says it better than I can ever explain, and she does just that on this video. WATCH IT NOW.

*   *   *

Before we get into their deals, let me share the email Sara sent me about their background, how they met me, and her message to you (in her own words.)

Your Background: *(Sara writing ...)*

I am a Realtor in Riverside County, CA, and my husband Rick is a licensed contractor. We both grew up and went to school in Southern

California and received our graduate degrees here. We have loved real estate our entire careers and have bought homes and fixed them up the traditional way. We were concerned about the personal risk and liability, and we wanted to find a way to buy real estate without using our own cash or credit. For a long time I talked to my colleagues I knew in the industry, asking them how to buy without using my cash and my credit, and they couldn't help us.

How you met Marko:

We (Sara and Rick) met Marko at an Apartment Investing seminar where he was one of the speakers talking about his ProfitGrabber program. We were impressed with Marko, his background, his real estate experiences with single-family housing, and his marketing program—Profit Grabber. We bought his program and received an invitation to his 4-day Foreclosure Training seminar. We attended the training and were "blown away" with Marko's step-by-step "complete" method of investing in foreclosures and ultimately building wealth. We thought we knew a lot about real estate and investing, given our backgrounds, but Marko's seminar was a huge eye-opener for us and was exactly what we had been trying to find. At that training, we applied to his Inner Circle coaching and its benefits.

Your Message to Reader:

If you are truly serious about building wealth using real estate, Marko is the answer—PERIOD. His methods work, and his training materials are the most complete systems or guidelines we have ever found. Everything is provided in his courses and has been laid out in a step-by-step manner. Nothing is missing or left to chance or to figure out on your own. His methods work in any market or any state and can be done over and over, year after year. This is a real business that can change your life and your plans for your retirement.

Don't get tempted with these other slick TV or radio info-commercials where the guru claims real estate fortunes for you without much work or effort. From our experiences with these other programs, they are mostly hype with little substance and have slim to no chance of generating true wealth with real estate either now or in the future.

I can say this to you because **we spent $80K** *and two years of researching real estate investing systems that were garbage or unworkable before we found Marko. If there really were some super easy or secret method out there for building wealth with real estate like these other gurus claim they have, trust us, Marko would be teaching it and have it in his Niche2Wealth system.*

Marko's Unlimited Funding Methods are the real deal if you are serious about using real estate to build wealth with minimum risk. We can say this to you, without reservation, because we now have received the BIG checks to prove Marko's methods worked for us, as well—many of his other successful students from around the country have these checks, too. What is exciting for us is we have more checks coming in our future as our other properties we have purchased or control work themselves through Marko's Niche2Wealth system.

This business works if you work it. No pain, no gain! For the effort and learning you put into this, the rewards are tremendous. We now look forward to our future and where this business is taking us.

Thank you Marko.

*   *   *

Let's look at two of Sara's deals and see what she did to make them happen.

Deal Example #1:
Unlimited Funding Method #2 – Get Paid to Buy

Here's a picture of the house that the seller paid $9,000.00 dollars to Sara and Rick to buy. That was after he fixed it up, put a fresh coat of paint on it, and put in some new appliances. As part of the purchase price, the seller was paying Sara and Rick to buy it, but when they asked for the money, they found out he didn't have any cash. So what were they going to do to make this deal? How did they get paid $9,000.00 if the seller didn't have any money?

157

That's simple. The seller was not behind on his payments, but when asked, he still didn't have the $9,000.00 necessary to pay to his buyers, Sara and Rick. So she got creative. She got the seller to use some of the equity in another property that he owned to secure a loan against that property in favor of Sara and Rick. You'll see a copy of the addendum to the purchase agreement that specifies that.

A good learning point here is—It always pays to be a good listener and to keep your mind open, so you can be somewhat creative if necessary. If you do that, you'll figure out the solution by knowing the seller's situation/pain and evaluating your options to make the deal happen. If you can't figure it out, your coach will (if you have a good coach). If you are in front of a truly motivated seller, the solution is always possible; you just need to create the answer.

Here are the deal specifics:

Fair Market Value: $380,000–395,000

Purchase Price: $342,929.73 <u>minus</u> $9,000 paid outside escrow

Down Payment: $10 to seller to make agreement legal

Loan Balance at that time: 1st loan of $267,784.49 & 2nd loan of $75,135.24

Loan Terms: 1st loan @ 4.875%; 2nd loan @ 2.74%

Marketing Used: mailed Check Letter to expired MLS listings in the seller's area

Seller's Motivation: Seller had partially moved to a new home out of state and didn't want to make two mortgage payments.

Selling Price: $415,000

Down Payment Received: $15,000 as option consideration

Selling Terms: Niche2Wealth Lease Option

Cash Flow Amount: $296/mo.

This deal, like any other real estate deal we talk about, started with a simple mailer and then a phone call from the seller.

It is very important for you to know what to say on the phone, so you know how to handle your incoming calls. My team and I teach our students to use a special form we call the "Phone Form," which I've mentioned earlier, so when you're talking to a motivated seller, you can build the proper rapport and get all the critical information that the seller is giving you.

You have two goals when you are on the phone to a motivated seller—one is to build as much rapport and credibility as possible.

Your second goal is to gather as much information as possible. And to do that you need to write down everything they say, regardless of whether you think it's relevant at the time. I can tell you it's likely going to be very useful in the future, whether you think it will be or not. If you need it later, you'll have it.

→ **Go to the online resource I've provided for you and download my special PHONE FORM.** This is a very useful tool that my students and I use every day. The questions on the form are very straightforward, strategic, and will position you as the authority. The important thing is to not change the sequence of the questions on the form. It works.

By the way, Bill and Elaine from Case Study #4 will give you some key points about using the Phone Form, so make sure you watch their video from start to finish when you get there.

One of the important things that has allowed Sara and Rick to do so well in real estate and in our PRIVATE Inner Circle coaching program is that they are great students of the system. They learn something, and then they implement it. They don't reinvent the wheel. They just move forward. Look at how detailed the Phone Form was that Sara completed on her initial call with this seller. This is how your form should look after you hang up with the seller:

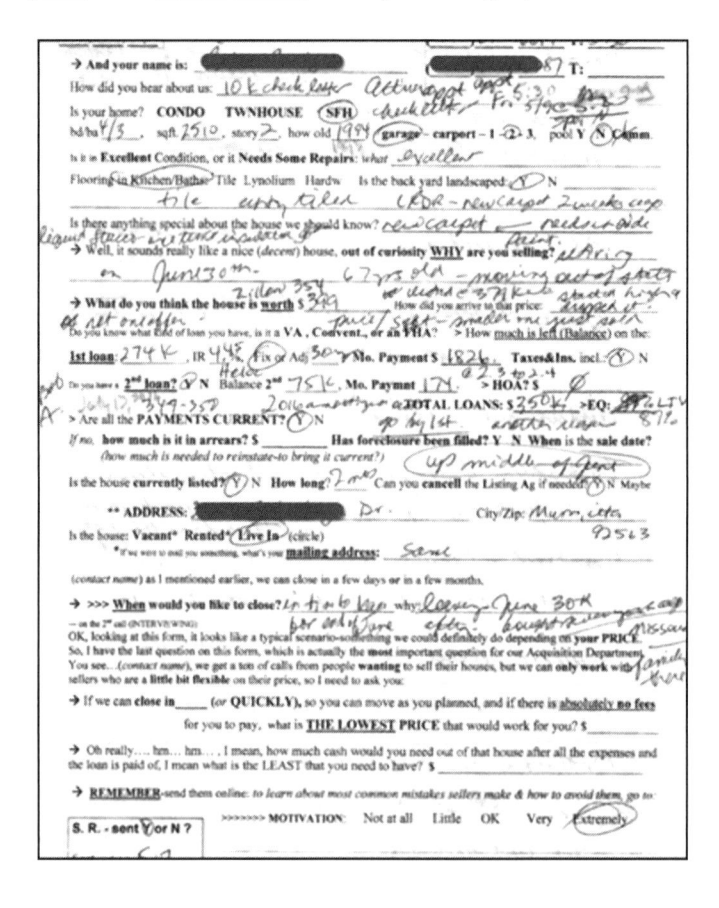

I know you can't read everything that it says, but that's not the point. The point is for you to notice how the form is filled out completely. You can never collect too many details when talking to a motivated seller. Write down everything you hear, and you can sort it out later.

Here's the purchase and sale agreement price breakdown:

```
2. PURCHASE PRICE. Buyer to pay the purchase price as follows (check all that applies):
   ☒ EARNEST DEPOSIT, receipt of which is hereby acknowledged in the sum of.......... $    10.00
   ☐ CASH DOWN PAYMENT at closing in the amount of.......... $    0
   ☒ TAKE TITLE SUBJECT TO AN EXISTING FIRST TRUST DEED NOTE
     held by  Nationstar   with an approximate unpaid amount of .......... $ 267,784.49
     payable $ 1,794.18  monthly until paid, including interest not exceeding 4.8 %.
   ☒ TAKE TITLE SUBJECT TO AN EXISTING SECOND TRUST DEED NOTE
     held by  Bank of America  with an approximate unpaid amount of .......... $ 75,135.24
     payable $ 174.85  monthly until paid, including interest not exceeding 2.74%.
   ☐ A PROMISSORY NOTE in the principal amount of .......... $    0
     See the Attached Addendum for the terms of the note.
   TOTAL PURCHASE PRICE IS THE AMOUNT OF .......... $ 342,929.73
```

Here's paragraph 11 of this purchase agreement that specifies "Other Terms." This is where Sara disclosed that she is a "licensed agent" acting as a principal in the transaction and not as an "agent":

```
11. OTHER TERMS: Sara_____ licensed CA Real Estate Agent acting as Principal and
    not as an agent for the seller. See Addendum to Purchase
    and Sale agreement.
```

A few days later, after verifying the values, Sara went back and explained to the seller that the only way for her to buy his house—was if he paid her. He said, "Okay," and they proceeded. They both agreed that he would pay them $9,000.00, and then he signed another addendum specifying that.

You may be wondering, "Wasn't Sara bound by the original contract?" Yes, she was, but her liability was limited to just $10 dollars, so if she didn't want the property, she could walk away and lose her $10 dollars. The seller didn't want her to do that, so he agreed to pay her the $9,000.00 dollars. As you can see below, the seller secured the note with a property they owned in another state:

Additional Terms:

1. Seller Note for $9,000 explained in previous Addendum to be secured by a note and Deed of Trust on Seller's property located at: 15~~   ~~, Fulton, MO 65251
2. HELOC w/ BofA to be closed and converted Principal of 75,135.24 to a fixed rate not to exceed 6% interest prior to close of Escrow.

Marko's Money Tip: Whenever you're buying a property "subject to" a second loan in addition to a first, you need to pay attention to what type of loan the second is. If the second loan is a Home Equity Line of Credit (HELOC), you should have the seller close it. This is what I instructed Sara to do, and as you can see, it specified that in Item #2 in the addendum.

I advise my students to do that for one reason only—to prevent the seller from calling the bank and borrowing more money against your property. Closing a **HELOC** may be as simple as having the seller call the bank and asking them to close it.

As we teach our Inner Circle coaching students, when you have a great deal, close right away, so Sara and Rick closed this deal within days of getting the agreement signed, but the seller needed more time to completely move out. Sara and Rick used our holdover occupancy agreement to rent the seller's home back to them until they could move, which was just another 8 days later. See the HUD1 Closing Statement from the purchase and the holdover occupancy agreement the seller signed to pay rent for the house back to Rick and Sara.

DESCRIPTION	DEBITS	CREDITS
TOTAL CONSIDERATION	343,065.10	
Initial Deposit		1,205.60
BALANCE ASSUMED ▊▊▊▊ Nationstar Mortgage		267,784.49
BALANCE ASSUMED ▊▊▊▊: Bank Of America		75,270.61
PRORATIONS/ADJUSTMENTS:		
Seller rent back from 7/1-7/8		546.40
Buyer EMD paid to seller outside of escrow		10.00
TITLE CHARGES		
Deed Recording Fee: Lawyers Title	35.00	
Binder Fee for 343,065.10: Lawyers Title	111.00	
ESCROW CHARGES TO: Cornerstone Escrow, Inc.		
Escrow Fee Escrow Fee	1,086.00	
Archive Fee	25.00	
BALANCE DUE YOU	495.00	
TOTALS	344,817.10	344,817.10

*The seller secured Sara the $9,000 dollars outside of escrow, before the closing. This way the closing agent didn't need to pull the title for a property out of state. That property had a lot of equity, so Sara's risk of preparing the note and the deed of trust herself was minimal.

HOLDOVER OCCUPANCY AGREEMENT

This is an addendum and part of the PURCHASE & SALE AGREEMENT dated ▊▊▊▊;
and entered into by:

Buyer/Landlord ▊▊▊▊ Solutions, Inc.
Seller/Tenant Robert ▊▊▊▊
Regarding occupancy of real estate premises known as: 39▊▊▊▊ ta, Ca 92563

This holdover occupancy agreement regards occupancy of this real estate after the ownership has transferred (or after close of escrow on the underlying agreement).

AGREEMENT: This occupancy is for a term commencing midnight on the date of the close of escrow (or the ownership transfer date), and terminating on ▊▊▊▊.

1. The following funds are to be withhold from Seller/Tenant's proceeds and handed to Landlord/Buyer: PITI of
   Security Deposit: $ 10.00   Rent: $ 68 30/day + 2049 prorat
   Tenant to pay rent in the amount of $ 2049.00 per month during the tenancy. ×8 days = 546.40 for 8 days
   Rent to be prorated to the date this tenancy is terminated. July

2. Rents to be payable to Landlord in advance on the 1st day of each month. Checks to be made payable to
   ▊▊▊▊ Solutions and mailed to ▊▊▊▊ Riverside, Ca 92503

3. If Tenant continues to occupy and possess premises AFTER termination of this tenancy, Tenant to pay on a day-to-day tenancy the rental rate of $ 150.00 per day.

> **Marko's Money Tip:** The holdover occupancy agreement is used when you are renting a house back to the sellers <u>after</u> the closing. This is basically done to allow you to close the deal quickly, so the sellers don't change their mind over time. Plus it allows them to pack and move out <u>after</u> the closing. It's important to note, if working with a seller in default or foreclosure, you will not want to use a holdover agreement because you shouldn't let the seller stay in the home <u>after</u> closing. **Why?** If they are not making payments to the bank for the home, why would they start making payments to you? The only exception to this is if there is a significant payment coming to them at a later date, so they have a reason to move out as agreed. In that case, you will specify the *"daily rent after termination of tenancy"* to be some larger payment, so if they don't move out on time, that money will be deducted from the money coming to them (i.e., from a note you owe them).

Once Sara and Rick took possession, they "sold" the property on a one-year lease option for $415,000, getting $2,345 per month. They gave the tenant/buyer the ability to **renew** the option for an additional year and took a $15,000 option consideration.

Look at the images below, which show the lease option terms and the lease option deposit breakdown:

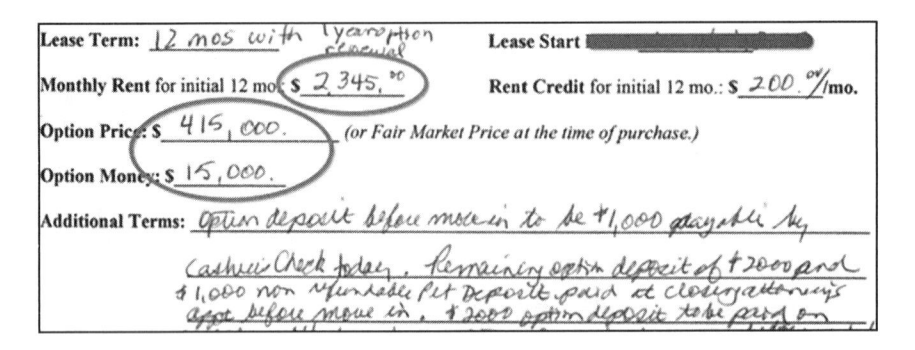

Lease Term: 12 mos with 1 year option renewal	Lease Start:
Monthly Rent for initial 12 mo: $ 2,345.00	Rent Credit for initial 12 mo.: $ 200.00/mo.
Option Price: $ 415,000	(or Fair Market Price at the time of purchase.)
Option Money: $ 15,000	
Additional Terms: Option deposit before move-in to be $1,000 payable by Cashier Check today, Remaining option deposit of $2000 and $1,000 non refundable Pet Deposit paid at closing attorney's appt before move in. $2000 option deposit to be paid on ___	

Another thing we teach our coaching students when selling on lease option is to use a "variable" option price clause in the option agreement. In a market that is flat, there is no need to use that clause, so you just set the option price to be 5–10%

above the current FMV. However, if the market is rapidly appreciating, then I always have my students use that one-page legal clause. Here's the important part of that clause:

> 3. **OPTION PRICE**: The OPTION price ("strike price") is: **$415,000.00**; provided, however, if OPTIONOR concludes at any time before OPTIONOR has received proper notice of exercise of the OPTION from OPTIONEE that the fair market value of the property exceeds the foregoing strike price, OPTIONOR may (but is not required to) propose to OPTIONEE that the Option Price be increased to the fair market value of the property as determined by a professional fee appraiser selected by OPTIONOR.

So as you see, this was a NO LOSE proposition for Sara and Rick, and the tenant/buyer gets into a house that they otherwise wouldn't qualify for. They get to live in the area they want to live in and in the school district where they want to be.

In conclusion, for this deal, Sara and Rick got paid $9,000.00 upfront to buy (secured by another property and paid at a later date) and another $15,000 from the new tenant/buyer for a total of $24,000, and make almost $300 a month passive cash flow and another $50,000 or so when the tenant/buyer exercises their option. And the best part is, if the tenant/buyer doesn't exercise their option, then Sara and Rick get the benefit of appreciation and can do it all over again. Is this a great country or what?

You get to hear the entire conversation with Sara. You'll get to hear her talk about these deals and their overall business. DON'T WAIT. Go to **www.MarkoRubel.com/book/Sara.**

> **Marko's Money Tip:** 70–80% of the time, lease option buyers will NOT exercise their option to purchase because of a lot of reasons. They can't get the financing, they decide to move, they don't have enough money saved, or some type of family event or some other reason that makes them decline the option comes into play. In that case, you get the house back and keep the non-refundable option consideration, and then, like I said, you do it all over again.

Deal Example #2:
Unlimited Funding Method #3 – Note4Equity – Seller Carries

* * $115,393.52 – The first 6-Figure Check for Sara & Rick * *

As you can see, this is another "pretty" house in a nice neighborhood.

I just realized that I have not talked much about my marketing machine—ProfitGrabber PRO software. This is the exact tool that Sara and Rick used to market to "expired listings" using our special <u>check letter</u>. All of my students use it, so I know it works, and it's a required tool if you're going to do this type of real estate.

The ProfitGrabber PRO software prepares and automates direct mail, keeps track of your scheduled sequential mailings, analyzes your deals, and provides "live" data like property profiles and comparable sales to help you determine the fair market value, and much, much more. You can learn more at www.ProfitGrabber.com

Sara and Rick use it every day.

In this case, they used the ProfitGrabber PRO software to enhance their expired lists by having ProfitGrabber PRO find the names and mailing addresses based on Site Address (a house's location).

As a side note, Site Address is the only thing that's provided by MLS when your friendly agent is downloading expired listings for you.

Using the above process, they found their MOTIVATED sellers. The sellers were motivated, were moving out, but weren't sure on exactly when they would have to move.

After using my techniques for negotiating, Sara and Rick agreed on the following terms:

Fair Market Value: $370,000–380,000 (at the time)

Purchase Price: $296,650

Down Payment: $100 Seller carried back a note for $28,550.

Purchase Terms: bought "subject to" the existing loan with seller carryback note with no interest and no payments until the house was resold—UFP#3

Loan Balance at that time: $268,000

Selling Price: $419,550

Selling Terms: sold outright to new buyer 12 months later

Gross Profit: $115,393.52

Sara and Rick agreed on a price of $296,650 with the seller, as evident from the purchase and sales agreement below:

2. PURCHASE PRICE. Buyer to pay the purchase price as follows (check all that applies):	
☒ EARNEST DEPOSIT, receipt of which is hereby acknowledged in the sum of	$ 100.°°
☐ CASH DOWN PAYMENT at closing in the amount of	$
☒ TAKE TITLE SUBJECT TO AN EXISTING FIRST TRUST DEED NOTE held by *Green Light* with an approximate unpaid amount of payable $ 1298.56 monthly until paid, including interest not exceeding 4.8%.	$ 268,000.°°
☐ TAKE TITLE SUBJECT TO AN EXISTING SECOND TRUST DEED NOTE held by _____ with an approximate unpaid amount of payable $ _____ monthly until paid, including interest not exceeding ___%.	$
☒ A PROMISSORY NOTE in the principal amount of See the Attached Addendum for the terms of the note.	$ 28,550.°°
TOTAL PURCHASE PRICE IS THE AMOUNT OF	**$ 296,650.°°**

Two important things to notice here are first, the seller agreed to take back a promissory note in the amount of $28,550 as part of the payment of the purchase price; and second, Sara and Rick only gave the seller a $100 earnest deposit. The balance of the purchase price in the amount of $268,000 was in the form of the seller's mortgage which Sara and Rick took "subject to."

> **Marko's Money Tip:** Don't write big checks to sellers. It is not necessary. <u>If you don't write big checks, you can't *lose* big checks.</u>

Sara and Rick controlled this house they bought for $296,650 with only a commitment of $100 dollars, and the seller would have accepted $10 dollars (as she tells you in the video).

Now this deal gets even better. Sara and Rick were able to negotiate with the seller on the terms of the seller carryback note. The seller agreed to <u>no</u> interest and <u>no</u> payments until the house was resold by Sara and Rick. Working with their coach, Sara and Rick got this included in the "Additional Terms" section of the purchase and sale agreement. In fact, look at all of the additional terms included in the picture below:

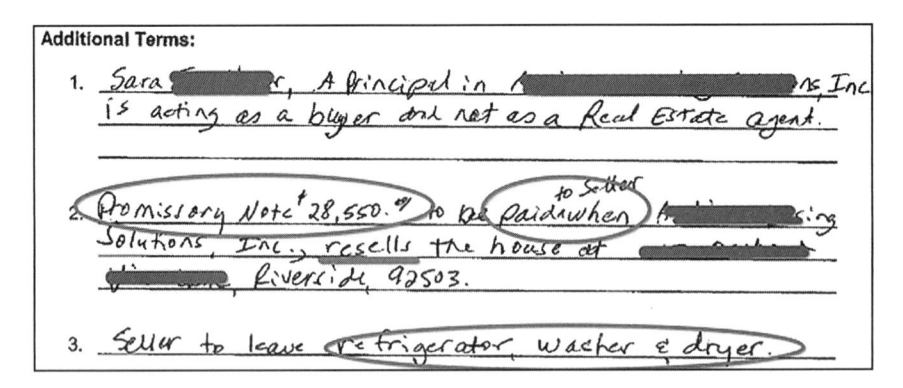

```
Additional Terms:
1. Sara ____, A principal in _____ Inc
   is acting as a buyer and not as a Real Estate agent.

2. Promissory Note $28,550.00 to be paid when to Seller
   Solutions, Inc., resells the house at
   _____, Riverside, 92503.

3. Seller to leave refrigerator, washer & dryer.
```

There are 3 important items to notice about the additional terms Sara and Rick added to the PSA. First, Sara acknowledged that she is a real estate agent but is not acting in that capacity.

This is important because some sellers will not deal with agents.

Second, Sara and Rick documented the terms of the note they were giving the seller to secure the $28,550 of equity that the seller agreed to take the note for.

Finally, they documented that the appliances they negotiated would transfer to them in the deal.

Here's where it gets even better. The seller's circumstances changed and dictated for the seller to stay in the area for another 10 months, so they asked Sara if they could rent the property back for another 6 months, with the right to extend month to month for another few months, if need be. They would be paying rent <u>equal</u> to the monthly house payment (PITI).

Now think about that. Who is better to rent the house from you than the previous owner who took care of it? So Sara and Rick have NO payments on the house, but they get to build their equity due to the principal pay down and appreciation. Amazing, isn't it?

As I've said many times, creative real estate done the Niche2Wealth way **<u>always gets better.</u>** I love this business, and you'll love it more and more as well when you realize that you can do what Sara and Rick are doing ... without any hassles from lenders or tenants and without taking major risks with rehabs.

Later on, the tenants moved out and left the house in <u>perfect</u> condition. Sara and Rick put it up for an outright sale because the seller needed to get paid off on that note. If the seller was "fine" with waiting, I would have suggested to lease option the house out.

Anyway, they found a buyer who agreed to pay $415,000 for the property, and in a short time they had a check for $115,000 in their hands. See the photos of the HUD1 statement from the closing, the escrow company letter to Sara and Rick, and the photo of the check that came with the letter.

LOAN PAYOFF: U.S. Bank Home Mortgage		
Principal Balance	261,401.03	
Interest	886.26	
Recording Fees	25.00	
Fax Fee	20.00	
Sub Trustee Rec Fee	25.00	
Total Loan Payoff		262,357.29
LOAN PAYOFF:		
Principal Balance	28,550.00	
Total Loan Payoff		28,550.00
TAXES:		
Property Tax to: Riverside County Tax Collector 1st .... - 3		1,593.38
ADDITIONAL DISBURSEMENTS:		
Natural Hazard Report Fee: First American Natural Hazard Disclosure Svcs		65.00
Federal Express to be determined		35.00
Seller Credit Buyer For Transfer Tax:		460.90
Seller Credit Buyer For Owner's Policy; Seller Credit Buyer For Owners Policy		328.00
BALANCE DUE YOU		114,967.64
TOTALS	419,550.71	419,550.71

You will notice that the actual check they received is higher than the closing statement because the *actual payoff* came in a little lower than had been originally calculated. This meant an extra $425.00 to Sara and Rick.

As soon as they came home, they took a picture of the check on their kitchen table and sent it to me. Needless to say, they were excited.

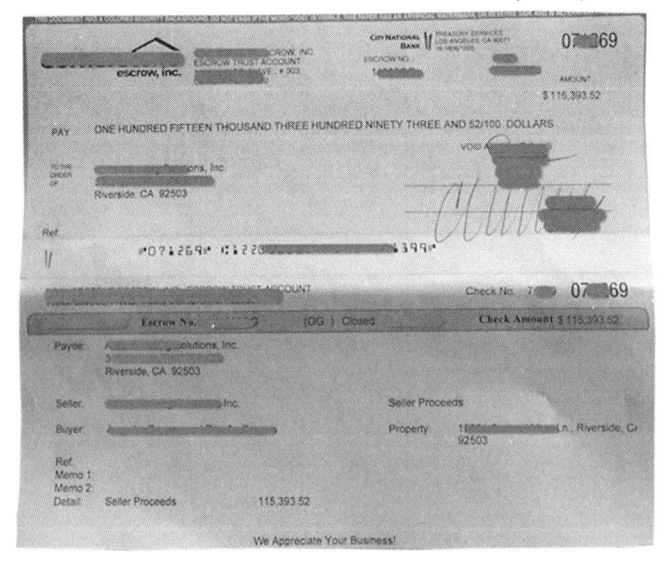

170

Here's a close-up of the check Sara and Rick got from the closing:

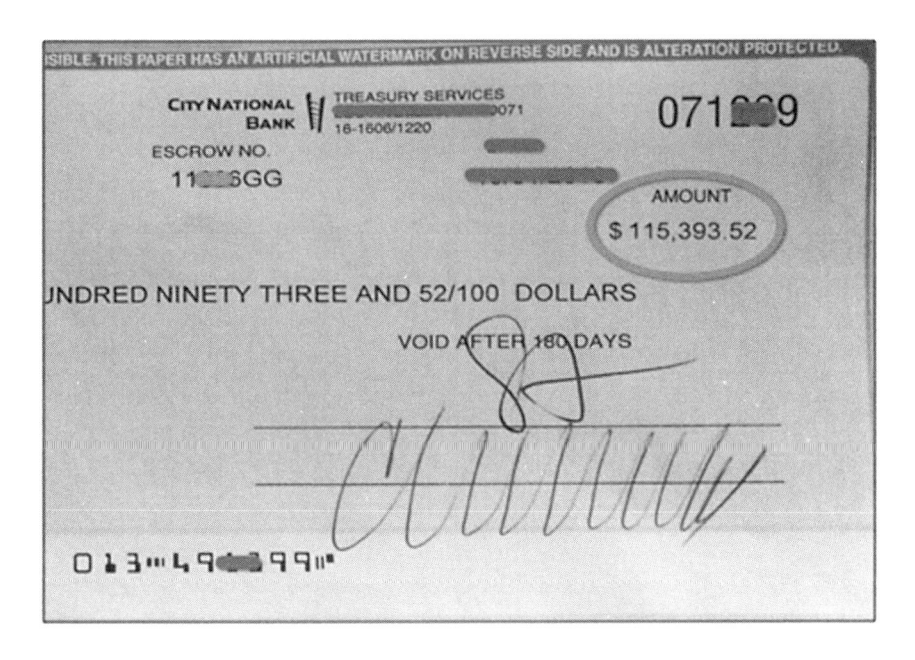

→ **If you want to start doing what Sara and Rick have done and start making money like they did with real estate deals that fill up your bank account, watch the video interview. You get to hear Sara express her feelings regarding this check and her real estate dealings.**

"You know Marko, this was the happiest day in my life except for getting married and having our son. I loved it!"

—*Sara*

*Results presented are not typical—read the Earning Disclaimer

Coaching Student Success #3

Kit, an Engineer, Left His Full-Time Job, so He Could Spend More Time with His Family & Pursue His Passion for Hunting. Discover How He Has Been Able to Do over 251 Deals and Learn From Him ...

In this video interview, Kit reveals a simple marketing piece that got him more than 150 deals. He uses it over and over again. Watch closely as you get to hear WHY the bomb squad came to his office after he first did it and what I told him to do ... It was effective but—scary. He's still doing it today.

Go to **www.MarkoRubel.com/book/Kit**

Kit Shares Two Foreclosure Deal Examples:
(1) 6-Figure P-J-L Short Sale (2) Reinstatement + LO

These two deals are interesting learning examples and are a little different than the examples you've read about so far. **Both of these houses were in foreclosure.** One house was **overleveraged** ("underwater"—with negative equity), and the other was in **foreclosure,** but luckily it had some equity.

Let me first give you Kit's answers to the 3 questions I asked all of these students to email me about.

Read it because it's important, and then we can go over the deals.

I really like the second part of his "message to you," so much that I even suggest you read it twice because it addresses the importance of your WHY, which is about your desire and your dream.

Once you're on the right course, you'll be working my proven system. Then it is your WHY that determines your success or your possible failure.

Your Background:

I had been a software engineer for 12 years. Things were going well, and the income from my job was great, but working for someone else and working on their dream was very frustrating. I always had a desire for something more fulfilling and something that could get me to financial freedom sooner. I began looking for an alternative way to create income from what I was currently doing. I wanted to live life on my terms.

How you met Marko:

As I started to research real estate investing, I went to a seminar in Los Angeles. At my very first real estate seminar I was lucky enough to see Marko speak and present his ProfitGrabber Pro office automation system. I purchased ProfitGrabber Pro at that event in July, went to his seminar in October, joined the Inner Circle coaching program at that same seminar, and then closed my first two deals in December. All of that happened in the same year. I feel extremely fortunate to have found Marko at the time of my life that I did.

Your Message to Reader:

First I would like to say that there is no doubt that Marko has the knowledge and experience to teach you how to make money in real estate. He is a master at finding deals and finding creative solutions to make them work. Marko is also one of the best teachers, speakers, and communicators I've ever met. However, as great as Marko is, you need to have a desire, a reason **why** that will have you put in the effort to learn the system, go on appointments, push through the hard times, and make it work for you. My message is to find your desire, have a dream, and keep your dream in sight. Know that it is possible and that it is possible for you!

* * *

→ **Watch the Skype video interview** and hear Kit share his dreams and motivations. Watch how Kit restates the importance of your WHY and why you need to find out what your why is. This is coming from a man who has gone on to complete over 251 profitable real estate transactions making significantly over $1M in profit since we met. If you want to make more money, it's worth your time to watch this 20-minute video. Do it now if you're finally ready to make the move and learn how to make money in real estate by going to **www.MarkoRubel.com/book/Kit**

You'll see that making money just for money's sake is boring. The real pleasure of success and making money is that doing real estate like I show you allows you to do things with your family. You build memories you will never forget.

Today, Kit has the ability to always be with his family at those important times, like school events, family outings, and long vacations. He gets those meaningful hugs from his daughters every day, and he doesn't have to wait until late at night to see his children. They can visit him in his home-office whenever they want.

In the picture below, Kit is on one of his many hunting trips he likes to take throughout the year (*by the way—he sends me some "crazy" hunting videos* J):

I know you may be building your own dream and that dream is as important a motivating factor as it was for Kit. That's why I really want you to pay close attention to the videos you are watching of all 10 students featured in this section.

Why?

You are the next Kit. Remember, they all started just like you. These are real people with an **above average desire** to be successful. They did a couple of things right. They took action using my system and my coaching. They persevered. This changed their lives and their families' lives forever. You can do the same.

Now let's review the deals from Kit.

Since joining our Inner Circle coaching program, Kit has done many successful "Payoff the Junior Lien" or P-J-L deals, as demonstrated in this first example.

Deal Example #1:
Unlimited Funding Method #6: P-J-L Junior Liens Discounted

Fair Market Value: $850,000
Owed Before Short Sale: $891,000*
*Owed on the first loan: $647,999.75 + $35,592.99 reinstatement
Owed on the second loan: $207,723.00

Purchase Price: $700,000

Selling Price: $812,000

Kit began marketing to people in foreclosure, meaning people who have missed 3 or more payments, so the bank has filed a notice of default (a.k.a. Notice to Foreclose or LisPendens, it is called different names in different states) and has begun the legal process to repossess the house.

Kit used the Check Letter that I developed specifically to appeal to people who might be in need of CASH immediately. Think about it. If you received a double window envelope and showing through the see-through window was a check reading, "Pay to the Order of …" with your name printed for you to see, wouldn't you open it just for pure curiosity's sake?

Of course you would and so would I. More importantly, so did the seller of this high priced, high-end home.

As you'll hear in the video interview, Kit believes that 60–75% of his deals have come from this "Ninja Check Letter." The Check Letter is very easy to send out, and you'll hear him explain how important it is to follow the marketing steps of the system exactly. Pay attention to that part of the interview because you could mess things up if you try and reinvent the wheel.

So Kit used my Check Letter, and a seller with a high-end home in Scottsdale, AZ called him. The seller had two loans on the property, and the loans were with different banks.

The first lender was foreclosing.

In this deal, Kit used the P-J-L strategy to acquire the property.

Now, while I did discuss the P-J-L strategy earlier in the book, let me remind you of a couple of key elements. The P-J-L is not the same as a traditional short sale.

To begin, the first loan balance must be below the fair market value of the property (at or below 80% of FMV).

Then the second loan must be with a different lender.

After all, a single lender won't give you a discount on the second loan and then let you reinstate the first if they are the same bank.

The next thing is that the second lender must feel at risk of loss because of foreclosure. This is key.

It is the second lender being at risk of loss that provides you, the buyer, the opportunity for deeper discounts.

If the FMV of the property is higher than the first and second loan combined, there is no real incentive for the second lender to discount.

Only when they are in a position of risk, will they consider the discount.

→ **In the video you'll get to hear Kit tell you about the secret advantages of the P-J-L strategy in his own words. By watching my interview with Kit, you'll get to listen to Kit give you some important real estate points that got him deals like this.**

Now the second loan was for $207,723, and Kit used the techniques we teach our coaching students to negotiate with the second lender who eventually agreed to take $15,204 as satisfaction for the second loan. (Some money is better than none.)

Now wait a minute—that is not a misprint, and I didn't miss a zero or a decimal place. The lender agreed to take $15,204 for the amount due of $207,723. I know you might find it hard to believe, but it's true. See the approval paragraph from the letter the second lender sent to Kit when agreeing to the discount:

> Upon receipt of certified funds in the amount of $15,204.00, we agree to release our lien interest in the above mentioned property. The payoff on the Account as of today's date is $207,723.00. After applying $15,204.00 to your Account, you will remain liable for the outstanding balance.

Basically what Kit was able to do was to create a huge amount of equity that came because he discounted the junior lien and paid off the balance when he closed on the purchase with the seller.

He had to also reinstate the first loan to STOP foreclosure. It needed a total of $35,592.99 to catch up on all the late payments plus the foreclosure legal fees. If you're wondering where you'll find the money to do that, let me say this.

SIDE NOTE: *This was a higher-end home, and it needed more cash to get the deal completed. So this is not where you start your real estate career, and Kit didn't start there either. This was not his first deal of this kind.* <u>You should still read </u>*everything I'm giving you because there are other P-J-L deals in the lower price ranges that you could start with.*

Here I am with Kit in that house discussing his options:

Back to the deal. The first loan had a good low interest rate on it, and as Kit explained, it was "built-in financing." Take a look at the picture of the HUD1 Settlement statement that Kit got from the purchase of the property:

400. Gross Amount Due To Seller:	
401. Contract Sales Price	700,000.00
402. Personal Property	
403.	
404.	
405.	
Adjustments For Items Paid By Seller In Advance:	
406. City/Town Taxes	
407. County Taxes	
408. Assessments	
409. HOA	
410. SEWER	
411.	
412.	
413.	
414.	*Reinstatement to 1st*
415.	
420. Gross Amount Due to Seller	700,000.00
500. Reductions In Amount Due To Seller:	
501. Excess deposit (see instructions)	
502. Settlement charges to Seller (line 1400)	35,592.99
503. Existing loan(s) taken subject to	647,999.75
504. Payoff of first mortgage loan	
505. Payoff of second mortgage loan	15,204.00
506.	
507. *P-J-L short sale of the 2nd*	
508.	

As you can see, Kit purchased this beautiful luxury home, which by the way needed only a light cleaning and vacuuming, for $700,000. He reinstated the first loan of $647,999.75 and bought the house "subject to" that reinstated mortgage. The reinstatement of the first loan is shown in line 502, and the amount of the first loan being taken "subject to" is shown in line 503. Line 505 shows confirmation of the payoff of the second mortgage loan in the amount of $15,204 dollars.

From $207,723 to $15,204 dollars. *When you have a system that works, real estate makes this a great country to be a part of.* Do you see why you might have missed some opportunity to create equity and do profitable deals on leads you might have previously thrown out?

Look, you can't cry over spilled milk or over what was lost yesterday. Just determine in your mind not to lose the next deal that comes from your marketing tomorrow, or in the very near future.

→ Don't Wait. Watch my Skype video interview with Kit, so you get to hear him explain why the sellers with such big second loans are the easiest to deal with and what's important when talking to their lien holders.

After closing on the purchase, Kit found a buyer, who incidentally was an investor, and Kit SOLD the house to that investor for $812,230.00 on short-term owner financing where the investor cashed him out shortly thereafter, giving Kit almost $100,000.00 in profit.

See the HUD1 Settlement statement in the picture below where Kit closed with his buyer:

100. Gross Amount Due From Borrower:	
101. Contract Sales Price	812,230.00
102. Personal Property	
103. Settlement charges to Borrower (line 1400)	1,701.47
104.	
105.	
Adjustments For Items Paid By Seller In Advance:	
106. City/Town Taxes	
107. County Taxes	
108. Assessments	
109. HOA	96.00
110. Impound Trnsfr on underlying	3,852.53
111.	
112.	
113.	
114.	
115.	
120. Gross Amount Due from borrower:	817,880.00
200. Amounts Paid by or in behalf of Borrower:	
201. Deposit or earnest money	
202.	
203. Existing loan(s) taken subject to	
204. Cash Payment & Closing Costs	25,650.00
205.	
206.	

Now it's important to know that Kit's deal we just reviewed did take some money to complete.

There are deals you can absolutely do with no money down. Then there are deals that take a few thousand dollars to do, and deals that if you have more money, like $20,000–30,000 or a money partner, then you can kill.

The point is not to *get scared off* by the numbers. Kit had done some deals by this time and had built some reserves for just such an occasion, but … he did not start out that way. The key is to start where you are and where your market is.

> **Marko's Money Tip:** A general rule of thumb is to market to 40–50% above and below the median-priced houses in your area and you should be safe. Now, if 50% below the median-priced home puts you in the war zone, then obviously you will raise the floor of your price range. The point is, eliminate the higher-end homes until you get good at this business.

IMPORTANT COMMENT: If you are confused by what you're reading, let me tell you that it is completely normal to not understand it all. This is a totally new concept to you, and I have to say, the P-J-L is on the side of the more complicated deal structures. If you decide to get into the business of real estate (and you should be about ready by this time), we may end up working together and then all of this will become as simple as it was for Kit and the many others I have helped launch their real estate investing careers.

Deal Example #2:
Unlimited Funding Method #5: "Reinstatement" – Foreclosure Reversal

Fair Market Value: $230,000
Purchase Price: $196,376
Down Payment: $0
Loan Balance at that time: $190,376 + $6,000 reinstatement

Selling Price: $239,000
Down Payment Received: $10,000 from tenant/buyer
Selling Terms: sold on Lease Option

Cash Flow Amount: $277/mo.

This was an OK deal, but not a super great one. I would not suggest a beginner do this kind of deal because it was purchased at over 80% of FMV, which is over what I suggest as a buying criteria. If you're a seasoned investor, like Kit is now, and you're in a good real estate market, then a deal like that is great. The most important benefit is that the loan is on a fixed LOW interest rate.

Here's the purchase HUD showing "subject to," as this is what we do:

201. Deposit or earnest money	0.00
202. Principal amount of new loan(s)	0.00
203. Existing loan(s) taken subject to	190,376.00
204. Promisory Note from Buyer to Seller	0.00

Kit didn't want to sell this house because he was in a rising real estate market, but he didn't want to rent it either and deal with tenants. (He follows the system.) So if you're in such a position, the perfect answer, as you already know, is to lease option it.

The tenant/buyer who put down $10,000 will take care of the property a lot better than a tenant with a $1,000 security deposit. Here are the other L/O terms:

Lease/Option Deposit Agreement
(L/O Earnest Deposit Receipt & Application)

Address Applied For: ▓▓▓▓▓▓▓ St, Mesa AZ 85205
Tenant(s)/Optionee(s)/Applicant(s): Jerry Thom▓▓▓▓▓▓▓

Lease Term: **36 moths**

Monthly Rent.: $ **1600**   Rent Credit for initial 36 mo.: $ **100** /mo.

Option Price: $ **239,000**

Option Money: $ **10,000**

And as you know, the L/O deposit is non-refundable, so if the tenant/buyer defaults, Kit will keep it and resell the house AGAIN:

4. OPTION CONSIDERATION: OPTIONEE has paid a fee of $ 10,000.00 as a *non-refundable* option fee which will be applied toward the purchase price of the property *if, and only if,* OPTIONEE abides by all of the terms of any other agreement between the parties, AND OPTIONEE actually exercises this OPTION timely and purchases the property. In the event OPTIONEE fails to exercise the OPTION or defaults under applicable terms of the attached lease, this OPTION will be automatically terminated and the OPTION fee will be retained by OPTIONOR.

While it won't be possible to go over even a small number of Kit's large portfolio of 250 deals in this book, this is another "bread and butter" deal where Kit made between $40,000 and $50,000, or even more, depending when or if the tenant/buyer exercises their right to buy and cash Kit out.

→ **Don't wait to make a decision. If you know real estate is the vehicle you want to use for improving your life and your family's life, then I encourage you to apply for our coaching. If you qualify and are accepted, then give it your all and you may become another Kit. I want you to be my next success story. If you have a strong "WHY," then I know that these proven and tested real estate systems can take you where you want to go.**

---

*Results presented are not typical—read the Earning Disclaimer

Coaching Student Success #4

Learn How They Created a <u>Million-Dollar Net Worth in ONLY 18 Months</u> Buying 25 Houses Using the Unlimited Funding Program—Read & Watch to Find Out How 50,000 Bees Changed Their Investing Career

Bill and Elaine reveal their BIGGEST REGRET, the one you need to avoid, in the first 5 minutes of this video. Watch today, take notes, and take action on their advice... you'll save money if you do!

Go to **www.MarkoRubel.com/book/Bill**

Bill and Elaine Share Two Deals:
(1) $30,000 Upfront Profit;   (2) $10,000 Upfront Profit

My coaching students Bill and Elaine have been in real estate investing for quite a few years. They had successful professional careers working in management for major corporations, so they understood the importance of investing in themselves and in their own education. From early on they hired different coaches and participated in different coaching programs. As you'll hear them clearly explain in the video, all of the programs they previously invested in lacked the precise direction they needed. It wasn't until they met me that their real estate investing exploded almost overnight. They created a few million dollars of net worth over a 2-year period of time, doing over 25 houses. That is remarkable! Here's the photo we took together at one my workshops:

In this example, Bill and Elaine will share two deals with you. In the first deal they gave the seller $2,200 in order to buy the property but quickly received $36,000 from their new buyer with a cash flow of $455/mo. The second deal was a $0 down deal, where they made $10,000 upfront and are getting $312/mo. in cash flow. Including the back-end profit, these two deals alone have a combined profit of over $100,000.

Now, before we get into these deals, let Bill tell you about their background, how they met me, and what their message is to you.

Your Background: *(Bill writing …)*

I spent many years in high tech in multiple management positions including a position as a senior manager for IBM in their Unix products division and ended my high-tech career as chairman of the strategic planning group for Sun Microsystems. We made all the major product decisions for Sun when Sun was the leading workstation provider in the world. My wife Elaine was vice-president of worldwide training and documentation for a multi-national high-tech company. Elaine and I then started and subsequently sold several small businesses focused on training students in high tech and office skills in the Greater Austin area.

How you met Marko:

Initially I watched Marko on YouTube and then attended a 4-day seminar where we (Bill and Elaine) signed up for the Inner Circle coaching program and mentoring. We attended a second 4-day seminar and plan to attend again.

Your Message to Reader:

Andrew Carnegie *said: "Ninety percent of all millionaires become so through owning real estate." So if your goal is to increase your wealth and secure your income long-term, then real estate investing is the way to go.* **The question we had when we started is how to do it.** *I have been interested in real estate investing for years and have paid many times what Marko charges for training and coaching from national and local REI training companies. None of them provided the detailed, practical step-by-step procedures Marko's training program provides. Marko tells you what to do, the exact order to do it in, includ-*

ing the critical selling procedures and all the documents you need. The coaching is from experienced real estate investors who are currently investing and profiting in the field unlike others who simply follow a script and have little to no actual experience or success.

* * *

The two deals they decided to share are the typical type my students do. Nice houses, in middle-class neighborhoods, generally in good shape. As you've already learned, we call them "pretty" houses because the most they usually ever need is carpet and paint. Rarely do the houses need more repairs, but even when they do, the repairs are still cosmetic in nature as you'll read below in Bill and Elaine's second deal.

Deal Example #1:
Unlimited Funding Method #4 – Cash4Deed Tiny Down

All this seller wanted in order to give up their beautiful 1.5-year-old house was $2,200 to pay for a professional packing and moving service. They loved their 4-bedroom, 2.5 bath home but hated the fact that their property taxes had skyrocketed and they couldn't afford it anymore. This house has over 2,900 square feet of living space. It was not a small property and almost brand-new.

The seller basically had two pain points causing them to want to sell the house. First was the husband's long commute to work, almost one hour, so he wanted to live closer to work. The second, and more complicated pain, was a dramatic tax increase caused by a reassessment of the property taxes from the original developer's pre-build tax estimate, which had been used in the mortgage payment calculation. They tried talking to the developer, agent, and mortgage company but got nowhere. They even hired an attorney who said there was little hope of winning a lawsuit based on a change in taxes because it commonly happens when building a home.

As you can begin to realize from this example, you can never guess someone's motivation and reason for selling until, like Bill and Elaine, you sit down with them. These people were not desperate and were not dumb. Bill and Elaine used the coaching and training they got from our Inner Circle coaching program and developed their brand to go out and identify the problem these sellers had and to solve it.

Many times sellers won't tell you their real motivation over the phone. I have said this for years at my seminars—your job is to find a reason to meet them for an appointment. Bill and Elaine said the same thing in our video interview, and this is critical to your success—if the numbers make sense, go on an appointment.

> **Marko's Money Tip:** Bill and Elaine used my Check Letter mailing, which we mostly use for marketing to people in foreclosure, but it also works for any other group of homeowners. It is a simple mailing piece. The check is printed on real check paper, and it's mailed using a double window envelope, so that the check will partially show through. The dollar amount we usually put on the check is the amount the earnest deposit would be for a house like that. However, practically speaking, no one ever asks about it, so it really doesn't matter what you put for the dollar amount. The important point to remember is that the check numbers are not real and the check is not signed. DO NOT SEND OUT your real account numbers. This is an advertisement, not a real check.

Bill and Elaine refer to this house as "Howard Lane" when you're watching their video interview, which by the way, has a lot of useful nuggets of investing advice. You definitely need pen and paper when watching.

Here's the deal summary:

Purchase Price: $192,000

Down Payment: $2,261 (+ Bill & Elaine paid closing costs)

Purchase Terms: "subject to" UFP Method #4

Loan Balance at that time: $189,660 @ 3.75% fixed 30-year.

Selling Price: $235,000

Down Payment Received: $36,377 ($29,177 at closing; $7,200 note with interest)

Amount financed by Seller/Bill: $198,623 @ 7%

Selling Terms: N2W AITD sold on owner financing in a few weeks

Cash Flow Amount: $455/mo.

Here's the Buying HUD statement from the closing:

115.	
116. Down Payment To Seller + Closing Costs	
120. Gross Amount Due From Borrower	$194,421.11
200. Amounts Paid By Or in Behalf Of Borrower	
201. Deposit or earnest money	$100.00
202. Principal amount of new loan(s)	
203. Existing loan(s) taken subject to	$189,660.12
204. Loan Amount 2nd Lien	
205.	
206.	

Bill and Elaine sold this property in six weeks by listing it on a MLS using a flat-fee listing broker.

> **Marko's Money Tip:** Using a flat-fee listing broker is an excellent way to get prospective buyers to notice your properties when you sell. A flat-fee listing broker will provide listing services for your property in the local MLS where you live for a fixed (flat) fee. This is usually from $99–1000, depending on the services provided. You will still pay a commission to the agent who brings the buyer, which when selling on wrap or lease option, is a lot less than the typical 2.5–3%. Plus, you save the full listing agent's commission when using a flat-fee broker to list it.

→ **Watch the Video:** Elaine also staged the house, like we teach in our Inner Circle coaching program, and she will give you a few tips in the video on how to do it for less than $100.

NOTE: The buyer put down a total of **$36,377**. Here's how this was paid: The buyer paid $29,177 at closing and promised to pay another $7,200 in the coming year. This $7,200 was secured by a note with interest and a deed of trust against the property. You will hear Bill talk about this in the video, explaining why the purchase was done this way. He brings up a good point.

And to conclude, these sellers were motivated, but not desperate. They were highly intelligent people, as you'll hear Bill explain in the video. He was a GS13 at a military base and she was a high school chemistry teacher. Why were they okay with leaving the loan in their name? It's simple—the sale of the house was more important. And as Bill says in the video, they were ecstatic with the outcome.

Deal Example #2:
Unlimited Funding Method #1 – $0 Down – Instant Ownership

Through their marketing efforts, Elaine answered a call from a seller who had a house that he had owned where his mother lived with him. The seller had married and moved out two years previously, and the mother was still living in the home by herself. The seller's mom was elderly and ill, so the seller and his wife wanted his mom to come live with them. They even added a room to their new house, so that the mom would feel more comfortable. The house had never been listed.

Below are the buying and selling HUD statements, and the deal summary:

Amounts Paid By Or In Behalf Of Borrower	
201. Deposit or earnest money	$10.00
202. Principal amount of new loan(s)	
203. Existing loan(s) taken subject to	$109,679.75
204. Loan Amount 2nd Lien	
205.	

120. Gross Amount Due From Borrower	$147,512.50
200. Amounts Paid By Or In Behalf Of Borrower	
201. Deposit or earnest money	$1,000.00
202. Principal amount of new loan(s)	
203. Existing loan(s) taken subject to	
204. Seller Financing Note	$135,000.00

Purchase Price: $109,690

Down Payment: $0

Purchase Terms: "subject to" UFP Method #1

Loan Balance at that time: $109,679 @ 5.5% fixed 30-year.

Selling Price: $145,000

Down Payment Received: $10,000

Amount financed by student: $135,000 @ 7%

Selling Terms: N2W AITD sold on owner financing in a few weeks

Cash Flow Amount: $312/mo.

Now remember earlier, I told you that most houses only need minor cosmetic repairs, like paint and carpet. This particular house needed a little more work than usual because of neglect in a few areas. The items that needed to be taken care of here were factored into the calculations that Bill and Elaine used when going through the Net Equity Worksheet with the seller.

→ **Watch the video interview I did with Bill and Elaine, and I will tell you how to get the Net Equity Worksheet we give our Inner Circle Students for FREE.**

The repairs included removing a backyard shed, adding some new fencing, painting the house, landscaping the front and back, and resurfacing a cracked back porch. While this might seem like a lot, Bill and Elaine, never lifting a finger, had it all done in a few weeks and ready to resell. All in all it was around $8,000. The buyer's down payment more than covered the out-of-pocket-expenses to fix up the property, so Bill and Elaine were cash flow positive in the deal.

→ **Watch the video as Bill and Elaine share many great investing points that could help you decide how to start improving your life. At the beginning, Bill explains the most important skill you need to acquire as an investor. In the middle, you'll hear about 50,000 "residents" they needed to evict (funny). Also pay attention towards the end when we discuss which deals are the best … and much more …**

*Results presented are not typical—read the Earning Disclaimer

Coaching Student Success #5

Ivan and Judy, a Retired Couple in Their 70s, Lost Everything When the Stock Market Crashed, $750,464.00. Learn How They Were Able to Buy 20 Houses "On a Limited Income" and Rebuild Their Legacy.

Ivan and Judy were in their seventies. They lost it all. So they had to come up with a viable strategy to rebuild their retirement fast. Listen how they were able to buy 20 houses on a limited income and how Marko saved their deal while on a boat in Croatia...

Go to www.MarkoRubel.com/book/Ivan

Ivan and Judy Share a Deal
Subject To + Seller Carry-Back = $70,000+ Profit

In telling you about one of Ivan and Judy's deals, I decided that I would show you an example of a **different kind of real estate deal**. So far, in the case studies you have seen: Get-Paid-to-Buy deals, Subject To deals, Seller Carryback Note deals, and even $0 Down deals. Many of Ivan and Judy's deals were NO money down or they got PAID to buy, as you'll hear in the video interview. But I don't want to talk about those either.

I want to share a deal with you that fully matured, meaning it was completed. It started in a rather unusual way, so that way you get to see the real breadth of what could happen with these deals and also what's possible in your business.

→ **If you're on somewhat of a limited budget or you just think you don't have the money to invest in a good real estate deal, it's very important that you watch the Skype video interview I've prepared just for you because this example is not only about deals, it's a story about an older couple's perseverance and determination.**

As usual, before we start, here are the three responses from their email to me:

Your Background:

As senior citizens, who were retired, we made some terrible investments and lost $750,000 of our retirement in the stock market. We were faced with having to find a business or some way to bring money in. We had our backs up against the wall. I had just had back surgery and had pins in my back, so my options were limited. Judy and I felt that real estate was something we could do considering our situation.

How you met Marko:

We decided that real estate would be the way to get us back on track. We started going to seminars, and after spending a lot of money, none of those systems were working. Then we attended a conference in Los Angeles, where we heard Marko speak for about 2 hours. It resonated with us, and we knew Marko was different. We later attended Marko's seminar and decided that he will be the last guy we'd need to follow. We joined his coaching, and the rest is history.

Your Message to Reader:

Marko always told us, "Success leaves clues." You don't have to learn the hard way. No matter where you are in life, his system can make the difference for you. The system Marko developed can be learned by anyone, and if we can do it at our age, with the challenges we faced, then you can do it with his guidance.

* * *

Most people dream of retirement. You know—that is the time of your life when you kick back and when you can do what you want, when you want. Well, as you heard, that should have been the case for Judy and Ivan until a few investing mistakes cost them $750,000 of their retirement. And if that wasn't enough stress, Ivan was partially disabled with back surgery and pins in his back. In fact, you can almost see the pain of his back surgery in his face as he is standing in the above photo. I can remember him telling me about the pins they had to put in his back and how painful it was every day. So many would understand if Ivan and Judy just gave up. But they didn't. Their WHY was stronger.

> **Marko's Money Tip:** Winners move forward in the direction of their dreams despite the circumstances. Losers wait for the circumstances in life to all line up in a row before taking action. Decide to be a winner and get started where you are with what you have right now.

Here's Ivan and Judy at our live training, which they attended many times:

After joining our program they immediately began studying and implementing the system exactly the way it was designed and used one-on-one coaching to keep on track. And now after a few years, they have done over 20 deals and have an average profit of about $50,000 per deal with some as high as $80,000, $90,000, or even $100,000 on a single deal. Ivan and Judy have a goal to get another 20 houses in the next year or so to round out their portfolio.

Deal Example:
Unlimited Funding Method #3 – Note4Equity – Seller Carries

The deal began when an investor friend approached Ivan about being his private lender on a deal he was trying to close. Ivan had some cash in one of his entities and after reviewing the numbers, decided he would move forward with $12,000 secured in the second position behind the seller's primary mortgage.

> **Marko's Money Tip:** One of the more advanced techniques of this business is to become the private lender for others on their deals as long as you are well-secured and in a good loan-to-value position. Remember, this is not a technique for beginners unless you are well educated about what you are investing in. You need to be careful.

Unfortunately the investor Ivan lent to could not make the payments and move forward with his plans for the house. At that time, I was in Croatia where I go every summer for a two-month vacation. In fact, I was in the middle of the Mediterranean on a yacht with some friends when I got a call on my cell phone. Here is a picture of where I was …

The caller ID showed a number from the United States. However, it wasn't my office number and my family was with me, so I knew it had to be a coaching student with a problem. I answered the phone, and it was Ivan calling. He was all stressed out; in fact, Ivan was almost yelling, and I remember him screaming, "The investor is not paying!" Because of this situation with the investor, Ivan used one of his emergency calls that are available for every one of my Inner Circle coaching students. I give them my cell phone number, and of course, they can't call me for any reason. It has to be a real emergency—for me to save their deal or make their deal. For Ivan, this was just such an emergency.

After 35 minutes on the phone brainstorming different ideas and yes, with the waves splashing in the background, we figured out the best solution. The truth is, I was excited when I got that call because I love finding creative solutions to real estate problems.

How did it turn out?

What was the result?

Are you sure you want to know?

Within one week Ivan got the deed from the investor and ended up "getting" the house "subject to" the first bank loan with Wells Fargo and the second loan extended to the investor by Ivan's own entity. Ivan and Judy used their Inner Circle coaching benefits to the fullest. Using my experience and their business savvy, we turned a losing situation into a deal that just recently closed, netting Ivan and Judy over $70,000 in gross profits.

Here's the summary:

FMV: $250,000–255,000

Purchase Price: $234,000

Down Payment: N/A ($12,000 was given as a loan to investor)

Loan Balance at that time: 1st loan of $198,000 with Wells Fargo; 2nd loan of $12,000 to Ivan's entity; 3rd loan of $24,000 that investor owed to original seller as part of original purchase price

Loan Terms: 4.75% on 1st loan, no payments & no interest on 3rd loan

Selling Price: $262,900

Down Payment Received: $20,000

Selling Terms: sold on owner financing at 7.4%

Cash Flow Amount: $517/mo.

How many of you have had that perfect deal, and then in the eleventh hour something happens and it starts to fall apart? I hear that story all the time. **What would it mean to you if you had a coach or even me in your corner when the deal got to this stage?** It meant $70,000 to Ivan and Judy. During the video interview, you'll hear Ivan and Judy tell you in their own words how stressed they were and what it was like to get support on that deal in that critical time and the relief it brought to them.

Once we got Ivan back in control of the deal, the next step was to resell it.

Ivan and Judy sold it to a doctor who gave them a $20,000 down payment on the house. The money came in as follows: a $1,000 earnest money deposit with the contract, $15,000 in the form of a cashier's check made payable to Ivan and Judy's company, and the remaining $4,000 at closing. Take a look at the HUD1 Settlement statement below:

116.		
120. Gross Amount Due From Borrower	$262,900.00	420. Gross Amo
200. Amounts Paid By Or in Behalf Of Borrower		500. Reductions
201. Deposit or Earnest Money		501. Excess Dep
202. Principal Amount of New Loan(s)	$242,900.00	502. Settlement
203.		503. Seller Finan
204. Commitment Fee		504.
205.		505.
206. Earnest Money	$1,000.00	506.
207.		507.
208. Cashiers Check to Preferred Housing Solu	$15,000.00	508. Cashiers Ch
209.		509.
Adjustments for items unpaid by seller		Adjustments for
210. City Property Taxes		510. City Proper
211. County Property Taxes		511. County Pro
212. Annual Ass		512. Annual Ass
213. School Property Taxes		513. School Pro
214. MUD Taxes		514. MUD Taxe
215. Other Taxes		515. Other Taxe
216.		516.
217.		517.
218.		518.
219.		519.
220. Total Paid By/For Borrower	$258,900.00	520. Total Redu
300. Cash At Settlement From/To Borrower		600. Cash At Se
301. Gross Amount due from borrower (line 120)	$262,900.00	601. Gross Amo
302. Less amounts paid by/for borrower (line 220)	$58,900.00	602. Less reduct
303. Cash From Borrower	$4,000.00	603. Cash To S

$20,000.00 down payment

Section 5 of the Real Estate Settlement Procedures Act (RESPA) requires the   Section 4(a) of

Marko's Money Tip: Notice that Ivan and Judy sold the home to a doctor who couldn't qualify for a bank loan at the time. My tip is don't disqualify people who could be potential buyers. You never know someone's situation, so treat everyone like you want to be treated. This doctor had a great salary (income) but couldn't qualify for a loan. That can be a perfect buyer for you.

After two years the buyer was supposed to refinance because Ivan and Judy had given him a 2-year balloon note. This means that the buyer would make agreed upon payments during the 2-year term, and then the unpaid balance of the loan would be due in full at that time. The doctor (buyer) could not get refinanced in time, so he was in default.

> Pursuant to the terms of the Note, the balance due and payable to Lender, as of today, is the total amount of $247,693.10 which is accrued but unpaid interest, principal, taxes, insurance, and late charges. In addition and pursuant to the terms of the Note and Deed of Trust, you are also liable for attorney's fees and expenses incurred by Lender in connection with collection of the Indebtedness. To date, attorney's fees and expenses in the amount of $750.00 have been incurred. Finally, because you have failed to tender payment in satisfaction of the obligation when due, past-due principal and interest is accruing interest at the default rate of eighteen percent (18%) per annum, which comes to a per diem rate of $119.51. You will continue to be responsible for additional interest and attorney's fees as they accrue.

To protect themselves, Ivan and Judy filed a demand for payment with an attorney in Texas. The demand payment notice is similar to a notice of intent to foreclose. Here is what it looked like, see the picture below:

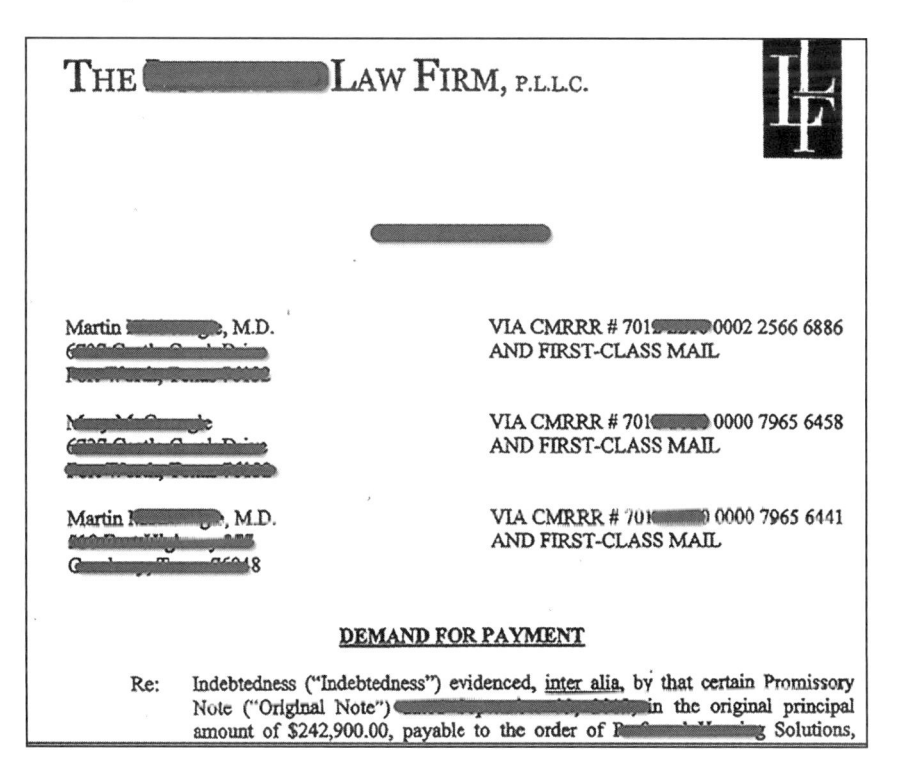

THE ▇▇▇ LAW FIRM, P.L.L.C.

Martin ▇▇, M.D.
▇▇▇▇▇▇
▇▇▇▇▇▇

VIA CMRRR # 701▇▇ 0002 2566 6886
AND FIRST-CLASS MAIL

▇▇▇▇▇▇
▇▇▇▇▇▇
▇▇▇▇▇▇

VIA CMRRR # 701▇▇ 0000 7965 6458
AND FIRST-CLASS MAIL

Martin ▇▇, M.D.
▇▇▇▇▇▇
▇▇▇▇▇▇

VIA CMRRR # 701▇▇ 0000 7965 6441
AND FIRST-CLASS MAIL

DEMAND FOR PAYMENT

Re: Indebtedness ("Indebtedness") evidenced, inter alia, by that certain Promissory Note ("Original Note") ▇▇▇▇▇▇ in the original principal amount of $242,900.00, payable to the order of ▇▇▇▇▇ Solutions,

Because the doctor had paid on time for two years up until the last payment and it wasn't Ivan and Judy's intent to harm him or leave him in a bad situation, they allowed him to stay and continue making the elevated payments called for by the note that he had signed.

Finally, after 90 days of paying $119 a day, the buyer was able to refinance and refinance the property out of the owner finance note that Ivan and Judy had created for him. Let me show you the profits on this one deal:

Down Payment: $20,000
Cash Flow: $517 x 24 months = $12,408
Cash Flow for 90 days @ 18% = $10,710
Financing Points: 3.5% of the original loan balance = $8,501
Back-End Profit = $19,838

Total Gross Profits: $71,457.00

How many deals like this would you need every year to change your life? What if you could do one a month? And remember, that is on a $262,000 house, not a $500,000 or $600,000 house as is the average in many areas of the country.

Plus, the ownership was recovered at 90%+ of the FMV ($234K / $255K).

Let me explain the financing points and the back-end profit. **Financing points** are what we sometimes charge for extending our financing to the buyers. In order to maximize the down payment we can get from buyers, we make these points payable at the end of the loan. Banks normally charge this upfront, reducing a buyer's down payment, and we charge it on the backend. In this case, $8,501—not bad, right?

Similarly, **back-end profit** refers to the amount of money that is the difference between the "subject to" note that Ivan and Judy were paying on with Wells Fargo at 4.75% interest and the note balance the buyer had with Ivan and Judy when they created the wrap mortgage at 7.4% for the doctor. Because the wrap mortgage interest rate is higher, that loan pays down slower, and the underlying loan that Ivan and Judy took "subject to" is paying down faster because it has a lower interest rate, so more money is being applied to the principal on a monthly basis. The longer the wrap stays in place, the bigger the difference and the more profit Ivan and Judy (or you, if this were your deal) would make. In this case, that was $19,838 in profit as shown on the wire transfer from the title company:

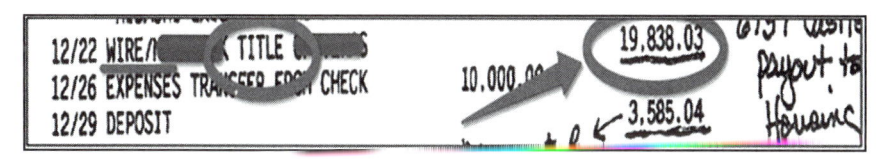

```
12/22 WIRE/        TITLE                    19,838.03
12/26 EXPENSES TRANSFER FROM CHECK  10,000.00
12/29 DEPOSIT                        3,585.04
```

> **Marko's Money Tip:** Small discounts can lead to big profits. We teach our students to have multiple sources of income on each property. Between upfront down payments, monthly cash flow, financing points, and back-end profits, small discounts on the property can lead to big profits.

How many of you would like to have a deal like this? Do you know it's totally possible. If you watched their interview, then you know it's possible.

Ivan and Judy did it and continue to do it, and you can too.

> **Ivan and Judy's Money Tip:** Do yourself a favor, put away all the other courses, unsubscribe from all those gurus' emails, and stop surfing the Internet. Take Marko's material, study it, take notes on it, and study it again. Then get out and do it because it will work for you if you have a big enough WHY.

The deal described above was just one of Ivan and Judy's deals. As I mentioned earlier, they completed many different deals. Here's the check when they got paid to buy for the first time. **See the email they sent me below.** They're holding the check on the way out from the title company. Hope it's not too small for you to read …

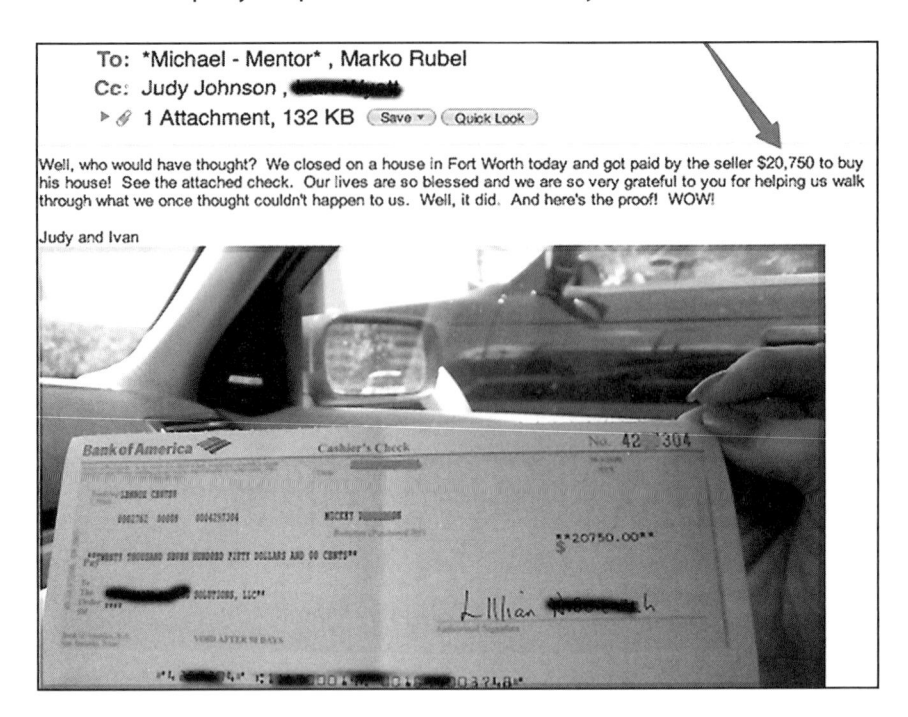

> **To:** *Michael - Mentor*, Marko Rubel
> **Cc:** Judy Johnson, ~~~~~
> ▸ 📎 1 Attachment, 132 KB (Save ▾) (Quick Look)
>
> Well, who would have thought? We closed on a house in Fort Worth today and got paid by the seller $20,750 to buy his house! See the attached check. Our lives are so blessed and we are so very grateful to you for helping us walk through what we once thought couldn't happen to us. Well, it did. And here's the proof! WOW!
>
> Judy and Ivan

I'd like to end this story with the following … It took more than the typical number of appointments for Ivan and Judy to land their first deal. However, as you witnessed, it's all been worth it for them. Their effort is best described with this quote from Michael Jordan:

I'VE MISSED MORE THAN 9,000 SHOTS IN MY CAREER.
I'VE LOST ALMOST 300 GAMES.
TWENTY-SIX TIMES I'VE BEEN TRUSTED TO TAKE THE GAME-WINNING SHOT AND MISSED.
I'VE FAILED OVER AND OVER AND OVER AGAIN IN MY LIFE.
AND THAT IS WHY I SUCCEED.

—*Michael Jordan*

*Results presented are not typical—read the Earning Disclaimer

Coaching Student Success #6

After 26 Years in the Air-Force, Butch Is On His Way to Becoming a Millionaire! Learn How He Was Able to Add 15 Houses to His Portfolio in the Last 16 Months Alone ...

Watch the Skype video interview as Butch talks about the painful mistake he made when he started in real estate investing. It got him in big trouble with the bank and with the IRS. You definitely need to avoid it, and now you can.

Go to **www.MarkoRubel.com/book/Butch**

Butch Shares Two Deal Examples:
(1) UFP with small down   (2) UFP reinstatement deal

The two deals Butch will share in a moment **have some great learning points.**

You will also notice that his deals are pretty typical compared to the ones we've covered so far in Section 2. If you remember, that's what I mentioned to you at the start of this section—all these deals are conceptually the same, and that's what makes this business pretty simple once you get it going.

Sure, every deal is unique on its own, has its own specifics, and that's why you should read about every deal explained in this section, and you should put a decent effort Into understanding the numbers presented and how the profit was calculated.

Butch's motivation to be successful in this business is little bit different than that of most of my students. He wants to get 30 houses and put them in an IRA that he plans to gift to his grandkids. He'll talk about it in the video.

Here's the email Butch sent where he's sharing his background:

Your Background:

I am a retired military Air-Force flight surgeon. I was living in Phoenix, Arizona and had always wanted to invest in real estate. I bought 4 houses at the housing peak using my own money and bank loans. I had to short sell two of the houses at a 40% loss. Then I met Marko. I've been following Marko's Niche2Wealth program the past two years. In the first year I bought 11 houses using Marko's Niche2wealth program. In this second year I have already bought 4 more houses using Niche2wealth here in Idaho where I live.

How you met Marko:

I met Marko at an AZREIA (Arizona Real Estate Investment Association) meeting. Marko did a presentation on his ProfitGrabber software. I purchased the ProfitGrabber office automation system and attended 2 of Marko's seminars. I bought Marko's advance course and studied it. I did my first subject 2 deal, making $20K. At Marko's next seminar I joined the Inner Circle coaching program. Now, my goal is to buy 1–2 houses per month using Marko's program.

Your Message to Reader:

Never sign for a bank loan and instead, follow Marko's methods! Lifting a pen is a lot easier than lifting a hammer.

Marko's Niche2Wealth program really works. There is studying required to pick up on all of Marko's way of planting seeds, etc. for effective negotiations. Marko will give you very explicit details on how to do the Niche2Wealth program.

Marko is an excellent instructor, he truly desires all his students to be successful with his bi-monthly conference calls, his quad yearly seminars, his web portal; he leaves no detail out of how to be successful.

* * *

Deal Example #1:
Unlimited Funding Method #4 – Cash4Deed Tiny Down

Here is one of Butch's deals. This particular deal came about as a referral from a prior client that Butch had helped not long before by buying her house. The client was so happy with Butch's service that she recommended that her friend call Butch and ask if he could help her too.

While this may not be the primary way that your deals come to you when you start your investing business, it certainly will be one of the ways that deals will come as you build your business one success at a time.

The seller was divorced and had moved in with her boyfriend. She didn't want the house anymore and was having trouble making the payments. She was perfectly happy for Butch to take over the loan and take care of the payments for her. See a picture of Butch with the house here.

The house was worth around $175,000 to $180,000, and Butch used our Unlimited Funding Methods #3 and #4 to negotiate a purchase price of $144,000 by getting the seller to agree to let him take over the existing loan of $140,000, giving the seller $2,500 cash to take care of some expenses, and getting the seller to agree to take back a seller carryback note of $1,500 for the balance of the equity. Then he "sold" the property using our Niche2Wealth Lease Option strategy, receiving a nice down payment and a few hundred dollars per month in cash flow. Here's a summary of that deal:

Deal Summary:

Fair Market Value (FMV): $175,000 to $180,000
Purchase Price: $144,000.00
Down Payment: $2,500.00 cash + $1,500.00 note
Loan Balance at that time: $140,000.00 @ 4.3%
Selling Price: $184,600.00

Down Payment Received: $9,500.00 +$500 deposit with application

Selling Terms: 1-year lease option

Cash Flow Amount: $323/mo.

Total Profit: $40,000+ if the tenant/buyer buys it. If they don't, then it will be more.

The seller carryback note was for a small amount, only $1,500. However, it did not have any interest. In fact, when you watch the video, you'll hear Butch tell you himself that he never pays interest no matter how big or small a note is—just like we teach our students.

I've included a copy of the purchase and sale agreement from the deal here:

```
2. TOTAL PURCHASE PRICE to be paid by Buyer is payable as follows:
   A. EARNEST DEPOSIT, receipt of which is hereby acknowledged in the sum of ............ 20.00
   B. DOWN PAYMENT BALANCE AT CLOSING, (not including Buyers closing costs, prepaid
      items or prorations) in U.S. cash or cashier's check. Approximately [ ]: Exactly [X] ............ 2480.00
   C. NEW LOAN. Proceeds of a new loan to be executed by Buyer to any lender
      other than Seller. ............
   D. TAKE TITLE SUBJECT TO AN EXISTING FIRST TRUST DEED NOTE
      held by ___ with an approximate unpaid amount of ............ 140,000
      payable $__ monthly until paid, including interest not exceeding _%.
   E. TAKE TITLE SUBJECT TO AN EXISTING SECOND TRUST DEED NOTE
      held by ___ with an approximate unpaid amount of ............ NA
      payable $__ monthly until paid, including interest not exceeding _%.
   F. TAKE TITLE SUBJECT TO AN EXISTING THIRD TRUST DEED NOTE
      held by ___ with an approximate unpaid amount of ............ NA
      payable $__ monthly until paid, including interest not exceeding _%.
   G. A PROMISSORY NOTE in the principal amount of ...To Be Paid within 3 mos... 1500
      Promissory note to Seller on terms set forth in Paragraph 2B.
   TOTAL PURCHASE PRICE IS THE AMOUNT OF ............ $ 144,000
```

As you can see the from the PSA, Butch used only $20 as his earnest money deposit and took over the seller's existing loan of $140,000. He never had his credit checked, never filled out a loan document, and just as important as this, the seller got what she wanted, most of which was relief from the loan payment she was having trouble making.

This was a lot simpler of a process than the one where Butch got a bank loan and later <u>lost his credit</u> and <u>owed money to the IRS</u>, as he describes in the video interview.

The way Butch got the seller to agree was by using our P-E-N method, which stands for Presentation – Education – Negotiation. And, within that process, we have a very powerful tool called the Projected Net Equity Worksheet. Using this tool, we teach our students to walk the seller through what they would likely get if they sold the home to a homebuyer using an agent.

→ **In many of my online webinar trainings I describe this tool and share a copy of it. Look for our next webinar training when you are in the online resource center watching these videos. You will want to get your hands on this tool.**

Let me show you the original Net Equity Worksheet Butch walked the seller through when he went on the appointment:

```
ALL AMERICAN HOMEBUYERS – STATE SPECIFIC WORKSHEET

              Projected Net Equity Worksheet

Realistic Sales Price of Property ............... $  158,000
> LESS:
   EXISTING FINANCING:
   1st Loan Balance: ........ 4.37% (927)  $  140,000
   2nd Loan Balance: .........................  $    0
   3rd Loan Balance: .........................  $    0

   BACK PAYMENTS, PENALTIES & COSTS .... $    0

   BACK TAXES & OTHER LIENS ............. $    0
   (add 10% penalty on the tax amount owed)

   LOAN PRE-PAYMENT PENALTIES ........... $    0

   SELLING COMMISSION (6%) ................. $  9480

   HOLDING COSTS (6-8mo. of Interim PITI payments) .... $  350

   CONTRIBUTION TO BUYER'S COSTS ........ $  4740
   (Buyer's market allowance of – 3%)

   TRANSACTIONAL EXPENSES ............... $  4700
   (Closing fees – 2 – 3%)
                                    TOTAL COST  $144,000
   COSMETIC FIX-UP:                 SALE PRICE  $84,600
        Interior Work ...... $ 250   PROFIT      40,600
        Outside Work ...... $         CASH FLOW  $3N/mo
        Yard Work ......... $
        TOTAL ............................. $  250

Projected NET EQUITY Proceeds ........... $  -1520
                                              2001
     2500+1500 (4000)                     (3500)
```

214

As you can see, Butch went through the Net Equity Worksheet helping the seller to see what would happen if they sold the home the traditional way, which could take months, and then Butch negotiated to buy the home giving the seller only $2,500 cash and a note the seller agreed to for $1,500. A perfect Niche-2Wealth deal!

And wait—that's not even the best part.

Then Butch marketed the house as a lease with an option to buy. He quickly found a buyer who loved the house "as is," so Butch had absolutely no repairs or other things to do to get the house ready.

Here are the terms of the option agreement, where he received $9,500 as the non-refundable option consideration plus $500 when they submitted their application. So with the $2,500 out-of-pocket Butch had paid to the seller as a down payment, Butch was still way cash positive.

Monthly Rent for initial 12 mo.: **$1150.00**
Option Price: $184,600 *(may be increased to Fair Market Price per Option Agreement)*

Option Consideration: $9,500.00 *(this is a non-refundable down payment)* including in the

Do you know the great thing about this deal? Butch sold it on lease option, so if the tenant/buyer decides not to go through with the purchase, Butch gets to keep the $9,500 option consideration (because it's non-refundable) and all the monthly cash flow he made along the way, and sell it again taking another non-refundable option consideration and making more cash flow. This is a great deal, and they are out there for you to get too.

How many deals making $40,000 and over $300 per month cash flow do you need to alter your life? To change what's possible for you and your family? To help someone you love in need?

Now that would be great if it was just one deal for Butch, but he's done MANY deals like that and many better deals than this one.

Let's look at this other deal he wanted to share with you.

Deal Example #2:
Unlimited Funding Method #5 – Reinstatement

This was the prettiest and most expensive house Butch has purchased thus far. It had 4 bedrooms, an office, and 2.5 baths. The seller was very motivated—and 5 months behind on payments, so the bank was foreclosing.

Deal Summary:

Fair Market Value (FMV): $245,000

Purchase Price: $193,290.42

Down Payment: $2,500.00 cash + $2,854 note

Loan Balance when purchased: $187,936.25 including $10,969.58 in arrears

Loan interest rate: 5.375%

FMV: $250,000.00

Selling Price: $263,900.00

Down Payment Received: $25,000.00

Selling Terms: sold on owner financing at 6% interest

Up-profit is $10,000+ and over $60,000 coming when the buyer refinances.

Now, while I won't go into every detail of this deal like I did with the previous one, it's important to note that the exit strategy you select may be different from deal to deal.

This deal Butch sold using the N2W Wrap strategy. *Do you know why this was the best strategy for this deal? What do you think was an advantage of the wrap instead of the lease option?*

The main reason was to get a higher down payment, so Butch could get his money out of the deal. As I mentioned earlier, you don't want to leave money in a deal if you don't have to.

What happens to your return on investment (ROI) when you have no money left in a deal? The answer is, it becomes INFINITE. So as you're learning, we're not looking for 10% or 20% ROI in this business. We're looking for a few hundred or a few thousand percent ROI, all the way up to infinite return.

As you already learned, the wrap buyer gets ownership, so he can take the interest tax write-off, which lowers his monthly payment.

NOTE: There are a few different methods involved with the Niche2Wealth Wrap strategy. The one that Butch used was an Installment Land Contract sale, and here's the agreement:

AGREEMENT FOR SALE OF REAL PROPERTY
(Installment Contract with Balloon Payment)
This is intended to be a legally binding contract.
If not fully understood, seek the advice of your attorney.

THIS AGREEMENT, made and entered into ███████████████, by and between **IDAHO HOUSING SOLUTIONS, LLC** hereinafter referred to collectively as Seller, and **OMOTAYO OLUBIYI** hereinafter referred to collectively as Purchaser.

Witnesseth:

WHEREAS, Seller agrees to sell and Purchaser agrees to purchase certain land, and all improvements thereon, on that certain real property located at ███████odhaven Ave. in the City of **MERIDIAN**, County of **ADA**, State of **IDAHO**, together with all buildings and improvements presently situated or hereafter placed thereon.

THE PARTIES COVENANT AND AGREE AS FOLLOWS:

1. **PURCHASE PRICE.** The purchase price of the property which the Purchaser agrees to pay and the Seller agrees to accept shall be the sum of $263,900 (Two Hundred Thousand Sixty Three Thousand Nine Hundred & No/100--------------- DOLLARS), payable as follows:

    A. The sum of $25,000.00 will be paid hereto as down payment to be applied toward the purchase price, the full receipt of which will be on or about June 1, 2015. With $5000.00 paid 11/10/14, $20,000 to be paid on or before 9/1/2015. A service charge of 2% per month will be applied to the unpaid balance

    B. The unpaid principal balance of $238,900.00 shall bear interest at the rate of **6.0**% per annum (amortized over 60 yrs.) from the date hereof, for the first 36 months after which interest will increase to **6.75** % thereafter for the following 36months after which the remaining principal balance will be due and payable . Principal and Interest payments of $1228.37 shall be made monthly with the first payment due the ███████ and a like payment due the 1st day of each month thereafter, for a period of 36 months (thirty six) after which the Balloon balance of the principle is due, however this may be extended another 36 months. Interest shall accrue from the date hereof. In addition, Purchaser shall accrue with his/her monthly installments equal to 1/12th of the annual obligation for said taxes, hazard insurance, and homeowner's assessments, if applicable, in monthly installments equal to 1/12th of the annual obligation for said taxes, insurance and assessments. The current annual estimate for said taxes, insurance, and assessments is: Taxes; $1,741.00/yr or $145.00/mo, Insurance; $863/yr or $71.92/mo, Association Fees; $400.00/yr or $33.33/mo.
    Purchaser understands that the taxes, insurance and association fees are subject to adjustment up or down and agrees to pay the actual amounts thereof. Purchaser further agrees and understands that should expenses for said taxes, insurance, and assessments be

SIDE NOTE: The Installment Land Contract is also called Agreement for Sale, Agreement for Deed, or Contract For Deed … it all refers to the same method.

Here's the part of that agreement zoomed-in:

> **THE PARTIES COVENANT AND AGREE AS FOLLOWS:**
>
> 1. **PURCHASE PRICE.** The purchase price of the property which the Purchaser agrees to pay and the Seller agrees to accept shall be the sum of $263,900 (**Two Hundred Thousand Sixty Three Thousand Nine Hundred** & No/100 ----------------- **DOLLARS**), payable as follows:
>
>   A. The sum of **$25,000.00** will be paid hereto as down payment to be applied toward the purchase price, the full receipt of which will ▓▓▓▓▓▓▓▓▓▓▓▓▓ With $5000.00 p▓▓▓▓▓▓▓▓▓▓▓▓▓ to be paid on or before ▓▓▓▓▓▓▓. A service charge of 2% per month will be applied to the unpaid balance

> **Marko's Money Tip:** Remember that knowing the best way to sell (using one of the 5 top selling strategies) depends on your situation and your objective with the home at the time you are doing the deal. Be sure to consider all of the relevant factors in your decision-making process.

As I have talked about in the book, there are many ways to market for motivated sellers. In Butch's first deal, the seller was referred to Butch because he had helped the seller's friend by buying her house. In this deal, the lead came from a pre-foreclosure lead that Butch contacted using the marketing tools he had. Here below is Butch in front of his **ProfitGrabber.com** automation tool that all of my students use.

Butch followed our system that we lay out step-by-step and used it to start his real estate empire—and you can too.

> **Butch's Tip:** Register for the local BBB as soon as you are able and when you get notarized testimonials, ask the sellers If they'd be willing to put their testimonials directly on the BBB site. See the video for more on this.

*Results presented are not typical—read the Earning Disclaimer

Coaching Student Success #7

Learn How a Mom with a Full-Time Job Got a FREE Loan from a Seller for $95,000 on Her Very First Appointment ... Was It LUCK?

Tara got her first deal on her first appointment and her second deal on her second appointment. That's 2 for 2 and is an unbelievable score! Watch this video as she shares her view on the real estate business ...

Go to www.MarkoRubel.com/book/Tara

Tara Shares Deal Example:
UFP with small down

Now for many of you who have read the title of this deal, you see that I mentioned LUCK. What do I mean by LUCK? Well, it's not the good luck you think of if you find a 4-leaf clover or a shiny penny on the sidewalk. To me LUCK means **L**abor **U**nder **C**orrect **K**nowledge or said another way, when preparation meets opportunity, and that is exactly what happened to Tara.

Tara's deal that I will describe to you came on the very first appointment she ever went on. Now I want to tell you upfront that this is not what typically happens; however, it is possible.

Let's first review her email with the 3 responses:

Your Background: *(This is Tara writing …)*
I was working and continue to work full-time as the CFO of a medium-sized company (after getting my MBA and CPA license). I was happy with my career, but I realized that I no longer wanted to be tied down and work full-time for the next 25 years until retirement. I wanted financial freedom and flexibility. I believed that real estate was the solution, so I purchased a short sale house, and then soon after that I began my real estate investing education.

How you met Marko:
In my quest to find the best real estate training program, I saw an advertisement on the Internet for Marko's program. After attending my first seminar, I joined his Diamond membership, and I truly regret not joining the Inner Circle at that time. I was hesitant because I was working full-time and was very busy with 2 little girls, trying to be supermom, and I didn't want to take any time away from my family. Then, while speaking to Marko at one of his seminars, he encouraged me to focus on his Inner Circle program by making small sacrifices now, so that I could have freedom in the future. So I took his advice, and I am so happy that I did.

Your Message to Reader:

I went through a few training programs before I found Marko's program, and I can honestly say that Marko's Inner Circle program is hands down the best. What Marko teaches is the most profitable niche in real estate, and he explains everything so specifically, there is no way to fail unless you don't put forth the effort yourself. I would recommend Marko's program to real estate investors at any level, especially beginners, because it is so detailed and easy to follow.

* * *

Let's talk about Tara's deal, but first let me show you a picture of Tara when she joined my Inner Circle coaching program.

Deal Example:
Unlimited Funding Method #3 – Note4Equity – Seller Carries

Tara found this deal by calling for-sale-by-owner ads. The ad for this house was on the Zillow website. She used the Phone Form that you've already downloaded from the online resource center at **www.MarkoRubel.com/book**. If you haven't yet, go there now.

How much did Tara spend to find this deal? $0—so if you don't have a lot of money, don't look for an excuse not to start. And if you don't have a lot of money, then you really need to start today, so you don't have to go through your whole life worrying about money.

In this deal, the sellers had already purchased another house and moved. Their house had been listed for a couple of months, and they wanted to get out of making two mortgage payments. The seller's motivation was not too strong, but Tara still got a great deal.

Here's a picture showing the house in great shape. Tara painted the inside and changed the carpet.

Tara purchased the house for $331,636 and "sold" it on lease option for $375,000. She bought it "subject to" the existing loan with a $5,000 down payment and a large seller carryback note with no interest and no payments. The tenant/buyer put down $10,000 as a non-refundable option deposit. The cash flow that Tara has is $454 per month.

Below is the summary of this deal:

Purchase Price: $331,636
Down Payment: $5,171
Seller Note: $95,800 for 3 years (no interest & no payments)
Loan Balance at that time: $230,665

Selling Price: $375,000
Down Payment Received: $10,000
Selling Terms: Sold on lease option with a 24-month term

Cash Flow Amount: $454/mo.

The most credit I give to Tara is for negotiating successfully such a large seller carryback note. It is not easy to get a seller to carry back such a large amount, and she did it without paying any interest and making no payments. Awesome!

Another important point—the note she created is a non-recourse promissory note.

Now what do I mean by non-recourse? It means that the only recourse the sellers have for collecting on the house is the interest in the property, and they cannot come after Tara personally if something happens and she never pays it off.

> **Marko's Money Tip:** Don't be afraid to secure a seller carryback note by giving the seller a mortgage on the property. If you use our non-recourse note, which we give you, then the seller cannot come after you personally; they can only come after the property. As you already know, those notes can be discounted as you've already learned from the previous examples.

Look here at the purchase and sale agreement showing the carryback note:

2. PURCHASE PRICE. Buyer to pay the purchase price as follows (check all that applies):

- ☒ EARNEST DEPOSIT, receipt of which is hereby acknowledged in the sum of .... $ __170.99__
- ☒ CASH DOWN PAYMENT at closing in the amount .... $ __5000.00__
- ☒ TAKE TITLE SUBJECT TO AN EXISTING FIRST TRUST DEED NOTE
  held by __Chase__ with an approximate unpaid amount of .... $ __230,665.28__
  payable $ __1,109.76__ monthly until paid, including interest not exceeding __4__ %.
- ☐ TAKE TITLE SUBJECT TO AN EXISTING SECOND TRUST DEED NOTE
  held by _____ with an approximate unpaid amount of .... $ _____
  payable $ _____ monthly until paid, including interest not exceeding ___ %.
- ☒ A PROMISSORY NOTE in the principal amount of .... $ __95,800.00__
  For the Terms of the Note, see paragraph 11 below. __Secured by house__
- **TOTAL PURCHASE PRICE IS THE AMOUNT OF** .... $ __331,636.27__

As you can see, Tara filled out the PSA with the figures provided by the seller, and then the seller agreed to the terms of the note that Tara outlined in the PSA's "Other Terms" section. See this section below:

11. OTHER TERMS: Principal $95,800 on note due at the end of 36 months from closing date, no interest, no payments. Buyer has option to extend the term 60 days by notifying, in writing, the seller 60 days prior to maturity.

Using the "Other Terms" section of the PSA confirms what you and the seller agreed to, and by Tara's getting that in writing, the seller cannot come back later and say that Tara owes them interest or payments.

So Tara closed on this transaction and got the deed and the seller's carryback note, and gave the sellers a deed of trust securing their $95,800 note with the property. And the best part is that the note has no interest and no payments for 3 years, as we've seen in the "Other Terms" section of the agreement.

→ Tara explains in the video why the purchase price was not a round number. Also she explains why this deal took only 3 hours of her time.

Let's look at some of the documents in the pictures below.

The first photo is a picture of the deed that the sellers gave to Tara at closing which gave Tara ownership of the seller's deed. Your title or escrow company will help with this, and you must make sure it is accurate.

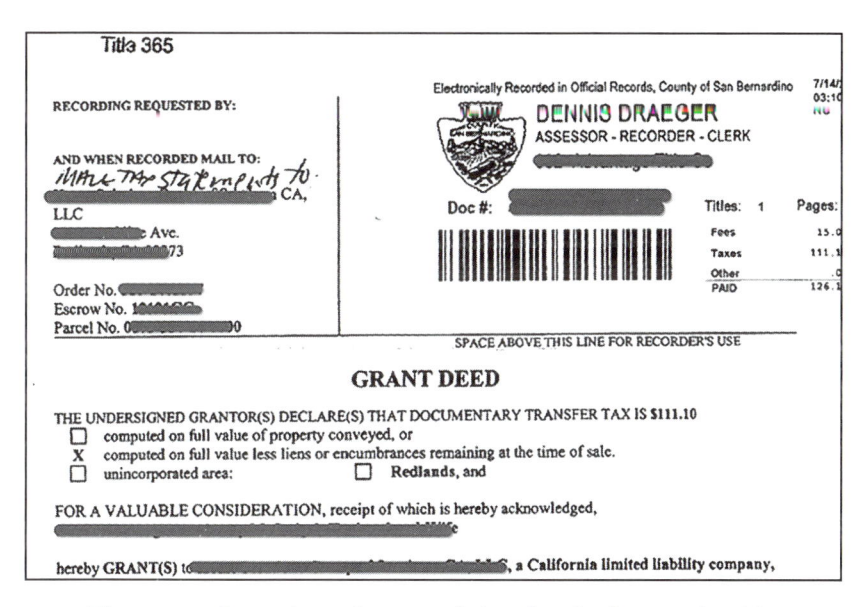

GRANT DEED

THE UNDERSIGNED GRANTOR(S) DECLARE(S) THAT DOCUMENTARY TRANSFER TAX IS $111.10
☐ computed on full value of property conveyed, or
☒ computed on full value less liens or encumbrances remaining at the time of sale.
☐ unincorporated area: ☐ Redlands, and

FOR A VALUABLE CONSIDERATION, receipt of which is hereby acknowledged,

hereby GRANT(S) to _____, a California limited liability company,

The next photo is a picture of the deed of trust that Tara created to secure the seller's carryback note:

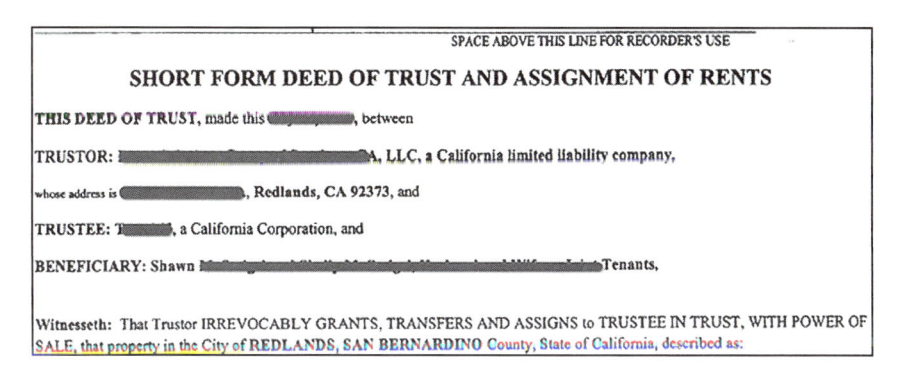

SHORT FORM DEED OF TRUST AND ASSIGNMENT OF RENTS

THIS DEED OF TRUST, made this _____, between

TRUSTOR: _____, LLC, a California limited liability company,

whose address is _____, Redlands, CA 92373, and

TRUSTEE: _____, a California Corporation, and

BENEFICIARY: Shawn _____ Tenants,

Witnesseth: That Trustor IRREVOCABLY GRANTS, TRANSFERS AND ASSIGNS to TRUSTEE IN TRUST, WITH POWER OF SALE, that property in the City of REDLANDS, SAN BERNARDINO County, State of California, described as:

This is a picture of the non-recourse note that Tara created for the amount of the seller's equity that they were leaving in the property:

PROMISSORY NOTE
(Balloon note)

[Date] ▓▓▓▓▓ [City] Redlands [State] Ca

[Note Amount] $95,800 [Property Address] ▓▓▓▓▓ 92374

FOR VALUE RECEIVED the undersigned without recourse, jointly and severally promise(s) to pay to the order

the principal sum of $95,800 being payable on or before ("balloon date"), in lawful money at the following address:

Within a short while, Tara sold the property on lease option, after touching up the paint, to a tenant/buyer who wanted 24 months to be able to buy. Here are the terms:

Lease/Option Deposit Agreement

Address Applied For: ▓▓▓▓▓ Ca 92374
Tenant(s)/Optionee(s)/Applicant(s): Eric and ▓▓▓▓▓

Lease Term: 24 months
Monthly Rent for ~~initial 12 mo.~~ lease term: $1,800   Rent Credit for initial 12 mo.: $ 0 /mo.
Option Price: $375,000 ~~(may be increased to Fair Market Price per Option Agreement)~~
Option Consideration: $10,000 (this is a non-refundable down payment)

228

> **Marko's Money Tip:** You always want the term with your tenant/buyer to be shorter than the term with your seller. In this case, Tara got 36 months no interest and no payments on her seller carryback note, so she gave her tenant/buyers 24 months to complete the lease option transaction with her and buy the property. This way you have some cushion in case your tenant/buyer doesn't end up actually closing on the purchase of the house.

The option agreement provided for an adjustable option price, ensuring that Tara benefits from any appreciation:

> 3. OPTION PRICE: The OPTION price ("strike price") is: $ *375,000* ; provided, however, if OPTIONOR concludes at any time before OPTIONOR has received proper notice of exercise of the OPTION from OPTIONEE that the fair market value of the property exceeds the foregoing strike price, OPTIONOR may (but is not required to) propose to OPTIONEE that the Option Price be increased to the fair market value of the property as determined by a professional fee appraiser selected by OPTIONOR. The OPTION price is not to exceed $ ~~400,000~~ *375,000*. **This Special Clause ensures that the investor captures any possible appreciation!!**

→ **As Tara shares in the video, lease option tenant/buyers never call and ask for repairs. She talks about this being very different from renters. Be sure to hear her explain.**

Our agreement ensures that tenant/buyers never call about minor repairs:

> 13. REPAIRS: Resident shall at his own expense, and at all times, maintain the premises in a clean and sanitary manner, including all appliances herein. Resident shall be responsible for all repairs not exceeding $100 per incident and in total not exceeding $1,000 per year. Management shall be responsible for any repairs exceeding the amounts specified herein. As the future purchaser of the Property, OPTIONEE accepts the responsibility to make all repairs and to maintain the premises in good, safe and working order.

Obviously, your attorney would need to make sure this clause complies with the local landlord-tenant law in your state.

There are a number of important pieces to a lease option transaction. One thing we teach our Inner Circle students is to use a separate lease and option agreement.

> **Marko's Money Tip:** I recommend that you always use separate lease (rental) and option agreements when doing lease option deals. The biggest reason is that this will help protect you in the case of a default by your tenant/buyer, so you can evict them as renters instead of having a judge force you to go through a foreclosure because a tenant claims equitable interest in the property. This is especially important in states where the foreclosure timeline can be more than a few months.

In all, Tara had a good spread on the equity, great monthly cash flow, got enough of a down payment on the lease option, so she wasn't in the negative with the money she gave to the seller, and was totally protected in her agreement with her new tenant/buyer. Not bad for your very first deal from your very first appointment …

How many of you would like to have a first deal like this where you live? You can if you follow our teachings.

→ **TARA'S SECOND DEAL:** Shortly after this first deal was completed, Tara closed on her second deal and invested only 2 hours of her time from start to finish. Another amazing fact is that Tara never met the seller in person. However, there's an important mailing piece that she sent which made a world of difference. Listen to her as she explains it.

The deal numbers were very similar, and the strategy was exactly the same—purchased "subject to," and "sold" using lease option.

To find this deal, Tara used ProfitGrabber Pro and mailed to MLS active listings in her target area, and an out-of-town seller who'd received the mailing called her.

Using a system like ProfitGrabber Pro allows investors to spend the maximum amount of time working with sellers and buyers and not in the administrative tasks of marketing, tracking, and evaluating leads. If you want to invest 2 or 3 hours per deal as Tara did, check out how ProfitGrabber Pro can make a real difference and take your business to the next level!

> **Tara's Tip:** I didn't need an accounting background or an MBA to do this business, and you don't either. The Inner Circle coaching is very specific and designed for beginners who don't know anything about real estate, and if you put forth the effort, you will get the results because it is straightforward, simple, and all laid out for you. If you follow the system, you can't help but be successful!

*Results presented are not typical—read the Earning Disclaimer

Coaching Student Success #8

Tire Salesman in Ohio Gets 5 Deals While Working over 50 Hours per Week at His Full-Time Job. Find out How He Is Planning to Escape His Job of 29 Years …

Watch this candid video interview where Chris reveals one thing he did that helped him to get his wife to support him in his real estate venture. Also watch to hear his "escape" plan …

Go to www.MarkoRubel.com/book/Chris

Chris Shares Three Deal Examples:
(1) UFP with small down (2) UFP reinstatement deal

It's very rare these days that you find someone who has been with the same company for 29 years and counting. Chris Smith is one of those rare men. Chris has been a store manager of a local branch of a national automotive tire and service company for over 29 years. At one point, he drove almost two and a half hours a day to go to work and worked over 50 hours a week. Add to that a family and other concerns, and you can see how Chris could easily have an excuse not to get into our business.

> **Marko's Money Tip:** Winners don't make excuses. Winners turn what could be excuses into reasons and then take action in the direction of their dreams and goals. What excuse have you been giving yourself for not starting in creative real estate? There has never been a better time than now because all we have is now.

Let's have Chris tell us about his background and how we met ...

Your Background:

I am currently working the automotive industry in management and have been for 29 years. This is a full-time job, and I have been doing real estate investment part-time for 10 years. Prior to using Marko's system, I was purchasing properties for rental purposes to use as a retirement tool. I have 4 grown daughters and 3 granddaughters. My wife and I love to travel and go boating, and we spend as much time as possible pursuing this activity but would like to be in a position to have more free time for it. I used to drive two and a half hours a day, and I was tired of working for someone else. It was a good income, but working for over 50 hours a week left me no time for other things, the important things.

How you met Marko:

I was maxed out on purchasing rental properties the traditional way (qualifying for loans and using my own personal funds) and was looking for other ways to continue to purchase properties and found Marko on the Internet. I decided to attend his foreclosure seminar training in Chicago. I was impressed by what I learned at that seminar and joined the Inner Circle coaching program that weekend. The Inner Circle coaching program is just invaluable. Being able to have contact with someone who is knowledgeable to answer questions and guide you is invaluable and has made the difference.

Your Message to Reader:

Marko's system is very easy to use. Everything is in a step-by-step learning process. Multiple teaching vehicles such as videos, workbooks, webinars, seminars, and personal coaching make this system well worth the investment of money and time. This is a way of investing in real estate that you won't hear about in the mainstream. It has worked well for me, and I am now considering doing this full-time.

* * *

Here's a picture of Chris and I at one of our workshops:

After joining the Inner Circle coaching program, Chris started taking action and began to market to MLS expired listings in his target area. Chris used our special Transferred Engineer series of linked letters in his marketing campaign to find this deal.

> **Marko's Money Tip:** Mailing to sellers one time is often a waste. I have found that multiple mailings give the best opportunity for a message to market match, where the message in my letter (or postcard) matches the seller's concerns at the right time.

Deal Example #1:
Unlimited Funding Method #4 – Cash4Deed Tiny Down

A seller who had moved to Colorado answered one of Chris' letters. Chris learned that the seller had moved in hopes of finding a new job and relocating his family to that area. The family was separated as they were still in Ohio, waiting for their house to sell. The husband had been out there for four months while the house was listed but not selling. The seller had gone to Chris' website and seen the testimonials of other people that were helped in his situation, and he called Chris. The seller's biggest motivation was to get rid of the house and to reunite the family.

I have said it before, no one will ever give up what they have unless they get something in return that they want more, and what the seller wanted most was to be reunited with his family in Colorado. He wanted his family, he wanted peace of mind, and he wanted those things more than he cared about leaving the loan in place.

> **Marko's Money Tip:** Don't rationalize why someone would be motivated. You are not in their shoes, and I can't tell you how many times I was wrong. Sometimes the sellers will tell you, and sometimes they will not. The important thing is not to judge them or think you know and cause it to change your finding a solution to their problem. Help the seller find a solution, and their reason will appear.

→ Take time to listen to Chris tell you about his life and this deal in his own words in the video.

Here is a picture of the purchase and sale agreement that Chris negotiated with the sellers:

2. TOTAL PURCHASE PRICE to be paid by Buyer is payable as follows:	
A. EARNEST DEPOSIT, receipt of which is hereby acknowledged in the sum of	$ —
B. **DOWN PAYMENT BALANCE AT CLOSING**, (not including Buyers closing costs, prepaid items or prorations) in U.S. cash or cashiers check. Approximately [ ]: Exactly [✔]	$ 3,000
C. NEW LOAN. Proceeds of a new loan to be executed by Buyer to any lender other than Seller;	$ 0
D. **TAKE TITLE SUBJECT TO AN EXISTING FIRST TRUST DEED NOTE** held by Fed Cr____ with an approximate unpaid amount of ... payable $ 1200.00 monthly until paid, including interest not exceeding 6.2 %	$ 125,000
E. TAKE TITLE SUBJECT TO AN EXISTING SECOND TRUST DEED NOTE held by ___ with an approximate unpaid amount of ... payable $___ monthly until paid, including interest not exceeding ___%	$ 0
F. TAKE TITLE SUBJECT TO AN EXISTING THIRD TRUST DEED NOTE held by ___ with an approximate unpaid amount of ... payable $___ monthly until paid, including interest not exceeding ___%	$ 0
G. A PROMISSORY NOTE in the principal amount of ... Promissory note to Seller on terms set forth in Paragraph 2B.	$ 0
TOTAL PURCHASE PRICE IS THE AMOUNT OF	$ 128,000

Here's a summary of this deal:

Purchase Price: $128,000
Down Payment: $3,000 down to seller
Loan Balance at that time: $125,000 @ 6.5%.

Selling Price: $159,900
Down Payment Received: $20,000
Selling Terms: N2W Lease Option

Cash Flow Amount: $150/mo.

In essence, the seller sold their house for the balance of the loan plus $3,000 cash. After the sellers moved, Chris refreshed the paint, put in new carpet, and used the techniques we teach in the Inner Circle coaching program to work with his coach to market for a lease option tenant/buyer. He listed the property using a flat-fee MLS broker in his area and used yard signs in front of the house (as you can see in the house picture above).

Within two weeks Chris had a tenant/buyer who gave him a check for **$20,000**:

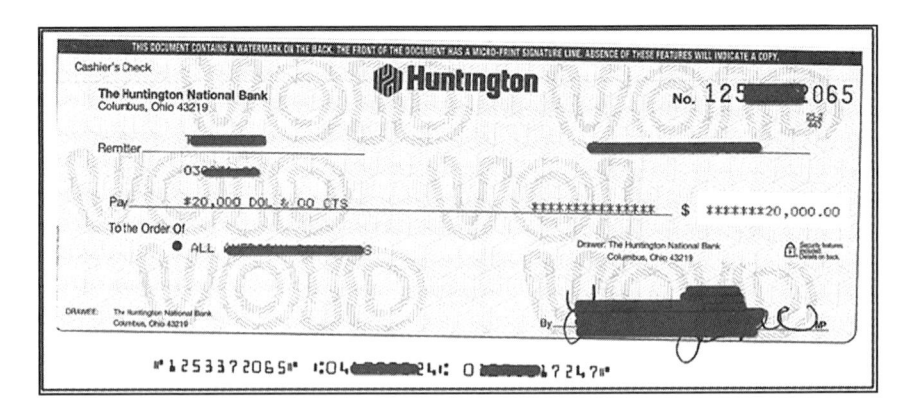

You already learned that this $20,000 is non-refundable if the tenant/buyer doesn't buy the property within the term given, as stated in the option agreement:

> **4. OPTION CONSIDERATION:** OPTIONEE has paid a fee of $ __20,000.00__ as a ***non-refundable*** option fee which will be applied toward the purchase price of the property *if, and only if,* OPTIONEE abides by all of the terms of any other agreement between the parties, AND OPTIONEE actually exercises this OPTION timely and purchases the property. In the event OPTIONEE fails to exercise the OPTION or defaults under applicable terms of the attached lease, this OPTION will be automatically terminated and the OPTION fee will be retained by OPTIONOR.

Now, it's important to tell you that it took a little while to find a title company that would do Chris' deal. In fact, he had to call 8 before he found one. Chris even had a couple of title companies tell him that it was illegal to buy a house "subject to" an existing loan. Chris just told them that it wouldn't be pre-printed on line 203 of the Federal HUD1 Settlement form if it was illegal, and he would just call the next title company.

One thing this shows you is that these techniques are a niche in real estate, not conventional, and not something every real estate investor knows. So the moral of this story is—Don't give up if you get a "no" the first time. Ask for referrals and keep looking. **Hear Chris tell you that story in our video interview.**

Deal Example #2:
Unlimited Funding Method #1: $0 Down – Instant Ownership

In his second deal, Chris used only $10 to buy. How many of you can afford to do that? Everyone! He also covered closing costs in the amount of $1,684. Now, this was a little more money than $10, but he quickly got it all back—and then some.

Here's the closing statement showing the purchase price that includes closing costs:

120. GROSS AMOUNT DUE FROM BORROWER	153,684.00	4
200. AMOUNTS PAID BY OR IN BEHALF OF BORROWER:		5
201. Deposit or earnest money		5
202. Principal Amount of New Loan(s)		5
203. Existing loan(s) taken subject to	*includes closing*	5
204.	*costs*	5
205.		5
206.		5
207.		5
208. Subject to Existing Mortgage	152,000.00	5
209.		5

The same as in his first deal, Chris found a tenant/buyer and quickly got $9,250. This more than paid back the closing costs he covered at acquisition.

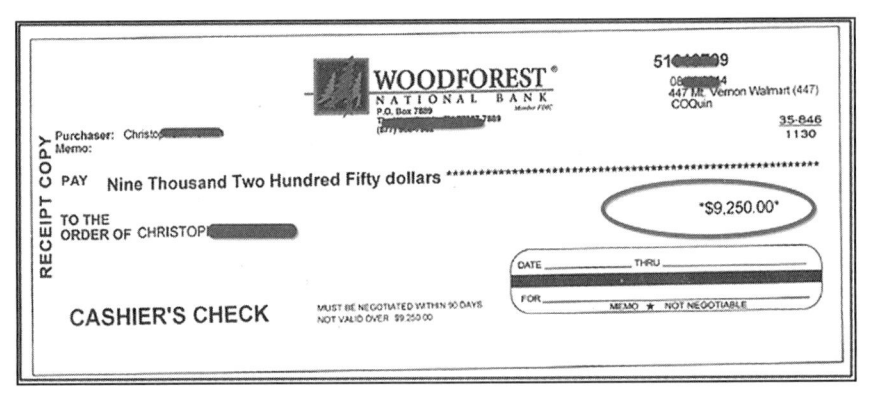

How many deals can you do like this? The answer is—as many as you can find. It doesn't take money to buy them.

Do you see what I mean when I say these deals are all the same? Do you see how drastically simpler this all becomes after your first deal?

That is the whole benefit of the Niche2Wealth system. It allows you to work smart, not hard, and make a lot of money.

Do you have a full-time job? Are you short on time?

With Chris being a business store manager, commuting over 2 hours a day and working 50 plus hours a week, that didn't leave a lot of time for answering seller calls. Chris used a **live answering service** we share with our Inner Circle coaching students that has a series of questions we provide that help pre-screen the sellers when they call. This allowed Chris to focus on his job, and sellers still got to talk to a live person, which definitely increases your conversion rate because sellers think you are a long-established company.

Here's what I did for my business and for my students. I integrated the live answering service we use with my, in this case, Chris' ProfitGrabber Pro automation system. Once a seller calls, the lead is captured and Chris gets an email telling him he has a new seller lead. Plus the lead is automatically put in Chris' CRM Profit-Grabber system, complete with all the answers the seller gave. Very cool, right?

Here's the email Chris received from the answering service about the above-mentioned deal. See the circled answer where the seller says that he'd sell the house for what's owed on it:

```
|1ST MORTGAGE BALANCE|:{152000       }
|1ST MORTGAGE LENDER|:{Chase                 }
|1ST MORTGAGE INTEREST RATE|:{        }
|1ST MORTGAGE PAYMENT|:{1135          }
|IS IT PRINCIPAL & INTEREST (PI) OR PRINCIPAL,|
|INTEREST, TAX & INSURANCE (PITI)|:{piti    }|TAB|
|2ND MORTGAGE BALANCE|:{               }
|2ND MORTGAGE LENDER|:{                      }
|2ND MORTGAGE INTEREST RATE|:{        }
|2ND MORTGAGE PAYMENT|:{               }
|ARE PAYMENTS CURRENT?|:{no }
|IF NO, HOW MUCH ARE YOU BEHIND?|:{1135     }|TAB|
|REASON FOR SALE?|:{Too big for them         }
|HOW DID YOU ARRIVE AT YOUR PRICE?|:{What is owed }
|IS HOUSE LISTED? (Y/N)|:{n }
|TAB|

|DOES THE HOUSE NEED REPAIRS?|:{no }
|IF YES, HOW MUCH? (IN $)|:{         }
|WHEN DO YOU WANT TO MOVE?|:{about a month }
|WOULD YOU SELL YOUR HOUSE FOR WHAT YOU OWE ON IT?|:
{yes}
```

> **Marko's Money Tip:** Whenever you can't answer the phone yourself, forward your calls to a live answering service. A live answering service has an operator who knows the seller is calling about your company and will ask the seller a set of pre-determined questions designed to gather information for you. .

→ Watch the video as Chris explains how he purchased a deal for cash and why he did it. Sometimes even when you reinstate a loan or just take the loan "subject to" an existing mortgage, it may still make sense to sell the property outright.

> **Chris' Tip:** If you're standing on the outside and looking in, it can be overwhelming. However, the system is laid out step-by-step, and everything you need to succeed is there. Get to the 4-day seminar, see the big picture, and then start where you are. If I can work 55 hours a week, drive 15, and still build this business, then you can too. Get started today.

Now Chris is considering going full-time as an investor and looking forward to giving up his 50-hour weeks for time with his family.

*Results presented are not typical—read the Earning Disclaimer

COACHING STUDENT SUCCESS #9

REAL ESTATE BROKER GETS THE SYSTEM, GIVES UP HER LICENSE, STOPS REHABBING, & GOES ON TO GENERATE $926/MO. IN POSITIVE CASH FLOW ON ONE DEAL …

Watch the video training to hear why Amy gave up on her broker license, why Jovy gave up on rehabs, why they only work with "hungry buyers," and how they got $25,000 without selling the house …

Go to **www.MarkoRubel.com/book/Amy**

Amy & Jovy Share Deal Example: Reinstatement

Amy and Jovy have a very interesting story. Both were ambitious professionals, both tried fixing houses, and now they are full-time working the Niche2Wealth system.

As you watch the video, you'll hear them say how different the N2W buyers are, as I've been telling you all throughout this book. They say it loud and clear on the video, which is another proof that this business is in fact a lot simpler than rehabbing.

One of those buyers gave them a $25,000 cashier's check and is paying them $926/mo. in cash flow. Wow!

I can't wait to share their deal with you and give you a few great tips. But let me first introduce them to you by sharing their email where they answered the 3 questions …

* * *

Your Background: *(Amy and Jovy writing …)*

We are both full-time in real estate now, using Marko's system. Before meeting Marko, Amy was a licensed real estate broker for several years, and she saw that working on commission was not the way to build lasting wealth. Jovy had been working for Los Angeles County as the volunteer coordinator for the Department of Public Health for several years as well, and was looking for more freedom and adventure in her work. When we met Marko, we saw his Niche2Wealth system as a way to achieve both freedom and financial independence together.

How you met Marko:

While attending a real estate seminar in Boston, Marko presented his ProfitGrabber Pro software system. While we enjoyed his funny and charismatic presentation, we immediately saw that it was powerful, simple to use, and held the key to our getting our real estate systems organized and consistent. We had no idea that our buying ProfitGrabber was the gateway to so much more for us!

Your Message to Reader:

We had some doubts in the beginning about this system and if it was too good to be true, but we could also see that it really could work and that it was the pathway to our real long-term goals of professional autonomy and financial independence. Also, Marko and his entire team are a great support and mentors, and they genuinely want us to succeed and show it consistently through their actions and availability to us.

* * *

Some of you reading this book are probably thinking the same—this is "too good to be true." Let me tell you, if you work the system, you will have the results. It's as simple as that. And the results could be huge.

If you're reading this book so far, then obviously you're intrigued by what I'm writing. Step back for a moment and decide if you agree with me on this—**the Niche2Wealth approach just makes a lot of sense, doesn't it?** It's like 1 - 2 - 3 to me … (1) if you want to get the maximum benefit, you have to own real estate; (2) you can't own a lot of real estate any other way than using the "unlimited funding," "subject to" approach; it's the only way; and (3) if you want to maximize the selling profit, sell to those who have no other choice and need you.

When you think about it, the benefit of my N2W system is revealed in these 3 rudimentary principles. If you understand that, you understand everything.

And if you understand that, then you'll never ask me questions about flipping or cash buyers. Let me address that, and then we'll get to our deal …

Some investors think they'll get rich selling to cash buyers. How wrong! Everyone knows "cash is king," and those who have the cash know it too. They look for bargains. So people with cash never pay full price. Why? Because they don't have to.

For that reason, you will not get rich selling to cash buyers. You will get rich by selling to people who are willing to pay you a premium price and premium interest because they don't have a lot of cash, so they don't have a lot of credit, so **they need you.**

→ **Listen to Jovy describe those "hungry buyers" in the video. They are so motivated, it's unreal. And they appreciate what you give them. Listen to Amy saying that the buyer who gave them $25,000 always pays early, and when they drive by the property, they are surprised at how nicely they are keeping it up.**

SIDE NOTE: *You could get access to cash buyers in your area via my Money Finder tool, but use it only for some ugly houses that accidentally come your way. I'll describe all of that in the bonus section.*

So let's review Amy and Jovy's deal—this house.

**Deal Example:
Unlimited Funding Method #5 – Reinstatement**

Here's the deal summary:

FMV: $345,000–350,000

Purchase **Price**: $291,950

Down Payment: $10.00

Loan Balance at that time: $285,000.00 plus 4 back payments totaling $6,940

Loan terms: 2% interest, adjusting to 4% in the future

Selling Price: $374,900

Down Payment Received. $25,000.00

Selling Terms: 3-year lease option

Cash Flow Amount: $926/mo.

As soon as Amy and Jovy joined our coaching program, we gave them the "90-Steps Implementation Program." Within a few weeks, they had their workflow and their systems ready to go.

They started mailing to houses for sale using our special "Transferred Engineer" letter. We use different marketing USPs (unique selling proposition) than most investors who tend to use the "We Buy Houses" USP. I feel that such a USP is fine if you're dealing with "ugly" houses, but for our business it sends the wrong message.

Their phone started to ring, and one of the calls was from a motivated seller who was 3 payments, and about to be 4 payments, behind on their mortgage and desperate to find a way to protect their credit.

Look at the Phone Form that Amy and Jovy completed as a result of their call with that seller:

> Well, It sounds really like a nice (decent) house, I'm curious WHY are you selling? Retired last year Oct. No longer can make payment
> What do you think the house is worth $ 340K   How did you arrive to that price? R.E.
> Do you know what kind of loan you have, is it a VA, Convent., or an FHA? > How much is left (Balance) on the:
> 1st loan: 235, IR 2%, Fix or Adj Loan Mod. Mo. Payment $ 1138   Taxes&Ins. incl.: Y N
> Do you have a 2nd loan: Y N Balance 2nd ____. Mo. Paymnt ____ HOA? S ____
> TOTAL LOANS: $ ____ >EQ: ____
> Are all the PAYMENTS CURRENT? Y N 3 payments NOD
> If no, how much is it in arrears? $ 3 pmts Has foreclosure been filled? Y N When is the sale date?
> (how much is needed to reinstate-to bring it current?) No Offers
> Is the house currently listed? Y N How long? 1 month Can you cancel the Listing Ag if needed? Y N Maybe
> ** ADDRESS: 26 ▓▓▓▓▓▓▓▓▓▓ ft   City/Zip: Long Beach

I suggest that you always have a stack of blank Phone Forms by your telephone. The Phone Form is a valuable tool because it allows you to build rapport with the seller and guides you on what to say when.

If you look at the form, it was very clear that this seller was motivated. See up there where it says, "No longer can make payment." Then "in arrears 3 pmts"... and notice the super low interest rate—plenty of reasons to go on that appointment.

But let me warn you, it's not always so clear. Many times the sellers don't tell you their real position and don't reveal their motivation. If you decide not to go on those appointments, you will leave a lot of money on the table. As a matter of fact, I think you will fail if you do that. Actually I don't think—I know.

> **Marko's Money Tip:** he purpose of the Phone Form is to build rapport with the seller and find a reason to go on the appointment. It is not to find reasons not to go on appointments. I can't tell you how many students have told me they couldn't find deals, and when I dug a little deeper, I found that they used the Phone Form as a way to hide their fears of actually going on appointments. Don't let fear stand in your way of going on appointments.

Once Amy and Jovy had set the appointment and hung up with the seller, they followed another one of our key steps in the sales process and sent out the "Special Report." The Special Report is a tool we make available to our Inner Circle coaching students called "How to Sell Your House in 7 Days or Less Without Realtors or Fees." It's a 16-page brochure which is in fact a carefully designed sales letter with testimonials designed to tell sellers how we buy homes.

→ **Watch Amy in the video share how the seller was sold on their service after reading that Special Report.**

In fact, our Special Report was so effective with this seller that when Amy and Jovy finally did get to meet her, she said that she wanted the "subject to" option as soon as Amy and Jovy sat down with her. How's that for a powerful marketing tool?—And more on that later.

But there was a problem. The night before the appointment, the seller called and canceled because the seller's agent had brought her a short sale offer. Now at that moment, most investors would have considered this a dead lead and forgotten about the seller, but that is not what we teach our Inner Circle coaching students and that's not what Amy and Jovy did. Amy followed up with the seller a few days later and learned that the seller didn't like the offer and decided not to accept it. Amy quickly set an appointment for the next day.

> **Marko's Money Tip:** It's important to pause here and ask you—What would have happened if we hadn't taught Amy and Jovy to follow up with the seller the evening the seller cancelled? You always want to follow up with the seller. I can't tell you how many times students have told me that their deals came from the 2nd, 3rd, or 5th follow-up with the sellers.

After Amy reset the appointment, both Amy and Jovy went to meet the seller, and that's when the seller told Amy and Jovy that she wanted to use the "subject to" option. After going through the P-E-N method (our exclusive Presentation, Education, and Negotiation method of meeting with a seller), they signed the deal giving the seller only $10 cash.

One of the key reasons that Amy and Jovy were able to get the deal is that they followed the P-E-N method to the letter. Among the many steps we teach our Inner Circle coaching students is to use a notepad to confirm all the terms of the purchase and get the sellers' verbal agreement before pulling out the purchase agreement. This restates the agreed and in a way creates the commitment, so you have higher chances of their not getting scared away when you start filling out the PSA.

Look at this picture of the notepad that Amy and Jovy used to make sure that the seller understood the offer, restated the agreed, and was okay with everything.

```
                                              NOTE PAD
    Close  Oct.  4
    Mae-Out   Oct. 21
    285,000
                              Bring
    PAY  4 Back payments  Current
    Pay    Oct. 1  Mortgage  /$6940
    Ceiling fans, stove, blinds, chandelier
```

So let's review the numbers of this deal and see how incredibly profitable it really was. First, they purchased the home for $285,000 plus the reinstatement balance of $6,940 and gave a $10 cash earnest deposit for a total purchase price of $291,950.

Yes, the seller got $10. I know it's hard to believe, so look at this photo that confirms what I'm telling you.

> **2. PURCHASE PRICE.** Buyer to pay the purchase price as follows (check all that apply):
>
> ☒ **EARNEST DEPOSIT**, receipt of which is hereby acknowledged in the sum of........ $ 10
> ☐ **CASH DOWN PAYMENT** at closing, in the amount .... $ /
> ☒ **TAKE TITLE SUBJECT TO AN EXISTING FIRST TRUST DEED NOTE**
> held by M&T Bank with an approximate unpaid amount of .... $ 285,000
> payable $ 1388 monthly until paid, including interest not exceeding 2 %. This includes $6940 reinstatement amount see 11 below
> ☐ **TAKE TITLE SUBJECT TO AN EXISTING SECOND TRUST DEED NOTE**
> held by _____ with an approximate unpaid amount of .... $ /
> payable $ _____ monthly until paid, including interest not exceeding ___ %.
> ☐ **A PROMISSORY NOTE** in the principal amount of .... $ /
> For Terms of the Note, see paragraph 11 below.
> **TOTAL PURCHASE PRICE IS THE AMOUNT OF** .... $ 291,950

Remember, $10 was all the cash they gave the seller, but they saved the seller's credit, which is priceless.

The $6,940 that Amy and Jovy used to bring the loan current could have been paid through the escrow at closing. See the clause Amy and Jovy used in the PSA to make that possible and to protect them from the loan balance being increased before closing.

> **11. OTHER TERMS:** At closing, Buyer will bring the loan in default current by paying the back payments in the amount of $6940. The principal of the 1st loan specified in paragraph 2, includes this reinstatement amount.

Once the seller signed the PSA, which she was so happy to sign, Amy and Jovy followed their coach's step-by-step instructions, opened escrow, and closed a week later. *Each one of our Inner Circle coaching students gets assigned one of my coaches that I trained personally many years ago, and their coach provides them with unlimited deal support during the program.*

> **Marko's Money Tip:** Never reinstate a loan prior to closing on a property that is in default. Paying someone else's reinstatement before you have the deed is throwing your money away.

The house was in good shape, but it needed some cosmetic touch-ups, which included some paint and flooring. Once complete, Amy and Jovy decided that the best exit strategy for them would be to sell the house on lease option because they want to keep as many properties as possible and benefit from the appreciation and future price increases if the tenant/buyer decides not to exercise their option.

> **Marko's Money Tip:** People who buy on lease option are more likely to not exercise their option on the property as people who buy on owner financing. The ratio is about 75–80% of the time tenant/buyers of lease option properties will not buy. Keep this important tip in mind when deciding on your exit strategy. It can be very powerful when used in the right market.

) Hear my conversation with Amy and Jovy about the house and their deciding to sell it on lease option in our interview.

Amy and Jovy showed the property many times and took 2 months to find a tenant/buyer because they were looking for the right combination of cash flow and a large enough down payment (option consideration).

They ended up selling the property on lease option for $374,900, taking $25,000 as the non-refundable option consideration.

> Special Close provides adjustment in price:
> 3. OPTION PRICE: The OPTION price ("strike price") is $374,900.00; provided, however, if OPTIONOR concludes at any time before OPTIONOR has received proper notice of exercise of the OPTION from OPTIONEE that the fair market value of the property exceeds the foregoing strike price, OPTIONOR may (but is not required to) propose to OPTIONEE that the Option Price be increased to the fair market value of the property as determined by a professional fee appraiser selected by OPTIONOR.

They received the $25,000 down, which allowed Amy and Jovy to cover the reinstatement, closing costs, cosmetic repairs, and holding costs of the property until the tenant/buyer moved in, so this was a profitable deal from the start.

4. OPTION CONSIDERATION: OPTIONEE has paid a fee of $25,000.00 as a *non-refundable* option fee which will be applied toward the purchase price of the property *if, and only if,* OPTIONEE abides by all of the terms of any other agreement between the parties, AND OPTIONEE actually exercises this OPTION timely and purchases the property. In the event OPTIONEE fails to exercise the OPTION or defaults under applicable terms of the attached lease, this OPTION will be automatically terminated and the OPTION fee will be retained by OPTIONOR.

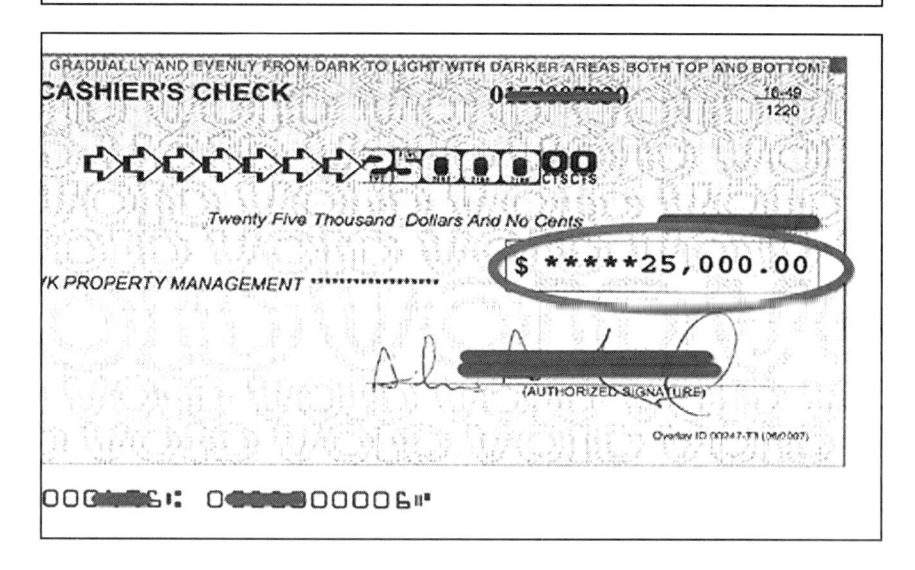

In the end, when all is said and done, with the $926 /mo. positive cash flow and the difference between the option price of $374,900 and the underlying loan balance after the reinstatement, Amy and Jovy will make in excess of $120,000 on this one house.

How many of you would like to have one deal like this every three months?

Now before I leave you with Amy and Jovy's last tip for you and your business, I just want to share with you that right before we published this book, Amy and Jovy did another "subject to" deal.

→ Hear Amy and Jovy tell you about their business in their own words. There are just too many gold nuggets of information to retell them all.

It's important for me to say that I personally had very little personal time involved in this deal because each one of our Inner Circle coaching students gets assigned a personal coach to work with who is a successful investor themselves and whom I have personally coached myself. In addition to their one-on-one coaching calls, all Inner Circle coaching students get unlimited email support and unlimited deal support.

Their coach Mike was on top of the deal every step of the way with Amy and Jovy, providing them all the support they needed to get it done. I love working with my team, they are topnotch, and I consider them my equal in expertise and experience. In fact, there is a synergy that allows us to deliver more to every coaching student.

> **Amy and Jovy's Tips:** Confidence with appointments comes with repetition, and having Marko and our coach in our corner has helped us to avoid mistakes and take action. Come see us at the next event. We learn something new at every one we attend.

*Results presented are not typical—read the Earning Disclaimer

Coaching Student Success #10

See What Happens When a Successful Rehabber Discovers the Potential of the Niche2Wealth System & Decides to <u>Stop Taking Unnecessary Risks</u> with Ugly Houses.

What if YOU could have a house paid off in 6.5 years? Watch the video interview with Peggy as she shares how she structured a purchase with a seller that will result in just that. If you're a rehabber, then listen why she's not anymore…

Go to www.MarkoRubel.com/book/Peggy

Peggy Shares 2 Deal Examples:
Got Paid to Buy & UFP #3/4

I almost couldn't wait to get to this part of the book to share about Peggy and her deals. **If you're a rehabber, you specially need to pay attention here.**

Peggy was like me, an immigrant from another country. Her family came here from Greece when she was young to give her a better life.

I almost wish all of you could be immigrants or at least have the mindset that you are coming to the greatest country in the world with nothing but opportunity in front of you.

On the first deal that she'll share, she got paid $10,000 to buy. And we're talking about opportunities—everywhere—even in your town!

Here's about Peggy…

Your Background: *(Peggy writing …)*

I came to the United States with my family consisting of my parents and three siblings when I was 11 years old from Greece. After getting a marketing degree and spending a short time in the corporate world, I was inspired to become an entrepreneur. I launched and ran a successful traditional business with locations and employees, and later sold it to start a family with my husband. After being introduced to real estate and doing fixer-uppers, I found Marko who taught me how to take my business to the next level, investing smarter with less effort and risk.

How you met Marko:

After going around the real estate seminar circuit for 5 years, I met two of Marko's students who were doing deals and kept talking about doing deals "Subject To" the existing loan. They told me that Marko didn't focus on rehabs and was a "genius" in creative real estate, and I wanted to meet him to find out for myself. ***I'm so glad I did!***

Your Message to Reader:

In life we have choices, and your desire to succeed has to be stronger and more powerful than your fear of failure. Make the choice to overcome your fears today. Don't try to do it overnight, but small baby steps each day are huge. You have the ability to be, do, and become anything your heart desires, don't let your fears stand in your way!

* * *

This is the house in nice condition, where she got paid to buy:

Deal Example #1:
Unlimited Funding Method #2 – Got Paid to Buy

Purchase Price: $363,900.00

Down Payment: The seller paid Peggy $10,000 to buy the house.

Loan Balance at that time: $374,000.00 (actually $370,656 at closing)

Selling Price: $435,000

Down Payment Received: $20,000

Selling Terms: 1-year lease option

Cash Flow Amount: negative ($509/mo.)

Principal Reduction: $900

This seller moved out of state and was making two mortgage payments and had been doing so for 4–5 months when he got Peggy's marketing letter to active listings. We teach our students if you see a sign for sale, send them a letter.

> **Marko's Money Tip:** Marketing to active listings is not allowed for agents. However, Peggy was not an agent. Marketing to active listings is a very targeted type of marketing you can do because you know 100% of the sellers are looking to sell immediately.

The seller had been listed, were making two payments for 4 months, and had the home listed for $425,000. After months of not being able to sell, he received Peggy's marketing and called her. Peggy told the seller that the most she could pay for the property was $363,900. Because the seller's loan was over $370,000 ($374,000 when Peggy and the seller signed the purchase and sale agreement), the seller agreed to pay Peggy the difference between the loan amount and the price Peggy was willing to pay, about $10,000 in this case.

The Loan Amount is Larger than the Purchase Price?!!

NOTE: Peggy sent out an Active Listing letter. The homeowner went to the special website that I give to all of my Inner Circle coaching students. What is so special about that website is that it is has my seller testimonials on it, so when the homeowner saw real proof of others who were helped in similar situations, they were willing to go ahead and call Peggy. Credibility and proof are important in any business.

> **Marko's Money Tip:** Having an opt-in buying and selling website with testimonials adds credibility to your business in a way that your explaining something about yourself cannot do. Make sure to add these powerful tools to your business.

Cash was tight for the seller, so Peggy agreed to take the $10,000 in the form of a **note secured by another property** that the seller owned free and clear. The seller agreed to pay Peggy $1,000 a month for 10 months.

This is an important point to bring up. This seller was not broke or destitute, and owned other real estate free and clear, meaning without a mortgage balance. It just goes to show you that the seller does not have to be desperate for you to get a great deal.

You will hear Peggy tell you about the deal in her own terms when you watch the video.

Here is my question for you—**Do you think there are sellers in your area who have property they don't want and would be willing to pay you to take off their hands?** There are.

In this case, the seller wanted peace of mind, and he was willing to give up the house and pay Peggy $10,000 to get it.

Remember what I always say: **No one will ever give up something they have unless they get something in return that they want more.**

Take a look at the actual HUD1 Settlement statement of the purchase and remember the actual numbers were adjusted for the date of closing just like yours will be.

	J. SUMMARY OF BORROWER'S TRANSACTION:		
100.	GROSS AMOUNT DUE FROM BORROWER		40
101.	Contract sales price	363,900.00	40
102.	Personal property		40
103.	Settlement charges to borrower (line 1400)	4,122.16	40
104.	HOA transfer fee	54.50	40
105.	HOA dues January/February, 2015	176.00	40
	Adjustments for items paid by seller in advance		
106.	City/town taxes to		40
107.	County taxes to		40
108.	Assessments to		40
109.			40
110.	Note from seller to buyer	9,425.00	41
111.			41
112.	**GOT PAID TO BUY!**		41
120.	GROSS AMOUNT DUE FROM BORROWER	377,677.66	42
200.	AMOUNTS PAID BY OR IN BEHALF OF BORROWER		50
201.	Deposit or earnest money		50
202.	New Loan and Note		50
203.	Existing loan(s) taken subject to		50
204.			50
205.			50
206.			50
207.			50
208.	Existing loan balance	370,656.35	5

Now, as if that wasn't exciting enough—Peggy then did some minor fixing up to the house, put it on the market, and within 2 months sold it on lease option to a nurse and her husband who had actually lost a very similar home to foreclosure.

Peggy sold the house at $435,000, taking $20,000 as a **non-refundable** option consideration from the tenant/buyer. *How many of you would like to buy a house and sell it, getting $20,000 from your buyer and being paid $10,000 from your seller?* Now that's a great deal.

NOTE: Remember how I told you earlier that the homeowner went to Peggy's buying website. Well, the tenant/buyer went to Peggy's selling website. This is another special site I have created for potential buyers and tenant/buyers to create credibility for my

Inner Circle coaching students, in this case Peggy. This buyer was willing to put down $20,000 for getting rights just a little greater than those of a tenant, no ownership, and no deed—so why would they do it? Why did they trust Peggy wouldn't run with their money? Because the special selling website has real testimonials that cover buyers in all situations, so it builds creditability and shows proof for Peggy's potential buyers.

> **Marko's Money Tip:** You need to join your local Better Business Bureau. It helps you get better deals with sellers and with buyers.

Let's look at the picture of the option agreement that Peggy signed with the tenant/buyers and a copy of the tenant/buyer's non-refundable option consideration check:

3. OPTION PRICE: The OPTION price ("strike price") is: $ __435,000.00__ Fixed for 12 months.

4. OPTION CONSIDERATION: OPTIONEE has paid a fee of $ __20,000.00__ as a *non-refundable* option fee which will be applied toward the purchase price of the property *if, and only if, OPTIONEE* abides by all of the terms of any other agreement between the parties, AND OPTIONEE actually exercises this OPTION timely and purchases the property. In the event OPTIONEE fails to exercise the OPTION or defaults under applicable terms of the attached lease, this OPTION will be automatically terminated and the OPTION fee will be retained by OPTIONOR.

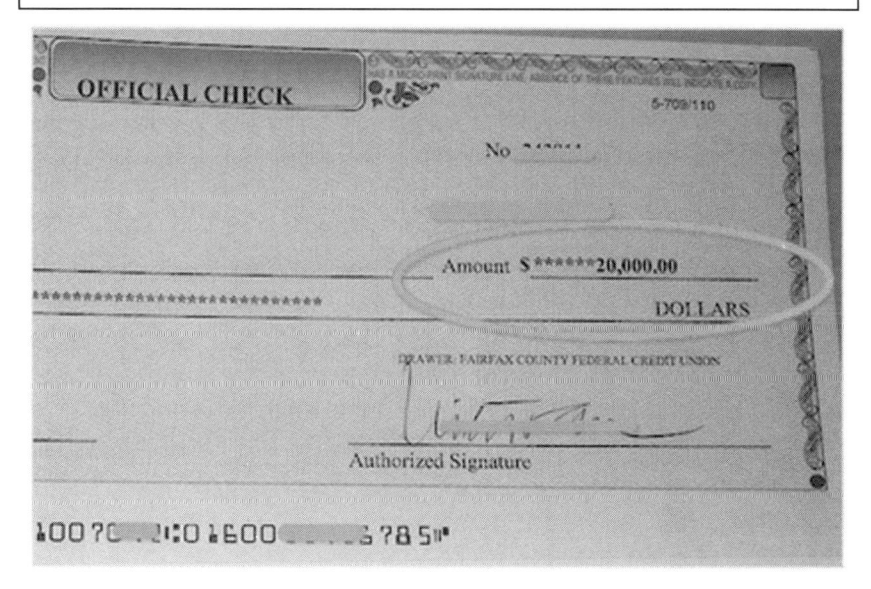

Now, since this property was higher priced, the rent for it was lower than the mortgage on the house (PITI). This created negative cash-flow in the amount of $509 per month. So you are probably asking, "Why would she do that?"

Great question, and here is why. Peggy knew that she got $20,000 upfront, so if she was $500 per month negative, in a year, she would still be cash flow positive by $14,000—do you follow me?

As you'll hear her explain in the video, when the mortgage payment is made every month, the loan balance is being reduced by over $900 (almost $1,000 a month) and that benefits Peggy. Finally, the seller is making $1,000 per month cash payments to Peggy to pay off the note the seller gave Peggy when he didn't have cash to close, so Peggy is in great shape on this deal. She is still way positive.

> **Marko's Money Tip:** Buying houses and having negative cash flow is not for the beginning investor. I recommend that you may want to consider buying your first couple of houses and then selling them outright to build cash reserves and a strong marketing budget.

After talking with Peggy about this deal, she shared with me the night and day difference between being a rehabber and buying houses the Niche2Wealth way.

She told me that while she loved taking something ugly and making it look pretty, **the pressure, risks, and trips back and forth weren't worth it** when she found out about the Niche2Wealth way to buy. And for all the rehab deals and fixer-uppers she did, she was personally liable for the deals and did not feel comfortable signing personal guarantees for each deal. **Hear Peggy tell you about it in her own words by going online. She will tell you how you don't have to buy houses at 60 or 70 cents on the dollar to make a profit. Listen how this busy mom of 3 kids does it.**

What would life look like if you could do just one deal where you could make $70,000 or more and have monthly cash flow?

And, the best part is that if the tenant/buyers decide not to buy, Peggy gets to keep the $20,000 non-refundable option consideration and turn around and sell it again. I think she is pretty happy to be in the US—I know I am.

**Deal Example #2:
Unlimited Funding Method #3 & 4 – Cash4Deed + Note**

Let's see another one of Peggy's profitable deals. **This house will be paid off in 6.5 years.**

FMV: $150,000

Purchase Price: $100,000

Down Payment: $16,585.32 cash + $100 earnest deposit + $65,000 noninterest-bearing note with seller

Loan Balance when purchased: $18,314.68

Loan Interest Rate: 5.00%

Loan PI: $507.60/mo. + $800/mo. payment on zero interest seller carryback note

Selling Terms: Kept as rental as home will be fully paid off in 6.5 years

Payment received: $1,200/mo.

Peggy owned an investment property in a subdivision when the neighbor of her property contacted her, asking if Peggy wanted to buy his home. While this isn't a method of direct marketing, you will occasionally get great deals that come from neighbors, tenants, and people you run into.

Let me describe what happened. When the neighbor contacted Peggy, she learned that the neighbor was preparing for retirement and was considering a move to a different area. The seller wasn't desperate and agreed to sell Peggy his property worth $150,000 for $100,000. Peggy took over the existing loan "subject to," giving the seller a modest down payment in cash and creating a seller carryback note for $65,000, which was the difference between the seller's equity and the agreed upon purchase price of $100,000, as shown below.

2. **PURCHASE PRICE** to be paid by Buyer is payable as follows (check all that applies):

- [✓] EARNEST DEPOSIT, receipt of which is hereby acknowledged in the sum of.............. $ 100.00
- [✓] DOWN PAYMENT BALANCE AT CLOSING. Approximately [✓]: Exactly [ ] .... $ 16,585.32
- [✓] TAKE TITLE SUBJECT TO AN EXISTING FIRST TRUST DEED NOTE held by M&T BANK with an approximate unpaid amount of.............. $ 18,314.68
  payable $ 507.60 monthly until paid, including interest not exceeding 5 %.
- [ ] TAKE TITLE SUBJECT TO AN EXISTING SECOND TRUST DEED NOTE held by _____ with an approximate unpaid amount of .... $ _____
  payable $ _____ monthly until paid, including interest not exceeding ___%.
- [✓] A PROMISSORY NOTE in the principal amount of .... $ 65,000.00
  Promissory note to Seller on terms set forth in Attached Addendum.

TOTAL PURCHASE PRICE IS THE AMOUNT OF .... $ 100,000.00

The best part of this deal is that because of the small mortgage, approximately $17,681 at closing, the home will be paid off in 6.5 years and worth around $185,000 or more.

How many of you would like to buy a $100,000 home and then 6.5 year later have it paid off and worth $185,000?

This would have never happened if the Peggy didn't have the proper training. One of the key moves here was to get the no interest loan—the $65,000 seller carryback loan was at 0% interest. Peggy never mentioned the interest. See the purchase agreement addendum below:

Additional Terms:

1. The buyer will procure a promissory note to the seller at closing in the amount of $65,000, payable monthly at the rate of $800.00 per month until paid in full.

See the picture of the closing settlement statement below:

120. GROSS AMOUNT DUE FROM BORROWER	103,099.98
200. AMOUNTS PAID BY OR IN BEHALF OF BORROWER	
201. Deposit or earnest money	100.00
202. New Loan and Note	65,000.00
203. Existing loan(s) taken subject to	17,681.00
204. + cash down payment	
205.	

Peggy has done many deals even though she's only been in our Inner Circle coaching program for about 18 months. This deal may not be your first because it took cash to do, but the first deal described didn't. In other words, you start where you can.

→ **On the video she talks about one more deal. Hear her tell you the story in her own words.**

Here's Peggy at one of our workshops…

> **Peggy's Tip:** Use the system that Marko has in place. It is so step-by-step that whether you have experience like I did or you are brand-new, anyone can do it. You have to have your desire to succeed be stronger than your fear of failure. Don't miss this real estate cycle.

* * *

Let me pause for a moment to acknowledge something—I'm sharing with you so many documents, so many numbers, so many deals … it could get confusing.

So you can get a more complete picture of the business, I've included so many details. It is in my nature to be thorough—and my students like that. However, because of my thoroughness, I'm sure you haven't fully grasped each deal or technique I've presented to you. And guess what—that's totally normal.

Please take my word for it … It is normal to not understand everything I'm telling you when you first hear it (or read it!). If you just get the concept down, you are doing well.

The good news is—the actual N2W business is a lot simpler.

Once it all settles down, you will then realize that **these strategies are in fact very simple, yet super powerful**. We've covered so many deals, but in the end they are all bought the <u>same</u> way. They are all sold the <u>same</u> way.

With determination and hard work on your part and support, tools, and custom advice on my part, I know you can be successful in no time.

*Results presented are not typical—read the Earning Disclaimer

– SECTION III –

Bonus Strategies for Deals that "Don't Fit In"

Let me start with the big picture.

As I mentioned previously, if you want to make as much money as possible in the shortest and most efficient way, you need to specialize in <u>one</u> business model.

The investing business model described in this book is the most profitable investing model I know of, unless you already have $1,000,000+ in your bank account. If you have that much cash, then there are other investing strategies you could add or do.

For most people, that's not the case.

Therefore, Niche2Wealth needs to be YOUR focus. You should not look into doing wholesaling, rehabs, etc. because those strategies aren't the best way to get to quick cash or to build long-term wealth. Why? Because they leverage only 1 wealth-building component out of the 5 of investing in real estate (remember the first part of this book).

In addition, those other strategies should not take an equal part in your investing game either. Why? It is because if you focus on Niche2Wealth business but you still want to do wholesaling, rehabs, etc., you will lose on efficiency and end up working hard, not smart. Remember, you don't want to be a "jack of all trades" and end up a "master of none."

So how do we focus only on the Niche2Wealth investing model?

It is by targeting our marketing to attract the type of deals that fit into 1 of the 7 "unlimited funding" acquisition strategies, which you can then turn around and sell to ANY credit buyers.

For example, if you're sending postcards targeting sellers in older lower-income neighborhoods, you will likely get calls from people with "ugly" houses. Most of those will not fit our business model.

However, if you target middle-class neighborhoods where "pretty" houses are, where pride of homeownership is evident just by driving by, you will have higher chances that most of the calls you get will fit our investing model.

Obviously, there are many other mailing or marketing criteria we use, but that's not the point of here.

In summary, by targeting your marketing to the targeted homeowners and by having a marketing message that resonates with them, you will get more efficient, which means you'll make more money faster and easier.

Now that we covered the big picture, let's get to our **bonus strategies** and why you need them. It is important to clearly define their purpose and the place they take in your overall investing strategy and investing game.

In order for a potential deal to meet our Unlimited Funding criteria and *not taking the "seller's motivation" into consideration here,* the house has to have:

1. Decent loan(s) against it—so we can use "subject to" to pay when buying
2. Equity—so we can meet our 75–80% of FMV acquisition criterion*
3. Should be a pretty house—with no, or only simple, cosmetic repairs

*As for #2—a house with no equity but with a big second loan where the first loan is foreclosing will meet the criteria, using the P-J-L strategy.

When your prospecting or marketing is properly targeted, 70% to 80%+ of the calls you get from homeowners will meet the above criteria. What about the rest?

The remaining 20–30% of the prospects will either have:

1. Loan(s) with a high interest rate or coming up to the maturity date (balloon)
2. Loan(s) but NO or low equity
3. Free & clear—no mortgage
4. An ugly house in need of a lot of rehab
5. A type of property you don't buy (i.e., condo, mobile home, etc.)
6. Other issues—code violations, neighborhood problems, etc.

In Section 3, I want to give you 3 strategies to monetize on some of these opportunities. In (1) above there's nothing we can do unless they have a lot of equity. There's nothing we can do with (5) or (6).

But let's see how we can monetize those that have no or low equity (2); those that have no debt against them (3); and those that need rehab (4).

Here are the 3 "side" strategies to address deals that are not your main game (and do not meet your main game criteria) but are useful to monetize.

1. Sandwich Lease Options
2. Free & Clear Acquisition Strategy
3. Wholesaling

Sandwich Lease Options – When a property has a manageable payment (close to the rent payment for the area) because it has a nice low interest rate loan, but does not have 15–20% in equity, we can still profit without getting ownership.

Free & Clear Acquisition Strategy – When a property has no loan, but the seller has some motivation, we can structure the seller financing in a way to still profit.

Wholesaling – You don't want to be anywhere close to fixing houses, so when you come across a "fixer" property in need of major rehab, you can still make some money with it by flipping it to a rehabber who doesn't know better and let him fix it.

<u>NOTE</u>: It is important for you to understand that NONE of these 3 strategies should be part of your <u>main</u> game because they have inherent flaws that cannot be corrected no matter what you do. That's why their purpose is as your <u>side</u> strategies and you need to use them ONLY as that.

I possess deep understanding of the above strategies and have a lot of experience doing deals using those strategies. However, I do not teach them as the main investing strategies because they would not serve you well as such.

In the next 3 chapters, I will explain each of these strategies and give you an example of a real deal we structured using them.

BONUS STRATEGY 1
– SANDWICH LEASE OPTIONS

Why do you think I picked Sandwich LO as the first bonus strategy?

It is because the **Sandwich Lease Option strategy is the MOST powerful strategy there is next to ownership via "subject to."**

Let's first learn how it works, and then I'll explain why that is.

Here's a slide from the home-study course I created for my coaching students that explains the mechanics of a Sandwich Lease Option deal.

Intro to Sandwich Lease Option Strategy

Motivated Owner → Lease + Option to Buy → YOU → Lease + Option to Buy → BUYER
Option Consideration & Mo. Payment ← → Option Consideration & Mo. Payment
CREDIT

FMV = $200,000
YOUR Option Price: $180k with $0 down
YOUR Mo. Rent: $1,200
SELLING Price: $200k with $7k down
Tenant's Mo. Rent: $1,400
TOTAL PROFIT (if T/B buys): $20k + Cash-Flow

SANDWICH LEASE OPTION WEALTH SYSTEM

As you can see, in this arrangement, the investor is the "middleman."

The investor uses an option agreement to control the property from the owner. That agreement gives the investor the **exclusive** right to buy the property at any time during the option term for the pre-agreed price. The owner has to sell under those terms and must not sell the property to anyone else during that term. The investor also has a lease agreement signed by the owners giving the investor the right to occupy the property.

There's one more important provision that the lease has to have—the right to sublet or sublease. In other words, the owner agrees that the investor may sublease the property to a third party.

That is how the investor controls the property under this Sandwich LO arrangement.

It is beyond the scope of this book, but it is very important for the investor to properly secure control of the property. For example, I guide my coaching students to open what we call a "long-term open escrow," where we get the seller to sign the deed at the onset of this transaction, so we don't need to chase them later on. The deed stays in that escrow. Then we record different documents, going as far as recording a special lien that allows us to foreclose in a worst-case scenario; for example, if the seller doesn't want to cooperate 3, 5, or 10 years later when my student wants to exercise their option and buy.

> **Marko's Money Tip:** Coaching is a tool used by the most successful people in all endeavors of life. A coach is someone who's been on the journey where the student wants to go and can guide the student there in a more efficient and faster way towards the goal. My Inner Circle coaching program takes all of the benefits that coaching offers and adds to it my complete arsenal of training, process, and office automation tools. Check out the video on Inner Circle coaching at MarkoRubel.com/coaching.

After the investor has secured his interest in the property, as mentioned above, he can start looking for a tenant/buyer who will then lease option the property from him.

The tenant/buyer will have their own lease and option to buy, but not with the owner, rather with the investor. They will have no rights to sublease.

So let's take an example from the above slide.

The property is worth around $200,000 (FMV) and the loan is $180,000, which is at 90% of the FMV. The owner had some offers for sale in the low $190,000s but refused them because he would have not been able to cover the cost of sale (commission, closing costs, etc.).

Out of his need to cover the payments, the owner started advertising the house as "For Rent." This is how the investor found him, and he agreed to let the investor "rent" the house from him as a "master" tenant. He also agreed to let the investor buy it as long as he, the owner, doesn't need to spend any money selling it.

As you realize, there are plenty of people out there who can't make double payments, but their house won't sell because they don't have enough equity. Their loan is at 90, 95, or even 100% of the FMV. There are also "tired" landlords who went through nasty evictions (plenty of those!) and would be happy to have an investor step in as a "master" tenant.

So in this example, the investor has negotiated these terms:

Investor's Option Price: $180,000 with $0 down
Investor's Mo. Payment: $1,200
Investor's Term: 5 years

Then the investor found a tenant/buyer who is a couple who wants to live in the area because of the school district but needs some time to improve their credit and save more money for the down payment.

The investor explained to them the benefit of their lease optioning the property versus renting somewhere else (i.e., fixed purchased price).

They moved forward and signed the lease and the option agreements with the investor. Note, their deal is with the investor and not with the owner.

The terms the investor gave them in this hypothetical example are:

Tenant/Buyer's Option Price: $200,000 with $7,000 down
Tenant/Buyer's Mo. Payment: $1,400
Tenant/Buyer's Term: 2 years

As you can see, if the tenant/buyer exercises their option after the first year, the investor will make $20,000 due to the difference in the option price between the price with the owner and with the tenant/buyer. Note: The $7,000 out of those $20,000 the investor received at the start, is a non-refundable option deposit.

The investor will also profit $2,400 from the 12 months of cash flow due to the difference in the monthly payments.

The transaction will be consummated via simultaneous or double closing, where the tenant/buyer's loan pays off the owner and the difference goes to investor.

If the tenant/buyer doesn't buy, the investor can raise the price or change the terms to make more money. If the tenant/buyer moves out, the investor keeps the option deposit and can do it all over again, as long as he is within his original term with the owner (in this example, 5 years). If in an appreciating market, every time a tenant/buyer moves out, the investor can raise the price and make more money with the next tenant/buyer.

As you can see, the investor makes money without ownership. So when the equity is not there or the seller doesn't want to sell the house "subject to," this strategy gives you control without ownership and allows you to profit.

Plus, there's also another benefit—the tenant/buyer is responsible for all minor repairs and the owner is responsible for all major repairs (roof leak, plumbing, A/C, etc.), making you responsible for nothing. Sweet.

Obviously, what I covered here is just an overview of the strategy. If we were coaching you on a deal like that, there would be other important pieces of the puzzle we would need to put in place. But you get the idea here.

Now, let's discuss WHY I said that next to ownership of the house "subject to," **this is the most powerful strategy.**

Let me say it this way… if one day, for some reason, "subject to" became unavailable to use, the only meaningful strategy for creating wealth would be Sandwich LOs.

There would be no other way to create long-term wealth. It is almost impossible to do it with wholesaling, and it would take decades to do it with rehabs or rentals.

Why is that? It is because the Sandwich LO Strategy (SLO) is the only strategy that leverages 3 or even 4 wealth-building components of real estate. Let's look at this important table again:

Wealth Building Component of Real Estate	Wholesaling Flip, or Fix & Flip	Ownership (UFP)	Control (S-Lease Option)
CASH FLOW	✘ Not Present	✔ Present	✔ Present
CAPITAL GAINS Buy Low – Sell For Profit	✔ Present	✔ Present	✔ Present
Equity Build-up Due to **Principal Reduction**	✘ Not Present	✔ Present	✔ Present
Equity Build-up Due to **Appreciation**	✘ Not Present	✔ Present	✔ Present
Tax Savings (Depreciation – IRS 167)	✘ Not Present	✔ Present	✘ Not Present

As you already know from the example we covered, with SLO you get **Cash Flow** ($200/mo. in the example); **Capital Gains** ($20,000 in the example), taxed as ordinary income though; and **Appreciation** in the case when the option is renewed or defaulted on.

You can also get **Equity Build-up due to principal reduction**, which is the loan pay down. We do that by defining the investor's option price as locked to the loan balance at the time of closing. This way the investor gets the benefit from the payments the tenant/buyer makes.

As you can see, with SLO <u>you do the work ONCE and get paid FOUR times</u>. This is a lot better than wholesaling.

Imagine if you had 20 properties locked in at 90% of today's FMV, on a 10-year term. They would probably double in value in 10 years, and you could just sell half of them and pay off the other half. You'd end up with 10 free and clear properties in 10 years.

It goes unsaid, but you don't need your credit to do this, nor do you need it for anything else I teach.

As with anything I teach, I give real examples and proof of the strategy. Here's one from our coaching student Mike in Ohio.

Coaching Student SLO Success

Using the Sandwich Lease Option Strategy, Mike Gets Control of 4 Pretty Houses <u>for 10 Years</u>, <u>Using ONE DOLLAR</u>.

The seller of a house in nice condition, located in a middle-class neighborhood in Ohio, has been unable to sell his house because he didn't have enough equity.

Mike met with the seller and negotiated to lease option his house on a 10-year term, with the option price being equal to the loan balance at the time Mike decides to buy it.

Then Mike turned around and found a tenant/buyer who paid him $20,000 as a non-refundable option consideration.

Here are the terms of this deal, on both sides:

	Acquisition	Exit
Option Price:	$156k*	$179,900
Option Term:	$10 y.	$3 y.
Down Payment:	$1	$20,000

As you realize, this is an amazing deal. Mike controls the seller's house for $1 and receives the benefit of a loan pay down and appreciation while the seller is still responsible for major repairs. Powerful strategy, isn't it?

Here's the part of the option agreement that seals this profitable arrangement:

> 1. **OPTION CONSIDERATION:** In consideration for the granting of this Option, the ($ 1), payable upon acceptance of this Option, and other good a the receipt and sufficiency whereof are hereby acknowledged by Optionor, the Op and exclusive Option to purchase property described herein.
> 2. **OPTION PERIOD:** The Option Period is for a term of 120 months commencing 12/1, 20__. Optionee may extend the option period under same conditions f
> 3. **PURCHASE PRICE:** The purchase price of the Property shall be:
>   A. ☐ Equal to the then current principal loan balance at the time of exercisir held by _____ loan # _____ with an app
>   or B. ☐ $_____ (_____), payab

You can see that Mike used only **$1.00** (Item 1) to get control of the property for **120 months** (Item 2), and the price is the "**then current principal loan balance at the time of exercise**" (3).

279

And here's the check in the amount of **$19,000** that Mike received, in addition to the $1,000 earnest deposit he got at the house when the tenant/buyer filled out the LO application.

How would you feel if you used $1 to make $20,000 without even owning a house?

You'd be very proud! And yes, you can do it!

As I said before, focus where you're going to be, not where you're now!

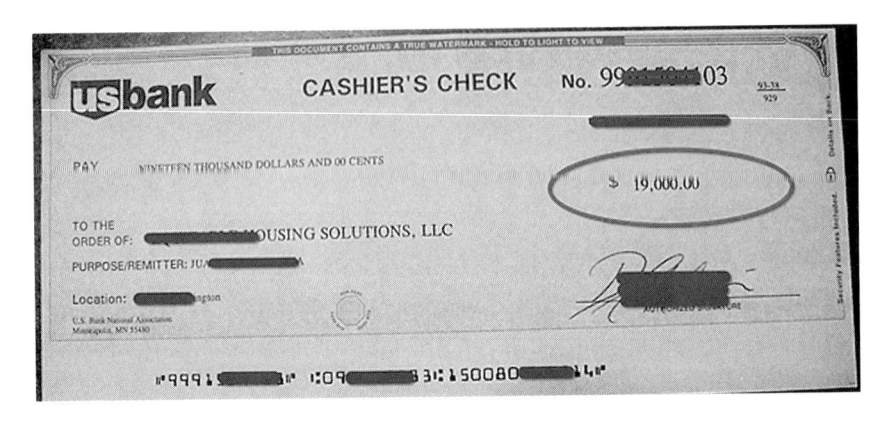

In addition to a few Unlimited Funding deals that Mike had done, he's added four of these types of SLO deals to his portfolio as I'm writing this book.

→ **Watch Mike's homemade video where he talks about this deal. You can find it inside our online resource center at MarkoRubel.com/book/Mike.**

Here Mike and I are at our workshop:

Mike is a super nice guy, very smart, and despite his tremendous success in IT, he decided to go full-time into real estate investing in order to expedite his retirement.

Here's part of the email Mike wanted me to share with you:

Your Message to Reader: *(Mike writing ...)*

Since joining Marko's Inner Circle coaching program and utilizing his systems, I have acquired 10 properties with an average profit potential of $31,048.12 per property, which isn't bad for a moderately priced city in the Midwest. Like any business, success in this one has required a strong personal commitment and a lot of work, but I see the potential of the program and am beginning to realize my own personal success. In addition to the vast amount of training, systems, and resource materials that Marko makes avail-

*able to his students**, it is his genuine interest in our success that continues to impress me**. Marko has given us a roadmap to success. In my opinion, the only way that one can fail is by not doing the work necessary to succeed.*

*Results presented are not typical—read the Earning Disclaimer

Bonus Strategy 2
– Free & Clear Acquisitions

There's another real estate niche that is <u>very small</u> but EXTREMELY profitable. It is investing in free and clear homes, which are homes that have no debt against them.

Below are the benefits of a properly structured Free & Clear deal as it compares to our standard Unlimited Funding deal:

Wealth Building Component of Real Estate	Ownership (UFP)	Ownership (Free & Clear)	Comment:
CASH FLOW	✔ Present	✔ Present	LARGER due to low or no Interest; and negotiated payment
CAPITAL GAINS Buy Low – Sell For Profit	✔ Present	✔ Present	SAME – depends on how well you buy
Equity Build-up Due to **Principal Reduction**	✔ Present	✔ Present	EXTREME – due to low or no interest rate; plus "note discount"
Equity Build-up Due to **Appreciation**	✔ Present	✔ Present	SAME
Tax Savings (Depreciation – IRS 167)	✔ Present	✔ Present	SAME

These types of deals can be structured to provide HUGE profit but **only** when the seller is really motivated. Since there's no loan, there's no "pain" of making payments, so in general <u>you don't come across these motivated owners very often</u>, or often enough to create a business out of it.

In addition, your proposals with these deals require them to either wait for a huge amount of cash for a long time or to take a substantial discount. Both provide a vastly different outcome for them than the one they'd have if they sold conventionally. Those challenges lower the number of potential deals you can do and the frequency you can do them at.

To the contrary, there are a lot more sellers in our core Niche2Wealth business that are motivated. Plus the outcome they get with you is very close to the outcome they would get if they sold it conventionally. In both cases they get relief from payments, which is what they want, and the cash difference is not that huge.

That's why buying free and clear homes should stay as your side strategy, but once you get good at using Unlimited Funding strategies, you should invest some time in learning it.

Let's cover the main strategies. When you have a motivated seller with a free and clear house, there are usually 4 strategies you can use to acquire ownership or control of that property. Which one of them will work in a particular deal depends on that seller's needs.

Here are the 4 ways to acquire interest in or ownership of a free and clear property:

Structure – For Most Profit

4 Most Common Structures:

1. All Cash at 65-70% minus Repairs
2. $0 Down - seller carry-back full purchase price
3. Up to 65% Down – seller carry-back the rest
4. Get seller to refinance and buy "sub2" (UFP#1)

Note: #3 could have an existing loan – it'd be the same.

THE ACCELERATED WEALTH SYSTEM

1. **All cash at discount** – In this case you need to buy at 65–70% of FMV in order to factor in the cost of cash. This kind of discount is harder to negotiate unless the property is in bad shape. As you know, buying with cash usually mandates the exit strategy to be the outright sale. As we know, that is the least profitable way to sell.

2. **Seller carries back the full purchase price** – In essence, you agree with the seller on the price, and the seller finances the whole purchase. There's a note that lists the terms of your repayment, such as the interest rate if any, monthly payments, and the maturity date by which you need to pay the seller completely off. The note will be secured by a deed of trust (or a mortgage) recorded against the property, in favor of the seller.

3. **Seller carries back part of the purchase price, with a cash down payment** – Most of the time the seller will need some money to move or just to feel more comfortable that you have some skin in the game. Other times the seller will need a sizable down payment to make it work. In both cases, getting a private lender on that type of deal can be very easy if you get the seller to subordinate—that means allow that lender to be secured against the house in the first position. That makes it a no-brainer for any lender, and thus it's easy for you to find one.

4. **Refinancing with "subject to"** – We have been successful in convincing some sellers to refinance and pull out their equity, and then we purchase their house "subject to." Typically in this case it would end up being UFP#1 with $0 down.

   Side strategy – Lease Option or Straight Option – If they don't need cash and they don't want to give you ownership without getting cash, you could propose a sandwich lease option. Or you could just get them to give you a straight option, which would allow you to find the buyer and in essence flip the house without ever owning it.

Now, the most profitable ways are 2 and 3:

2. **Seller carries back the full purchase price**; or
3. **Seller carries back part of the purchase price, with a cash down payment.**

We've helped our students structure some killer deals with those 2 strategies. Once we had a student who was buying a property at 80% of its FMV and the seller carried back the full purchase price at no interest (0%). The student "sold" the house on lease option and for 2 years 100% of the payment was going towards our student's equity (since it was a no interest loan). Then 2 years later the seller took another 10% discount on that note to get paid off early. *Screaming deal, isn't it?*

In a similar deal as the above, the seller asked to get paid an interest of 4% but he needed $50,000 cash, which was about 20% of the FMV. We got him to agree to "subordinate" his interest to a new first loan, so our student was able to get a private lender in the first position. We also got him to agree to wait for 6 months before we started making payments to him—this helped the student with the cash flow.

> **Marko's Money Tip:** You always want to limit your liability by having a "non-recourse" clause be part of every seller carryback note you're the borrower on. This is a must when you're coached by me.

Now I've mentioned coaching before, and throughout this book you have seen example after example of how my coaching students have used my systems and their one-on-one coaching to create what was possible in their lives. If you are person who is ready to take action, then consider hiring help. It's a shortcut to success.

There are 2 other clauses to mention that increase your profit (see slide below).

3 "Profit-Booster" Clauses - <u>Absolutely Necessary Clauses:</u>

1. **Non-Recourse** – makes the deal "zero" risk
2. **Subordination Clause** – helps you borrow / refi
3. **First Right of Refusal** – helps you later get a discount

* these are part of PSA Addendum

THE ACCELERATED WEALTH SYSTEM

I created an entire system for investing in these types of homes. It's called the "Accelerated Wealth System." It helps my mastery team and me when coaching students on these kind of deals. There are some tools needed to turn these opportunities into killer deals, like some special calculators to figure out hidden profits, special legal clauses, etc.

I want to share with you a deal example that is an average deal in this niche. Nothing spectacular, just average.

Coaching Student F & C Success

Dentist from Chicago Uses $20 to Get Full Ownership of a Beautiful House, Without Ever Talking to a Bank

Our coaching student Richard has multiple talents. He is great at crafting beautiful smiles in his dental practice, but he also excels in solving sellers' needs and creating win-win real estate solutions in his free time.

Richard and his son Joe started marketing and calling sellers as soon as they came home from the seminar. When they found a seller with a free and clear house, they called their coach and quickly figured out a few possible scenarios. Here's the result.

They purchased this house for literally $20.

→ Watch the video in the online resource center as Richard walks through this house and explains how they had no closing costs due to a property tax surplus.

The fair market value of the house was around $340,000. They purchased it for $293,020. Here's the purchase agreement:

> **2. TOTAL PURCHASE PRICE** to be paid by Buyer is payable as follows:
>
> A. **EARNEST DEPOSIT**, receipt of which is hereby acknowledged in the sum of.................... **$20.00**
>
> B. **DOWN PAYMENT BALANCE AT CLOSING**, (not including Buyers closing costs, prepaid items or prorations) in U.S. cash or cashiers check. Approximately [ ]: Exactly [ ] $0.00
>
> C. **NEW LOAN**, Proceeds of a new loan to be executed by Buyer to any lender other than Seller; .... N/A
>
> D. **TAKE TITLE SUBJECT TO AN EXISTING FIRST TRUST DEED NOTE** held by ___ with an approximate unpaid amount of .... N/A payable $___ monthly until paid, including interest not exceeding ___%.
>
> E. **TAKE TITLE SUBJECT TO AN EXISTING SECOND TRUST DEED NOTE** held by ___ with an approximate unpaid amount of .... N/A payable $___ monthly until paid, including interest not exceeding ___%.
>
> F. **TAKE TITLE SUBJECT TO AN EXISTING THIRD TRUST DEED NOTE** held by ___ with an approximate unpaid amount of .... N/A payable $___ monthly until paid, including interest not exceeding ___%.
>
> G. **A PROMISSORY NOTE** in the principal amount of .... **$293,000.00** Promissory note to Seller on terms set forth in Paragraph 10.
>
> TOTAL PURCHASE PRICE IS THE AMOUNT OF .... $ $293,020.00

The terms of the note are spelled out below:

> **10. OTHER TERMS:** A.) Standard Mortgage to be prepared for $293,000 at 4% annual interest rate, amortized for 30 years, balloon payment in 120 months. Prepayment penalty if paid off prior to 24 months. Prepayment penalty equal to remainder of interest that would have been paid if loan was paid off after 24 months.

Below is a summary of that deal in their own words from the email they sent me, followed by their message to you:

Deal Summary: *(Richard writing ...)*

In short, we bought a house that was valued at $340,000 for no money down, and we got the owner to take back a mortgage for $293,000, paying 4% interest with a 10-year balloon. We are currently renting out this house for $2,500 per month for this year and $2,600 per month for the next year. This is currently providing a $400 per month positive cash flow. The area is appreciating, on average 4.5%, and it is our intent to maintain ownership so that we are the ones benefiting from the appreciation. Our projected back-end profit on this deal after 5 years exceeds $130,000 conservatively. When principal reduction and cash flow are added, the total profit exceeds $180,000.

Your Message to Reader:

Marko gives it his all. He doesn't keep his secrets to himself but shares every little thing that makes his business work with his students. The Inner Circle program is like a franchise without franchise fees. Marko provides a step-by-step plan for implementing his system.

→ **As you realize, there are many deal structures available in this business, and even though every single one of you reading this book can succeed on your own, having an experienced coach will help you monetize on deals that you would, many times, not even recognize. Plus, there are a lot of other aspects where having a good coach can make a world of difference when it comes to succeeding or failing.**
To learn more about coaching go to www.MarkoRubel.com.

Here's Richard and I discussing the deal on a camera, at one of our live events:

→ this video is available at **www.MarkoRubel.com/book/Richard** .

*Results presented are not typical—read the Earning Disclaimer

Bonus Strategy 3 – Wholesaling

I want to start this chapter by saying AGAIN AND AGAIN that wholesaling is not the best way to start in real estate investing and it's not the best way to get your first check either. It is not a foundation of our Niche-2Wealth business and should not be for you either. However, it is an important strategy you need to know and in the right circumstances can be extremely powerful.

I had to reiterate this because some of you have been so brainwashed, for lack of a better term, with all those guru emails—flip this, flip that, flip, flip … Wholesaling, also called "flipping," is not even close to what it is hyped to be.

HOWEVER, wholesaling definitely has an important role as a **side** strategy, as I'll explain here.

Let's briefly review how wholesaling works, and then I'll uncover some wholesaling myths.

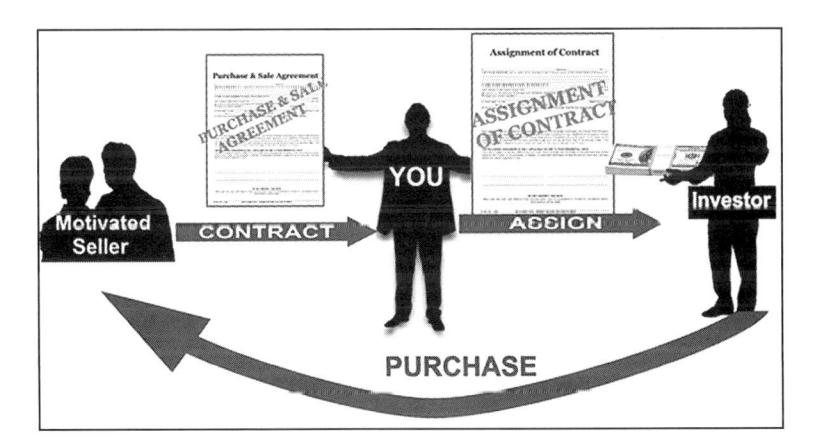

You are the middleman here as a wholesaler or flipper. You sign a purchase and sale agreement at a low price with a motivated seller of an ugly house that needs a lot of repairs. Then you turn around and try to find an investor-rehabber who will step in your shoes in that PSA and become a buyer.

Once you find the investor who is interested in buying that property and likes the terms you negotiated, you will prepare an assignment agreement. That agreement makes the investor officially the buyer and ensures that you get paid the fee for letting him assume your position in the original contract. After that, he closes the purchase directly with the seller.

So how do you get paid? You get paid an assignment fee for assigning that contract to the investor as explained above. Common assignment fees are from $3,000 to $10,000 and vary depending on the area of the country.

What's important here? It is important that the purchase price and terms you negotiated with the seller are good enough to allow the investor-rehabber to profit. Remember, if the price is not low enough, no investor will be interested and you wasted everybody's time.

Now, that you have a basic idea of how wholesaling works, let's dispel some common myths about the benefits of wholesaling. Here's a slide you should remember:

Wholesaling Myths:

❏ ~~Fast Cash~~ – First Deal
 - big discount requires a lot of marketing (formula)!

❏ ~~Build~~ Wealth
 - small profits taxed as ordinary income, no cash flow

Some of you will say, "Marko, your N2W strategies are powerful, but first let me just make a few thousand dollars with flipping and then I'll learn your strategies."

The problem with that is that it will take you longer to make your first check with wholesaling than it will with the other strategies that I have explained here. Why? Because in order to be able to wholesale a property, you need to contract it at 50–60% of its ARV (after repaired value). Unless you follow that formula, you won't be able to find a buyer.

Here's the universal **Wholesaling Formula** for your Maximum Purchase Price:

Max. Purchase Price = ARV x 0.7 – Repairs – Your Profit

As you can see, in order to put a property under contract at the price that allows your buyer-rehabber to profit, you need not to exceed 50–60% of ARV (depending on repairs). It is not easy to find a seller who will agree to such a large discount, no matter the condition of the property.

Consider this …

Is it easier to get a seller to agree to a 10–20% discount or a 40–50% discount? Which one is easier?

Obviously it's easier to get them to agree to a smaller discount. So that's your answer.

By the way, with N2W strategies it's easier to get a seller to agree to your offer because your offer requires a lot smaller of a discount.

That's why wholesaling will not get you to your first check any quicker.

Now, let's briefly review the **second myth** from that slide, *Building Wealth with Wholesaling*. You should already remember this table below.

Wealth Building Component of Real Estate	Wholesaling Flip, or Fix & Flip	Ownership
1. CASH FLOW	✗ Not Present	✓ YES
2. CAPITAL GAINS Buy Low - Sell for Profit	✓ YES, but... Taxed as Ordinary Income	✓ YES
3. EQUITY BUILD-UP Due to Loan Paydown	✗ Not Present	✓ YES
4. EQUITY BUILD-UP Due to Appreciation	✗ Not Present	✓ YES
5. TAX SAVINGS Depreciation - IRS 167	✗ Not Present	✓ YES

As we discussed at the beginning of this book, with wholesaling you **only** leverage ONE wealth-building component of real estate investing and that is capital gains or the profit that comes in via an assignment fee.

This assignment fee is a one-time payment that you receive basically for "selling your position" in that original purchase agreement with the seller. How is it taxed?

It's taxed as ordinary income. So you pay more in taxes than you would pay if you kept the property for more than a year.

I hope you realize, that **building wealth with wholesaling is next to impossible.**

* * *

Just as I stated in the previous bonus chapters on sandwich lease options and free and clear properties, wholesaling should <u>not</u> be your <u>main</u> strategy, but it is an <u>important</u> side strategy.

You always want your marketing to find you the deals that have the greatest potential for helping you achieve your investing goals. However, you will still get deals coming your way that do not fit our N2W criteria.

If a deal that falls in your lap is for an ugly house that needs a lot of repairs AND that house has enough equity for you to get the desired discount determined by the above Wholesaling Formula, you should go on appointment and try to get it under contract.

You should not pass on it because it doesn't meet your N2W criteria. If it has equity and the seller is motivated, try to make some money with it.

I prepared a database of cash buyers for my coaching students. It is part of our **Money Finder tool**, which connects to multiple data depositories around the country and enables you to find the cash buyers right in your own backyard with a click of a mouse.

> **Marko's Money Tip:** Do NOT get tempted to fix an ugly house. For the time you'll waste with a major fixer, you can find a few N2W deals and make more money with a lot less risk.

Now you know the basics of how to use wholesaling <u>as a SIDE strategy.</u> Keep it in your back arsenal, but remember you won't get rich selling to cash buyers—cash is king, and they will want a bargain. You will though get rich selling to any-credit buyers who NEED you.

So now that you have the basics of wholesaling, I want to introduce you to someone who's really motivated me. I just have to share his story with you.

Coaching Student Wholesaling Success

Hear How Joe Closed a $70,000 Wholesaling Deal, Survived a Brain Aneurysm, & Closed 2 More Deals While in ICU …

I know that you have already seen 15+ students and deal case studies, but I promise you this one is worth your time. Joe and Nami have an interesting story, and I have to tell you upfront that this is a very special story for me.

Joe was born in Baltimore, MD and left home after high school to join the Navy. He got married to Nami 8 years later, and they were blessed with a son. Joe quickly realized that Navy life and married life do not mix well, and so after 4 more years, he was honorably discharged.

Trying to make ends meet for his family, Joe tried selling life insurance and products from several network marketing companies, but all failed to produce the promised income.

Then Joe thought, "I'll try real estate investing," and started by buying books, attending expensive seminars, and playing a "board game." It was during this time that Joe spent tens of thousands of dollars on real estate gurus without any results.

Then one day, Joe attended the local RE Investor Club meeting where I was invited to be a guest expert. I was talking about working smart, not hard by using automation in a presentation on my ProfitGrabber system.

Joe was so excited, instantly seeing the value in ProfitGrabber. In fact, I think he was the first person in the room who invested in it. Then Joe attended my seminar, joined the Inner Circle coaching program, and has never looked back.

→ **After you're done reading this book, go to ProfitGrabber.com to review the 4 essential business processes that ProfitGrabber automates. We have over 4,000 investors using it, and they claim that with it they can do in 30 minutes per week what used to take 5–10 hours.**

Here's Joe and his lovely wife at one of our live workshops:

The deal I'm going to share with you is a wholesale deal where Joe made more in this one deal than he made in the same year at his job. I thought that might get your attention.

Shortly after joining our coaching, Joe started calling sellers and then received a call from a motivated seller with an upper-middle-class home that needed a lot of rehab work.

Since Joe traveled for work and knowing that the house required a lot of work, he thought he should throw the lead away but decided to mention it on the scheduled call with his coach.

His coach, like my whole team, including me has a mindset to never give up easy. So the coach asked Joe to email him the Phone Form (below).

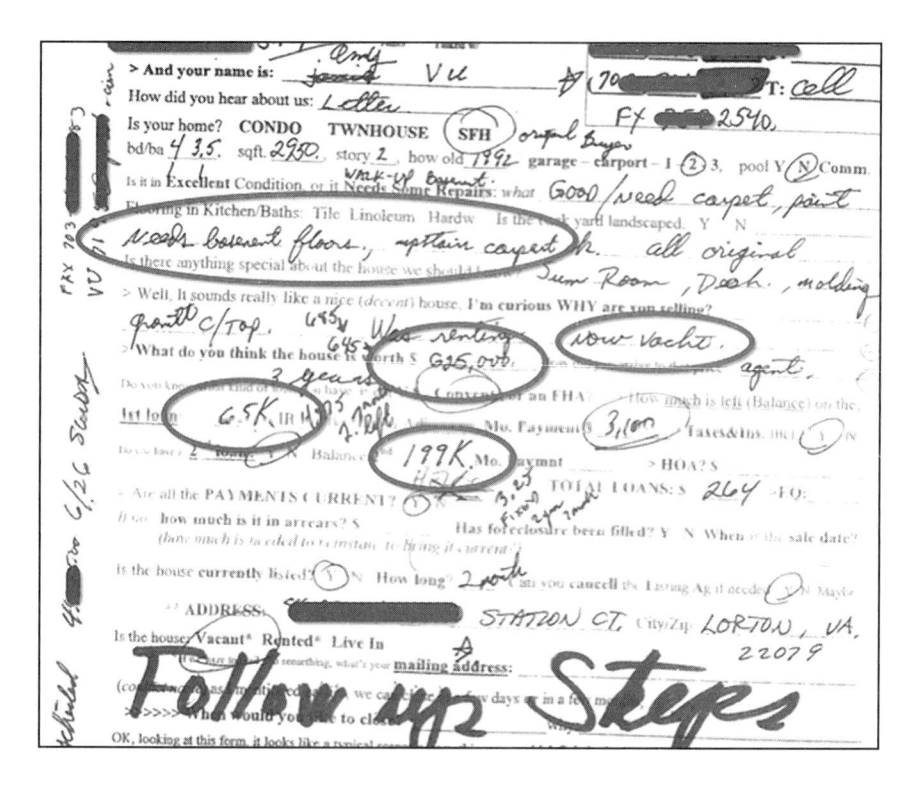

SIDE NOTE: As soon as I see a Phone Form with that much information, I immediately know that the student had a great call with the seller. A lot of writing indicates a longer call and good rapport.

The two IMPORTANT facts you can see right away on the above form are:

(1) Worth = $625K
(2) Owe = $65K + $199K

Would you be excited if you got a deal like that, based on those two facts?

Absolutely, it means that the house most likely has A LOT of equity.

There's nothing better than a deal with a lot of equity and a motivated seller.

However, this house needed a lot of work. Joe's coach encouraged him to go on an appointment and planned a strategy for Joe.

At the meeting, Joe got the seller to agree to sell the house "subject to" the first and second loans, plus cash.

Here's what Joe sent to our office after the meeting:

This property had a lot of drawbacks as Joe marked on the picture above. Plus, it needed more than $88,000 worth of repairs, and we would not let him do the rehab himself. However, he already had the house under the contract.

Here's what we advised him and what he did next. He found a contractor and had him give him a repair estimate. Then he went back to the seller and renegotiated the contract. He managed to get even better terms as you can see below.

From the above agreement, you can see that Joe contracted the house at a $399K purchase price paid as:

$10 – Earnest Deposit

$0 – Cash Down Payment

$50K – Subject To the 1st Loan

$199K – Subject To the 2nd Loan

$90K – Seller Carryback Note

Long story short, Joe found a contractor who had cash and assigned the agreement to him. Due to all the favorable terms that Joe was able to pass on, he got a huge **assignment fee of $70,200.**

Within 72 hours of closing on the deal, Joe had $70,200 wired to his account, which was more than Joe was making in a whole year. *How many of you would like to have a deal like that as your first?*

→ **Watch the video Joe sent by going to www.MarkoRubel.com/book/Joe .**

Balance	Description
$76,193.29	CHECK NUMBER 1096
$76,293.29	INCOMING FEDWIRE FUNDS TRANSFER &
$6,093.29	WEB PMT CHASE (Slate)
$6,193.29	WEB PMT CARDMEMBER SERVICES
$6,893.29	CHECK NUMBER 1081
$7,093.29	WEB PMT NAVY FEDERAL CREDIT UNIO

Now you need to realize that this is NOT a typical wholesaling deal. This was an unusual deal with a great Unlimited Funding type of structure. Frankly, those deals you can't find. You can only stumble on them.

*Results presented are not typical—read the Earning Disclaimer

*   *   *

Now I have one more story to tell you about Joe.

Remember I told you Joe sometimes traveled for his job.

Sometime after this deal, Joe had another house under contract with a closing in two weeks. Everything was looking good, but Joe had to go out of town for a business meeting. While in the hotel room, Joe had the worst headache of his life. He called the front desk and yelled for an ambulance.

Later, Joe found out he'd had a major aneurysm in his brain and was in the ICU for three weeks. I was shocked, my office was shocked. We were all sad but hoping and praying for Joe.

Here are some pictures of Joe in the hospital. Be advised—these are some detailed pictures, so they may not be for the faint of heart.

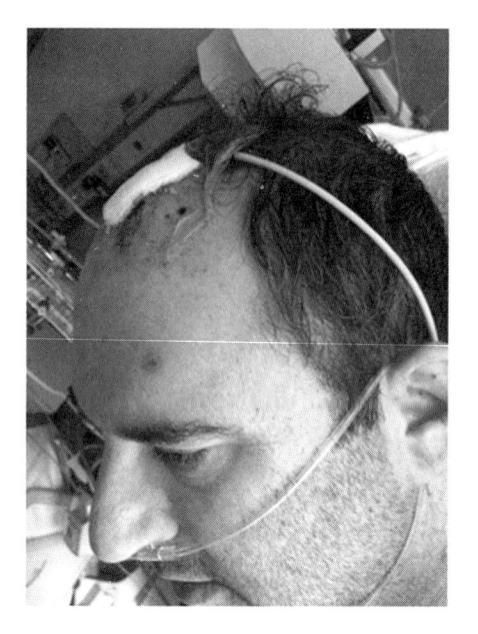

We all were extremely happy when we heard he fully recovered. Even weeks later when he emailed me these pictures, I was still shaken ... Here's one more:

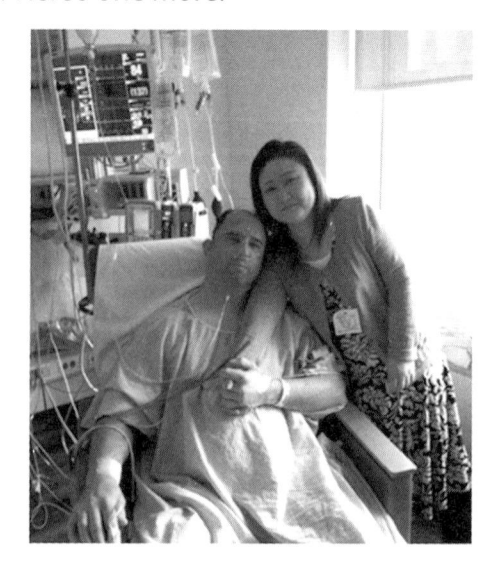

On a positive note, during his 3-week stay in the hospital, with ProfitGrabber and my coaching team, Joe's wife was able to complete all the forms, and Joe's son, then 22 and a partner in his parents' business, went to the closing and bought the house "subject to" using **UFP Method #1–$0 Down**.

Here's his GREAT reaction when he heard that the deal closed:

Joe was making money while lying in a hospital bed. Wow! Now Joe is all better, and they still own that house, currently with cash flowing at $415/mo.

About 6 months later when he recovered, he came back to our seminar. Here's the picture:

I have to tell you—with tears in my eyes (and I am not what you would call an outwardly emotional guy)—that I am so glad I put up with all the no's, the rejection, the people at my job who told me I'd never make it, and that I learned to do this business.

And I really am grateful to see how if God forbid, something were to have happened to Joe, that his wife and son were able to carry on this business.

Folks, we are not guaranteed tomorrow, so let me encourage you to find your reason WHY to build this business—and do it while you still can.

It's in your hands—and we can help.

The Next Step Determines Your Destiny ...

There are three types of people in this world.
Firstly, there are people who make things happen.
Then there are people who watch things happen.
Lastly, there are people who ask, what happened?
Which do you want to be?

–Steve Backley

You are at the end of this book, and this is the moment of decision.

There are 3 groups of people described in the above quote. Now's the time to decide which group you think is the largest.

I'm not sure which one you chose, but unfortunately, most people who are given a chance ... "watch things happen" or "ask what happened"...

Most people don't act quickly and decisively when they see something that requires some learning. They see it as an effort ... and therefore, do nothing. I would like to know, *what are you going to do?*

Here's what I find. Most people simply let the days pass them by as they just go through life ... half-awake.

Leading most of them to living a life like this …

They had dreams when they were young, replaced by responsibilities as they matured, and then they were left with nothing but regrets when they were old.

Sure they'd hoped to be happier, wealthier, and stronger. Deep down, they wanted to be successful. But what happened was every day was the same, and therefore nothing ever changed for them. They didn't feel like they had the time, the discipline, the money, the fortitude, or the resources to take the necessary steps.

Let me ask you this simple question: If not now, when?

When are you going to take that first step and make a life-changing decision?

If you are reading this, I am pretty sure that you want to improve your life, make more money, help your family, have less stress, and even enjoy more vacations. If you want to pursue your dreams and fulfill your aspirations, why don't you make a decision to do that right now?

<u>If not now, when?</u>

In Section 1 you got the bird's-eye view of this amazing real estate business. In Section 2 you got to see the deals. Sure you had questions, but as I said, that's normal—but really, that's not the obstacle here. The obstacle here is you moving forward and making that life-changing decision you've always thought you were capable of.

You also got the PROOF that the system works, so again, **if not now, when?**

What else do you need to move forward?

You got undeniable PROOF that people from various backgrounds are doing exactly what you can do. So with that said, what are you going to do, and **if not now, when?**

<u>**If you're going to take that first step, it has to be NOW**</u>, or nothing will ever change.

If you lay this book down and don't take the step suggested on the next page, nothing will ever change and you have basically wasted your time reading it. That's the truth. We both know it.

Again, you can choose the next step in the following pages, or you can continue to do what you've done in the past, and that is to make excuses—"*I don't have a lot of money, or the credit, or the time.*"

Those, my friend, are nothing but excuses because you've seen ordinary people getting paid to buy houses, and you already know that your credit doesn't matter if you follow this system.

I've shown you ordinary people with full-time jobs doing exactly everything I've shown you in this book, like the tire salesman from Ohio who works 50 hours and commutes another 15 hours every week. So as far as I'm concerned, you really DON'T have an excuse to not move forward. So I am going to ask you again,

If not now, when?

If you understand the importance of **this** moment in YOUR life, then I know you're going to do the right thing. If you want to have more money, have lots of properties, be a real **estate** mogul, get respect from your peers, and finally have the life and money you deserve, I can help you achieve those goals in a few ways. We can start with more education and add one-on-one coaching, so you get your goals accomplished as fast as humanly possible. When you've taken that all-important first step, we have different levels of affordable entry programs available to you. Simply call my office now and ask for a business advisor. If you would rather do it quickly and not wait, go to my website and click on "coaching."

Call 1-800-600-7997 or Go to:
www.MarkoRubel.com

Importance of Coaching

> ALL COACHING IS—
> IS TAKING A PLAYER WHERE HE CAN'T TAKE HIMSELF.
>
> —*Bill McCartney*

What do Tiger Woods, Oprah Winfrey, and John Travolta have in common?

Most people don't realize this one point, but it's an important one. Think about it. TIGER WOODS didn't start playing golf by just reading books about golf and watching golf instructional videos. No, he invested heavily in direct access to the best golf swing coaches on the planet. Here's where a lot of people miss the boat. Even when you hit the jackpot, you never stop growing. Same for Tiger. He still hires the best coaches to help him with his game to this day. It's his secret formula.

So what about OPRAH WINFREY? She's a billionaire. If you pay attention, she often expresses her gratitude to her coach and mentor in life, Maya Angelou, for showing her *the connection to the heart* that made Oprah famous.

It is the small tip that Maya Angelou gave to Oprah, summarized in a sentence, that completely changed Oprah's career and consequently made her a billionaire.

Maya Angelou said: *"People will forget what you said, people will forget what you did, but people will never forget how you made them feel."* If you think about it, Oprah really did follow her coach's advice.

Then there is JOHN TRAVOLTA. When John started his career 30 or so years ago, he was just a face on TV, a "sweat hog" on *Welcome Back Kotter*. Unlike virtually everyone else who appeared on the show, who have all but disappeared at this point, he did something different than all his co-workers. He invested heavily in publicity. It is this investment in a publicity coach that landed him the lead role in *Saturday Night Fever*, and the rest is history. *How different do you think his life would have been if he had opted out to save some money and never invested in a coach?*

As I've shown you, even famous people like TIGER WOODS, OPRAH WINFREY, and JOHN TRAVOLTA have NOT done it on their own. They became famous and successful, and they did it with the help of their coaches. Having a coach that has your back is having everything in my books. To me, this is just one of the big shortcuts to becoming wealthy.

These famous people's success (and wealth) was **not lucky or random**.

So what separates them from the rest of their peers is THE SAME THING that separates the students you've read about in this book from you.

They were in the same spot as you are right now, and the only difference from them and you is this: They made a conscious decision to invest in themselves. They made an investment in themselves, so they could have access to the sharpest minds and top experts in their fields.

If you want the same kind of results, shouldn't you do the same?

These examples of Tiger, Oprah, and John are just three real-life examples of famous people. In addition to reading about 15 of my coaching students, there are countless others who could tell you about their wins, especially among the Inner Circle members, but I'm out of time and out of room.

To be blunt—when it comes to creative real estate investing, the best and the brightest minds you can hire to help you make your move in real estate investing are my Mastery Team and me.

Here's why I say that.

I know just about every real estate guru out there. I'm friends with a few of them, I've actually coached a few of them, and here's what I discovered.

When it comes to "smart" investing approaches that go beyond regular flipping or fixing-and-flipping, I don't know anyone more qualified than my team and me. The combined number of transactions that we've participated in with our clients and coaching students is in the thousands, which means one thing—if it's happened to someone, it's probably happened to one of our students as well—which means we have a lot of experience.

We've had the opportunity to guide countless real estate investors, from the novice beginner to the seasoned pros, and we've helped them achieve successful, large deals—beyond their wildest dreams.

Will you be next?

And… **If not now, when?**

If you're ready to make your move, stop sitting on the sidelines watching everyone else make money, while you work at a JOB. You're finally ready to step up and get your own real estate investing moving in the right direction, APPLY for our one-of-a-kind, take-you-by-the-hand Coaching Program by calling 1-800-600-7997 right now. If you can't make the call, fill out an application at www.MarkoRubel.com

Here's the process:
1) Get an application and fill it out.
2) Once you've filled it out, my team and I will review it.
3) If we have any follow-up questions, we'll contact you.

The reason we do this is because we carefully screen people we believe want to succeed. In essence these are the people who have their WHY.

If we end up working together, you'll have access to **all the exact same tools** that the investors you've read about in this book had.

As a coaching client you get private access to one of my 4 wealth-building coaches. They'll be working with you exclusively, one-on-one.

My coaches have done lots of real estate deals, and many years ago I coached them personally. Once you're IN, you're IN. You'll be with the best, and that way you'll get the quickest results.

Here's a short list of just a few of the things you'll receive:
- All of the necessary training materials from the Unlimited Funding system, Lease Option Wealth system, Free & Clear Accelerated Wealth system, the Short Sale Insider system, and much, much more
- The best automation tool ever—the ProfitGrabber PRO software
- The Buying Deal Conversion website with my very own seller testimonials you can use to create instant credibility with your motivated sellers. (This is something you can't be without if you want to build authority and respect instantly)
- My Any Credit Selling website that allows you to get the highest down payments—due to its credible look and direct-response design.
- My very own Presentation Binder that I take to a seller's house and use at the first point of contact to get them to say YES!

But beyond all of the above, beyond all the **personal one-on-one calls** with your coach, and even beyond the **unlimited deal support and guidance we offer you**, you also get **my personal and private cell phone number for real estate emergencies.**

This is the magic number you dial … when you think I can save your deal or make your deal when everything you've tried, didn't. Saving you can equate to hundreds of thousands of dollars if you're a highly motivated student.

With any program of this magnitude, you most likely realize that we are limited on the number of coaching clients we can support (and give my personal cell phone number).

That's why if you are finally ready to stop working for everyone else and are ready to make money, spend more time with your family, get out of the rat race, and finally make a real difference in who you are, I strongly advise you to apply now. **If not now, when?**

Call 1-800-600-7997

or

Apply by going to Coaching Section at:

www.MarkoRubel.com